Radical Children's Literature

Also by Kimberley Reynolds

GIRLS ONLY? Gender and Popular Juvenile Fiction in Britain 1880–1910

VICTORIAN HEROINES: Readings and Representations of Women in Nineteenth-Century Literature and Art (*with Nicola Humble*)

CHILDREN'S LITERATURE IN THE 1890s AND 1990s

CHILDREN'S BOOK PUBLISHING IN BRITAIN SINCE 1945 (*with Nicholas Tucker*)

REPRESENTATIONS OF CHILDHOOD DEATH (*with Gillian Avery*)

FRIGHTENING FICTION (*with Geraldine Brennan and Kevin McCarron*)

CHILDREN'S LITERATURE AND CHILDHOOD IN PERFORMANCE

CHILDHOOD REMEMBERED

MODERN CHILDREN'S LITERATURE: An Introduction

Radical Children's Literature

Future Visions and Aesthetic Transformations in Juvenile Fiction

Kimberley Reynolds

First published in 2007 by
PALGRAVE MACMILLAN
Houndmills, Basingstoke, Hampshire RG21 6XS and
175 Fifth Avenue, New York, N.Y. 10010
Companies and representatives throughout the world.

PALGRAVE MACMILLAN is the global academic imprint of the Palgrave
Macmillan division of St. Martin's Press, LLC and of Palgrave Macmillan Ltd.
Macmillan® is a registered trademark in the United States, United Kingdom
and other countries. Palgrave is a registered trademark in the European
Union and other countries.

ISBN-13: 978–1–4039–4696–6 hardback

This book is printed on paper suitable for recycling and made from fully
managed and sustained forest sources.

A catalogue record for this book is available from the British Library.

Library of Congress Cataloging-in-Publication Data

Acton, Carol, 1958–
  Grief in wartime: private pain, public discourse / Carol Acton.
    p. cm.
  Includes bibliographical references and index.
  ISBN-13: 978–1–4039–4696–6 (cloth)
  ISBN-10: 1–4039–4696–5 (cloth)
    1. War and society. 2. War and literature. 3. War – Psychological
  aspects. 4. Grief. I. Title.
HM554.A26 2007
155.9'3708835502—dc22   2006051709

Printed and bound in Great Britain by
Antony Rowe Ltd, Chippenham and Eastbourne

For Peter

Contents

List of Illustrations

Acknowledgements

I owe a great deal to Peter Hunt and Nicholas Tucker, who both kindly read drafts of this book as it emerged and gave wise advice, strategic feedback and encouragement as needed. The book is much richer for their contributions; any errors are mine alone. My husband, Peter Reynolds, also read the manuscript as it evolved and bore the brunt of my excitements and anxieties. He also made it possible for me to leave the everyday world behind for some concentrated writing weeks. These were times of great quiet and pleasure and I would not have had them without him. The Faculty of Humanities and School of English at the Newcastle University gave me a period of leave to write this book, and my colleagues there were immensely supportive throughout. Matthew Grenby in particular was uncomplaining about the extra work my absence created for him – and a wonderful host while I was between homes as well. Mark Vasey-Saunders was generous with his time and knowledge of the world of role playing games. Without Kate Chedgzoy and Linda Anderson's determination to create a place for children's literature in the School of English, there would have been no book. My mother, Bobbie Griffith, and Mary Nyman, from the Westbrook Library in Connecticut, were tireless unpaid research assistants. David Rudd read, commented on and carefully corrected the final manuscript.

This book has grown out of several years of teaching and research. Many colleagues and students – not least those at the National Centre for Research in Children's Literature and the MA in Children's Literature at Roehampton University – have contributed to the thinking it contains at various stages. There is not space to mention them all by name, but some have played a particularly important part in this book's genesis and I want to thank them for their time, companionship and unfailing interest in children's literature. Special thanks, then, to Noga Applebaum, Laura Atkins, Sandra Beckett, Clare Bradford, the Children's Literature UK ListServ, Valerie Coghlan, Nadia Crandall, Marie Derrien, Alison Evans, Michele Gill, Susan Hancock, Vanessa Joosen, Gillian Lathey, Tomoko Masaki, Kathy Meyer, Okiko Miyake, the NorChilNet group – both students and leaders – Lisa Oakden, Emer O'Sullivan, Lissa Paul, Pat Pinsent, Lisa Sainsbury, Liz Thiel and Akiko Yamazaki. Lynne Vallone was great at making sure it got written!

Finally, Paula Kennedy, my Editor at Palgrave, has been a steady support throughout. I appreciate her belief in the project and her efforts in helping it take shape.

Parts of Chapter 7 and 8 first appeared in 'Frightening fiction: beyond horror' in *New Review of Children's Literature and Librarianship*, vol. 11, no. 2, November 2005.

Parts of Chapter 4 first appeared in 'Alchemy and Alcopops: Breaking the Ideology Trap' in Mary Shine Thompson and Celia Keenan (eds) *Critical and Theoretical Responses to Children's Literature*, Dublin: Four Courts Press, 2004.

Author's Note

I have tried to draw my examples from beyond the English-language tradition of writing for children and to be aware when I am making assumptions based on Western (and sometimes specifically Anglo-American) situations. As someone who has lived all my life in the West and who is effectively monolingual, I have been limited in the extent to which I can use and comment on texts from other cultures though I have also been fortunate in being introduced to a wide variety of children's books by colleagues and students from many countries. Despite my limitations, this book would have been the poorer if I had left out some of the hugely challenging, beautiful, and aesthetically rich books for children that have been produced around the world.

1
Breaking Bounds: The Transformative Energy of Children's Literature

G.K. Chesterton once observed, 'in everything that matters, the inside is much larger than the outside' (*Autobiography*, 41). Whether you are thinking about individual children's books or the whole domain of children's literature, the inside often turns out to be surprisingly larger than the outside might suggest – sometimes literally so as when material pops out and unfolds from apparently flat pages. Usually, however, it is the words and images of often physically small texts that turn out to be capable of filling the minds of generations of young readers with experiences, emotions, and the mental furniture and tools necessary for thinking about themselves and the world they inhabit.

This surprising quality can be hard to detect in studies of children's literature. As the field has developed, these have tended to take five forms, often in combination: those that trace the history of children's book; attempts to define children's literature and identify its characteristics; works that consider the relationship between children's literature and critical theory; studies that explore what children's literature does to its readers by, for instance, encoding ideological assumptions or disseminating strategies for resisting them; and analyses focussing on the ideas of the child and childhood inscribed in children's texts and critical works about them.[1] This book owes something to all of these approaches, but its overall project is rather different: it attempts to map the way that children's literature contributes to the social and aesthetic transformation of culture by, for instance, encouraging readers to approach ideas, issues, and objects from new perspectives and so prepare the way for change. This is the sense in which I see writing for the young as replete with radical potential.

Although quite a wide range of material is covered in the following chapters and I hope to show that children's literature, since its inception, has been implicated in social, intellectual, and artistic change, this is not primarily a historical study. I do not, for instance, look at the way children's books were

1

called into the service of the Puritans, the Abolitionists, or the Nazi party. My focus is broadly contemporary: the book begins with a discussion of the way children's literature has responded to ideas associated with literary modernism – arguably one of the most influential and widespread periods of creative activity in the modern age – then focuses on a selection of genres, topics, and media where fictions for the young can be seen to be contributing to thinking and debates associated with changes to narrative and culture. I hope the map it provides gives a sense of the vast inside created by this area of writing, and suggests ways in which children's literature matters beyond the pedagogic and historical explanations that are now so well established.

Jack Zipes has pointed to the way that fairy tales, and by extension children's literature, are implicated in acculturation – in transmitting cultural values and 'civilizing' children (1991: 9), a view elaborated by Robyn McCallum (1999), who sees much of children's literature as part of an ideological trap that seduces readers into accepting a liberal humanist world view. While children's literature is undeniably implicated in cultural integration, such explanations overlook an important and contrary impulse in many of the fictions we give to and make for the young. Childhood is certainly a time for learning to negotiate and find a place in society, but it is also about developing individual potential suited to a future in which societies could be different in some significant ways – for instance, in the organisation of families, the distribution of resources, or the circulation of power. It is not accidental that at decisive moments in social history children have been at the centre of ideological activity or that writing for children has been put into the service of those who are trying to disseminate new world views, values, and social models. The influence of Puritan beliefs and values extended far beyond the relatively small number of Puritans, and one means by which this came about was through their efforts to address the young on the page. In the same way, children's literature was used in the eighteenth century to help establish and promulgate the thinking and behaviour of the rising middle class in England (O'Malley, 2003).

Growing up involves making choices and shaping an identity. As a general rule, choosing one path, whether this is educational, cultural or social, closes down options. Much of the symbolic potential of childhood in culture derives from the fact that children have most of their choices before them: they represent potential. As a group, the fictions of childhood emphasise this view of childhood because they tend to be narratives in which the future is still an unknown and the self is in formation though, as I have argued elsewhere (Reynolds, 1994), the realistic 'problem novels' that started to appear in the 1960s have a tendency to foreclose on childhood by requiring readers to engage with events such as rape, death, and family breakdown. By the end of such novels, characters are shown to have matured, and by implication, readers too will have moved a step closer to adult knowledge and experience.

As the following chapters will show, children's literature provides a curious and paradoxical cultural space: a space that is simultaneously highly regulated and overlooked, orthodox and radical, didactic and subversive. It is a space ostensibly for children – and certainly in the fictions created for them, children encounter ideas, images and vocabularies that help them think and ask questions about the world[2] – but children's literature has also provided a space in which writers, illustrators, printers, and publishers have piloted ideas, experimented with voices, formats and media, played with conventions, and contested thinking about cultural norms (including those surrounding childhood) and how societies should be organised. Because writing for the young has a future orientation, there is often a freshness and urgency to the storylines of children's fictions that correspond to the fact that their target readers are generally encountering ideas and experiences for the first time. Many children's books offer quirky or critical or alternative visions of the world designed to provoke that ultimate response of childhood, 'Why?' 'Why are things as they are?' 'Why can't they be different?' With this in mind, children's literature can be equated with the 'monster child' that Jean-François Lyotard associated with creativity and the potential for change: 'The monster child is not the father of the man; it is what, in the midst of man, throws him off course [*son dé-cours*]; it is the possibility or risk of being set adrift' (in Burman, 72).

The aesthetic of childhood innocence

This study is in many ways a response to two very different accounts of writing for children that have done much to encourage scrutiny of children's literature as an area of cultural and aesthetic activity. The first and more influential of these is Jacqueline Rose's *The Case of Peter Pan, or, The Impossibility of Children's Fiction* (1984). Despite the fact that it was written nearly a quarter of a century ago and has been discussed often and at length (see, for instance, Lesnik-Oberstein, 1994 and Rudd, 2004, 2006), its centrality to this study makes a brief recapitulation of Rose's central arguments as I read them helpful. Many of her insights into the forces at work in children's literature are valuable, and I will be drawing on them in the chapters that follow. However, there are also aspects of her thesis with which I cannot agree and which I feel distort the way children's literature is received in culture. Of particular concern to me is the fact that Rose sees the child in children's literature (and by extension, children's literature itself) not as embodying the disruptive and creative force of Lyotard's monster-child, but as having an innately conservative effect on what can be written for children.

One of Rose's central activities in *The Case of Peter Pan* is the identification and interrogation of the impulse to set boundaries around what children's literature 'should' do and be. Since the beginnings of commercial publishing for children in the eighteenth century, she says, there has been 'a set of barriers constructed which assign the limits to how far children's literature is allowed to go in upsetting a specific register of representation – one which ... is historically delimited and formally constrained' (139). Rose's formulation implies that the barriers she identifies are agreed and stable. In fact, although since at least the seventeenth century, religious thinkers, parents, philosophers, educationalists, and critics have attempted to define what kind of writing is suitable for children (for an overview and indicative sample of such critical material, see Tucker 1976) and to make informed choices about what constitutes 'good' children's literature (see, for instance, Hunt, 1991: 7), the boundaries around children's literature have always been in dispute. Often these disputes arise from different understandings of what children are like and what children's literature is and does, differences at work at particular historical moments and arising from changing attitudes over time.

Ted Hughes's initial attempts to become known as a children's writer provide a useful illustration of such differences and changes and their potential consequences for children's literature. In the 1950s, when publishers of children's books were increasingly turning to formulaic, 'I Can Read' series, with their emphasis on the acquisition of reading skills and vocabulary,[3] Hughes was producing short fables and creation stories which were then deemed to be 'too sophisticated' (Paul: 2005) for children. Subsequently they were published as *How the Whale Became* (1963) and accorded high status in the field of children's literature.[4] So, while at one point Hughes's work fell outside the boundaries of what was deemed suitable for children, later it was so firmly inside and reflected so strongly the aspirations of those involved in the production of children's books for children's literature that his writing became a benchmark against which much other work for the young was measured.

As the case of Ted Hughes shows, the boundaries around children's literature are neither rigid nor agreed; nevertheless, those involved in creating, producing, and studying children's fiction have for long acknowledged that they exist. For much of the twentieth century, a combination of received wisdom and a strong sense of what the main purchasers of children's fiction (librarians, parents, and teachers) wanted to see in the books they gave to children resulted in an unwritten code of practice: no sex, no violence, and no 'bad' language (meaning that the writing should refrain from swearing, slang, and most aspects of colloquial or idiomatic use, and be grammatically correct).[5] In *The Case of Peter Pan*, Rose argues that the purpose of these boundaries has much less to do with children's tastes and development than with adult needs, and specifically the desire for an image of childhood based on children's relationship with language that, she claims, results in children's literature being arrested as a literary form.

For Rose (who in 1984 was herself pushing at the boundaries of academic criticism as they were then set with her interest in Lacanian psychoanalysis and poststructuralist critical theories), writing for children is committed to taking its readers (and writers and critics) back to a mythical time when the world was knowable and could be expressed in language (9). As she sees it, children's fiction has tended to be regarded as a cultural safe-house which preserves an ideal of the innocent child dating back to Locke and Rousseau. Rose maintains that adults need this image of the child – she pointedly does not claim that this is how children are or how they read – to keep a sense of themselves intact. According to *The Case of Peter Pan*, children's literature reassures and stabilises adults by refusing to disturb their views of childhood at the levels of language, content (specifically content that could disturb at psychic and sexual levels) and form (20; 142): these comprise the barriers around children's literature to which she refers and result, she claims, in an aesthetic of childhood innocence that she feels dictates what children's literature is and does.

But Rose's argument sits uneasily with evidence both from within children's literature and from other aspects of Western culture. As art historian Anne Higonnet (1998) demonstrates in *Pictures of Innocence* (1998), images of children and childhood have become deeply conflicted, with the entrenched but essentially residual allegiance to the innocent child (Higonnet, like Rose, associates this image with Locke, Rousseau, and the Romantics) giving way to what she terms the 'knowing' child in the course of the twentieth century.[6] Rose overlooks the ambivalent nature of many images of childhood, including in children's literature, past and present. On the basis of a very limited sample of material she comes to the conclusion that because it is specifically addressed to and works to secure an audience of children, the child in children's literature (by which she means both the idea of childhood it contains and the implied notion of the child reader outside the book) plays a central role in an 'impossible' collective fantasy about childhood.[7] Moreover, because this image is imbibed by children during the primary stages of language acquisition, with all that entails for the development of self and social understanding, it persists into adulthood, informing and shaping subjectivity, responses, and decision-making at a number of levels.

According to *The Case of Peter Pan*, this cycle stifles innovation. However, many writers – and particularly writers for children – have specifically acknowledged the way fictions encountered in childhood inspired them to think in new ways and to break free from prevailing views of childhood. The extent to which children's literature participates in redirecting writing and thinking is one of the central ideas explored in this study. Inevitably, with the advantages of hindsight and historical distance, it is easier to identify transformative discourses, ideas, allusions, and influences in writing produced for earlier generations, but in the following chapters I also attempt to see in what ways contemporary writers and illustrators from several countries are interacting with current debates, responding to new media and artistic tastes and formulating visions of the future.

Whether their aesthetic and social visions are regressive, conservative or progressive, at the heart of all works of juvenile fiction is an implied child reader who will encounter an image of childhood on the page. *The Case of Peter Pan* makes it clear that what is at issue for Rose is not the real lived experience of childhood or actual relationships between adults and children – these are not 'impossible'. Rather, she argues that children's literature creates the illusion that the early stages of language acquisition in the individual recapitulate an originary moment in culture when language was not the inadequate and evasive medium it is now experienced as being; particularly in a post-Freudian, postmodern world.

> It is assumed that children's fiction has grown away from this moment [a time when conceptualization of childhood was dominated by the philosophical writing of Locke and Rousseau], whereas in fact, children's fiction has constantly returned to this moment, repeated it, and reproduced its fundamental conception of the child. Children's fiction has never completely severed its links with a philosophy which sets up the child as a pure point of origin in relation to language, sexuality and the state. (8)

In Rose's analysis, this demand that writing for children assumes children's relationship with language is simple and pure – that it shows words as being able to say what they mean – is not about meeting the needs of children, though it does tell them what the culture in which they are growing up thinks children should be like. For this reason, her discussion of language is not concerned with the aspects that have traditionally exercised editors – swearing, slang, or grammar (except insofar as the acquisition of Standard English was a social marker transmitted and measured by the education system and so affecting the life choices of children, as discussed in her chapter on '*Peter Pan*, Language and the State'). Rose is interested in the more metaphysical understanding that the self is constructed through language, and so, if language is acknowledged to be unstable, arbitrary, and inadequate, the self is put at risk. As Rudd puts it, Rose conceives the child in children's literature as 'a fetish, functioning to disavow an adult's lack of completeness ... a being that seems to stand apart, coherent, outside the defile of the signifier and immune from the general slipperiness of language' (2006: 13). While she makes her case for the destabilising influence of language well, as I show in Chapter 3, she also ignores key areas of children's literature where the nature of language is explored, including the large and impressive body of nonsense writing. Since literary nonsense is precisely about the kind of wordplay that destabilises meaning and so could be argued to be putting the self in jeopardy, this is a significant omission.

The innocence of the child-figure that Rose places at the centre of children's literature is derived from its assumed inborn access to language that has not been contaminated by adult understanding.[8] The pervasiveness of this image and our dependence on it is what makes images of evil children or objects that represent childhood (dolls, toys, miniatures) so powerfully uncanny. Rose's interpretation of what the child represents in children's literature can also be extrapolated to explain why, even when many adults fear the young and when children under sixteen are responsible for rising proportions of contemporary crimes including violent robberies and murders,[9] there remains a conviction that children as a group should have special rights, including the right to a childhood. It sheds an equally useful light on the high levels of emotion and vitriolic rhetoric directed against high-profile juvenile offenders.

Having postulated an association between a time of linguistic purity, the possibility of meaning, and childhood, Rose goes on to look at children's literature as a body of texts. On the basis of her highly selective sample of books and authors, she concludes that writers for children have consciously rejected literary modernism (and presumably she would have included post-modernism if she had written the book a few years later) as part of a strategy to maintain the status quo and to resist cultural change. This involves what she sees as a refusal on the part of those who create children's literature to explore the extent to which subjectivity is created in and through language (1984: 141–2). In fact, as Rudd points out, 'it was not so much that children's fiction resisted modernism as that modernism deliberately distanced itself from what it saw as the restrictive world of children's [and women's] writing' (2006: 8). While some modernists were determined that their work be recognised as the antithesis of what they felt children's literature stands for, as Chapter 2 shows, this was not universally the case. Not only are there many examples of modernist writers and artists who created books for children, but there are also numerous children's books that are fully engaged with modernist debates and experimentation. Why the rejection of modernism should be identified as a defining characteristic of children's literature by Rose is also unclear given that much popular adult fiction also rejects modernist (and subsequently postmodern) writing.

Another problematic aspect of Rose's work is her failure to consider how children's books are understood in relation to other kinds of narratives children encounter, including picturebooks, despite the fact that by 1984 most children would first have encountered her focus text, J.M. Barrie's *Peter Pan*, on stage or through the Walt Disney animated film and related merchandise rather than in the form of the book or play script. Presumably she regards language as less central to other narrative forms than it is to fiction, which is where she locates the drive to secure, for the future reproduction of culture, 'the child's rationality, its control of sexuality or of language (or both)' (10).

To support her case, Rose cites distinguished writers who have been drawn to children's literature because they feel alienated by developments in adult fiction, and specifically by modernism. Their views are typified by Nobel Prize-winning (1978) writer Isaac Bashevis Singer, who in the 1970s explained why he wrote for children: 'I came to the child because I see in him the last refuge from a literature gone berserk and ready for suicide' (in Rose: 10). This view of children's literature as an antidote to and reaction against elitist trends in adult fiction has not disappeared. Philip Pullman made much the same point in his 1996 Carnegie Medal acceptance speech in which he castigated the literary establishment's antipathy to story, the elevation of 'technique, style, literary knowingness', and those adult writers who 'take up their stories as if with a pair of tongs' because they are 'embarrassed by them'. In a book for children, he maintains,

> you can't put the plot on hold while you cut artistic capers for the amusement of your sophisticated readers, because, thank God, your readers are not sophisticated. They've got more important things in mind than your dazzling skill with wordplay. They want to know what happens next. (http://www.randomhouse.com/features/pullman/philippullman/speech.html)[10]

Children's literature does much more than offer an environment where story is sacrosanct and the strategies of the classic realist text predominate, however. By, for instance, incorporating visual elements and narrative devices adapted from other narrative forms and formats which tend to be associated with less self-consciously literary modes and conditions of reading, and responding to changes and debates in society, it can offer new points of view or understandings of what constitutes a story. Thus, you may not be able to 'put the plot on hold', but you can, while it is unfolding, extend and question it, which is precisely what many of the books discussed in the following chapters do. Of course, these qualities are not exclusive to children's literature, but for several decades in adult fiction narrative experimentation tended to be at the expense of strong and satisfying plots while, because of its commitment to story, children's literature made room for both.[11]

Ultimately, based on what has been said about children's literature rather more than on the evidence of the texts themselves, Rose's argument is that the primary function of children's literature is to secure the child in culture: it is coercively normalising. To show how it does this, she identifies a number of demands that shape what writing for children's literature should and should not do: 'there should be no disturbance at the level of language, no challenge to our [adults'] own sexuality, no threat to our status as critics, and no question of our relation to the child' (20). While she accepts the demands are 'impossible' for an individual child, she claims they persist in the aspirations of those who mediate between children's fiction and child readers, holding at bay complex questions about sexuality, origin, and meaning.

While there is much of value in Rose's thinking, there is also much that is awry. The following chapters are particularly concerned with challenging the view that children's literature is conservative and creatively dependent by focusing on its demonstrable capacity for innovation. Since much of Rose's argument stems from her conviction that children's literature has rejected literary modernism – and must continue to do so if her interpretation of how it functions is to be sustained – this is an area that needs to be given specific attention. The first chapter approaches the topic from both textual and visual perspectives to demonstrate that children's literature was actively engaging with modernist thinking by the 1930s. One of the first critics to consider the relationship is Juliet Dusinberre, whose *Alice to the Lighthouse: Children's Books and Radical Experiments in Art* (1987) is the second work to which this study responds. Although it has not had the same kind of impact on the study of children's literature as *The Case of Peter Pan*, it makes many important and original observations about the place of children's literature in culture and deserves to be better known. Dusinberre's recognition of the relationship between childhood reading and creative innovation is central to the ideas developed in the following pages.

Children's literature and the aesthetic of transformation

> The impressions of childhood are those that last longest and cut deepest.
>
> (Virginia Woolf in *The Common Reader*, quoted in Greenway, xv)

Where Jacqueline Rose sees children's literature as largely regressive, arrested, and antipathetic to literary modernism, Juliet Dusinberre argues that children's literature plays a seminal role in bringing about cultural change, including preparing the way for modernism. Indeed, she credits a single children's book – *Alice in Wonderland* – with ushering in the modernist movement in all its forms. According to Dusinberre, for the generation to which her central subject, Virginia Woolf, belonged:

> ... cultural change was both reflected and pioneered in the books which children read. Radical experiments in the arts in the early modern period began in the books which Lewis Carroll and his successors wrote for children. (5)

There is, she argues, a 'symbiotic relationship between children's books and adult writing' (xv), or to put it another way, the books read in childhood lay the foundations of a writer's literary aesthetic; they provide the models, the anti-models, and the springboards for subsequent generations. This is not always conscious, but it is undeniable that the stories we encounter as children perpetually 'inhabit the landscape of childhood, what Bachelard calls "the oneiric house of memory" or the realm of dreams and imagination' (Natov, 2003: 6). Like childhood itself, these stories do not disappear, but continue to unfold and inform how we interpret the world. In the case of writers and other creative artists, they provide the kind of fund of remembered images that Dusinberre says Carroll's books provided for Woolf's generation. In this way they become seedbeds of creativity.[12]

Dusinberre attributes the importance of the Alices and the children's books they inspired to the way they challenged authority, released subversive energies, refused to condescend and preach to readers, and, particularly for modernists, foregrounded issues to do with language as the medium of meaning.

> The question of mastery over language, structure, vision, morals, characters and readers was to become the central concern, not only of children's authors, but of many adult writers – Virginia Woolf, Henry James, Joyce – in the shift of consciousness at the turn of the twentieth century. ... (xvii)

This is a far cry from Rose's account of the direct nature of language in children's literature.

As its title suggests, *Alice to the Lighthouse* is primarily concerned with the relationship between Carroll's Alice books and Woolf's writing, but in passing, Dusinberre points to other key children's texts and writers that demonstrably contributed to the rise of literary modernism and the modernist consciousness. Her list includes the influence of Frances Hodgson Burnett on D.H. Lawrence; *The Rose and the Ring* and *Black Beauty* on Roger Fry, and the Alices, *Treasure Island* and *Huckleberry Finn* on just about all the best-known modernists. The extent to which writers are aware of their debt to children's literature is in itself an interesting area of study (I should say that throughout this book I distinguish between books written for an audience of children and books that are read in childhood as this makes it possible to focus on the creative space specifically represented by children's literature and arising from the constraints associated with its audience at any given moment). A small amount of work has already been done on the relationship between writers and their childhood reading, beginning with Humphrey Carpenter's (1989) entertaining analysis of the role Beatrix Potter played in shaping the modern literary sensibility. Carpenter traces a line from Potter through W.H. Auden, George Orwell, and Evelyn Waugh to Blake Morrison, who uses two characters from Potter's *The Tale of Tommy Tiptoes* in a 1987 sonnet:

> They are holed up in some bar among the dives
> Of Deptford, deep in their cups, and a packet
> Of cashew nuts, like Chippy Hackee and cute
> Little Tommy Tiptoes hiding from their wives.

Carpenter notes particularly the debt to Potter acknowledged by Graham Greene:

> Of course there was Beatrix Potter. I have never lost my admiration for her books and I have often reread her, so that I am not surprised when I find

in one of my own stories, 'Under the Garden', a pale echo of Tom Kitten being trounced up [*sic*] by the rats behind the skirting-board and the sinister Anna Maria covering him with dough, and in *Brighton Rock* the dishonest lawyer … hungrily echoes Miss Potter's dialogue as he watches the secretaries go by carrying their little typewriters. (From *A Sort of Life* in Carpenter, 272)[13]

Greene was convinced that childhood reading (referring both to children's writers such as Potter and books read in childhood) is profoundly influential. His autobiography, *A Sort of Life* (1971), sums up his belief that creative writers are for ever in thrall to the visions and perceptions of childhood and adolescence: 'The influence of early books is profound. So much of the future lies on the shelves: early reading has more influence on conduct than any religious teaching' (in Sinyard, 2003: 23). Greene's essay 'The Lost Childhood' (1951) also explores this idea, concluding,

Perhaps it is only in childhood that books have any deep influence on our lives. In later years we admire, we are entertained, we may modify some views we already hold, but we are more likely to find in books merely a confirmation of what is in our minds already … But in childhood all books are books of divination, telling us about the future, and like the fortune-teller who sees a long journey in the cards or death by water *they influence the future*. (In Sinyard: 31; my emphasis)

Betty Greenway's edited collection of essays, *Twice-Told Tales: The Influence of Childhood Reading on Writers for Adults* (2005) similarly maintains that 'artists are made by the books they read as children' (xxiv). Greenway emphasises that it is not just the words in the books that shape future writers but books as objects, and the range of sensory and emotional responses evoked through their pictures, words, sounds, and even the weight, feel, and smell of their pages. Not every text necessarily has a physical form, and influences from oral sources can be as powerful and enduring as those from printed texts. For Sylvia Plath, the rhythms, images, and sometimes earthy language of nursery rhymes helped her articulate deeply ambivalent feelings about family relations, childhood, and the literary tradition (Castle, 2005: 114). In the case of Salman Rushdie, it was the 1939 MGM film adaptation of L. Frank Baum's *The Wonderful Wizard of Oz* (1900) that provided a seminal experience.[14] That childhood narratives are experienced in various forms and media is assumed in the approach to and selection of children's 'literature' in the following pages, though the handheld book is given primacy.

In a study of 'Adult Children's Literature in Nineteenth-Century Britain', Claudia Nelson looks at the rags-to-riches stories that comprise 'success literature' to construct an argument that can be used to support Dusinberre's observations about the impact of children's literature on writers and on culture beyond the modernist time frame of *Alice to the Lighthouse*. Nelson begins by highlighting what would now be called the crossover phenomenon in the Victorian period, noting that some contemporary critics saw the popularity of children's fiction with adults as a symptom of social degeneration (165).[15] The thrust of her argument, however, is on the influence of children's literature on Victorian writers, looking particularly at how writers of success literature, the best known being Samuel Smiles, adapted the techniques of the children's literature of their youth to appeal to and instruct adult readers (173).

Nelson calls attention to the way that Smiles in particular constructs his working-class readers in the same way as had writers of the children's books he would have known as a boy; notably Thomas Day, Maria Edgeworth, and the author of the anonymous 1804 work titled *The Renowned History of Primrose Prettyface, Who by Her Sweetness of Temper and Love of Learning Was Raised from Being the Daughter of a Poor Cottager to Great Riches and to the Dignity of the Lady of the Manor, Set Forth for the Benefit and Imitation of Those Pretty Little Boys and Girls Who by Learning Their Books and Obliging Mankind, Would to Beauty of Body Add Beauty of Mind* (175). Although his audience is assumed to be comprised of adults,[16] they are posited as *tabulae rasae* – characters in process – who it is hoped will ingest the simply written sketches, directed at inexperienced readers, that comprise a series of lessons designed with a view to encouraging them to reshape themselves according to middle-class (adult) formulations and so rise in the social hierarchy (173). In this way, Nelson suggests, writers of success literature consciously drew on writing for children as part of a project to transform individual lives and improve society.

Probably the most sustained and probing exploration of the uses and enduring impressions made by children's literature on an individual writer is Francis Spufford's *The Child that Books Built* (2002), an autobiographical account of himself as a young reader. As Spufford explains, he undertook the project because he recognised that in many ways he had read himself into the kind of adult and writer that he is:

> the words we take into ourselves help to shape us. They help form the questions we think are worth asking; they shift around the boundaries of the sayable inside us, and the related borders of what's acceptable; their potent images ... dart new bridges into being between our conscious and unconscious minds, between what we know we know and the knowledge we cannot examine by thinking. They build and stretch and build again the chambers of our imagination. (21–2)

While the detail in Spufford's reflections on himself as a consumer of fiction suggest that at some level he always understood himself in relation to what he was reading, the author Eva Figes did not realise that the fairy tales she encountered as a child were at work, shaping her thinking and behaviour, until she began to read them to her first grandchild. In *Tales of Innocence and Experience* (2003), she writes about how she gradually became aware that reconnecting with stories remembered – and misremembered – she had heard and read when young, was releasing and giving expression to lost, repressed or unacknowledged childhood experiences. In her case, sharing fairy tales with her granddaughter allowed her to realise that she had unconsciously used the tales to understand the experience of fleeing from Nazi Germany and resettling in an alien world. That insight has made it possible for her to write about both the events and the way the tales continue to shape them for her.

All the examples provided so far focus on the role played by children's literature on the formation of adult writers rather than why writing for children appeals to writers.[17] In an essay on Kipling's late short story, 'Fairy-Kist' (1928), Judith Plotz sets a series of interesting ideas in motion, ideas which support the notion that children's literature both directly influences the way its readers who become writers write, and represents a valuable cultural space for writers. (Inevitably this influence is recognised long after the first reading; it is never possible to recover initial responses to works read in childhood, though many writers testify to strong memories of being powerfully affected by what they recall as first encounters with particular books, comics and stories in periodicals.) In what at first appears to be a corrective to Dusinberre's claims for children's literature, Plotz carefully establishes that, publicly at least, the main figures in literary modernism dismissed children's literature, just as they did writing by women (Greenway, 2005: 183; see also Hughes in Hunt, 1990). She concludes that by the turn of the nineteenth century, male modernists had begun variously to 'appropriate, fear, obscure and diminish' children's literature as part of a lesser, female tradition that serves 'larger male cultural needs' (183).

The uber males of modernism might have derided children's literature (and envied its buoyant market), but Plotz's reading of 'Fairy-Kist' suggests that they also regarded children's literature as doing important cultural work. She makes her argument by showing Kipling to be yet another writer who drew on formative childhood reading. In his case, it was Juliana Horatia Ewing who particularly shaped his taste, style, and even the content of his work, as he acknowledged in the course of reprising his career. In *Something of Myself* (posthumously published in 1937) he says about Ewing's *Six to Sixteen* (1872), 'I owe more in circuitous ways to that tale than I can tell. I knew it, as I know it still, almost by heart' (in Plotz, 184). After comparing their oeuvres, Plotz concludes that Kipling was constantly rewriting Ewing's stories, but in the process making them 'insistently hyper-masculine, misogynist, and alienated' (185). More importantly, however, she shows that 'Fairy-Kist' is not just a masculinised retelling of Ewing's *Mary's Meadow* (1886), but an example of the way that Kipling used children's literature in general as a kind of 'common tradition, a folk tradition after the age of folk, freely appropriable, usable, cooptable by the children-turned-writers it has served' (193), and that this is how it is figured in the story.

In 'Fairy-Kist', a wounded, terrified, shell-shocked soldier listens to a female nurse reading him *Mary's Meadow*, and the story soothes him as drugs and doctors cannot. Although the healing process is not complete at this stage and involves uncovering his debt to the book some years later, the story's beneficial effects are profound and enduring. Plotz suggests that despite some ambivalence about the literary and artistic merits of children's literature – and especially that written by women – Kipling sees it as a restorative for an ailing post-war society. Peter Hunt develops Angus Wilson's suggestion that Kipling was caught between 'the anarchic, romantic, child-like force of his creative impulse and the ordered, complex, at times almost self-defeating pressure of the craft he imposed upon it' (2001: 82) to offer a reading that chimes in with Plotz's. Hunt proposes that in some ways writing for children toned down or even filtered out some of the opinions that to modern eyes have often seemed questionable in Kipling's work (2001: 82). Plotz extends this line of thought, claiming that he underscores the transformative potential of children's literature, seeing it as necessary to bringing about spiritual renewal and a shift from the individualistic, hierarchical old masculine world towards a collective community and new, more feminine world order (2005: 191). Kipling is a reluctant champion, however, as Plotz explains with reference to the story's title. Those who are kissed by fairies invariably become their prisoners and often go mad, thus, though 'Fairy-Kist' 'signals and celebrates the increased centrality and value of children's literature to the culture of modernism, it also pathologizes that celebration by representing children's literature as adult therapy' (195).

Dusinberre is not interested in the therapeutic value of children's literature, but she does point to the way writing for children releases visionary potential during periods of upheaval and uncertainty like that in which Kipling's story is set: 'in times of great change', she says, 'some of the most radical ideas about what the future ought to be like will be located in the books which are written for the new generation' (34). This ability to envisage and engage young readers with possibilities for new worlds and new world orders strikes me as central to the transformative power of children's literature, both socially and aesthetically. The stories we give children are blueprints for living in culture as it exists, but they are also where *alternative* ways of living are often piloted in recognition of the fact that children will not just inherit the future, but need to participate in shaping it.

New visions may operate primarily at the levels of plot and content, but as examples in the following chapters show, they may also inspire stylistic innovation, new narrative forms, and fresh explorations of the book as medium, resulting in intellectual platforms from which to build new thinking. Such platforms are necessary but rare. In the absence of new ways of thinking or creative alternatives to the way society works, writing for children may take up a diagnostic position, identifying problems as a first step towards formulating solutions. For instance, in the United Kingdom and the United States, the Thatcher–Reagan era coincided with (or provoked?) a wave of political dystopias and concerns about the environment, globalisation, and the ethics of some scientific/technological developments, a wave which has been gathering force as the extent of the problems becomes more apparent.[18] Whether intellectual, social or creative in their focus, as Graham Greene recognised, children's books have the potential to influence the future.

The uses of children's literature

Alice to the Lighthouse is specifically concerned with the radicalism associated with modernism, but Dusinberre's thesis can be applied more generally, and this is part of what I attempt to do in this book. This is not a question of tracing influences, entertaining as that can be, but of refuting Rose's claim that children's literature is becalmed as an art form, and demonstrating that many textual experiments are given their first expression in writing for children. Children's literature, then, is both a breeding ground and an incubator for innovation. There are certainly many very ordinary children's books – at least as many as there are banal books for adults – but there are also aspects about writing for children that result in a kind of wild zone where new ways of thinking are explored, given shape, and so made part of the intellectual and aesthetic currency of that generation of child readers.

Dusinberre's Introduction complains that children's literature has not been treated seriously – that the critical establishment perceives it as 'belonging to a separate sub-culture which has never been allowed a place in the discussion of high culture' (xvii). As I see it, however, this lack of visibility contributes significantly to the freedoms available to those who create children's literature – there is a clear distinction between the amount of regulation and scrutiny applied to narrative forms such as television, films, comics, magazines, and computer games, and that given to children's literature. *Learning from the Left* (2006), Julia Mickenberg's fascinating study of the role played by children's literature in the United States in disseminating and preserving left-wing thinking during the rigours of the McCarthy era and the Cold War, celebrates the fact that commercial children's literature (as distinct from textbooks) flies under the cultural radar and so is able to cross any number of official and unofficial boundaries. Precisely because children's books, then as now, were generally assumed to be good for children, she explains, they 'escaped the stigma attached to commercial culture and often maintained an aura of purity that could ward off would-be censors' (14). Although Mickenberg traces an enduring leftist legacy in American children's publishing – which largely holds for Britain too as the two publishing industries are closely allied – the cultural and aesthetic wild zone at the centre of children's literature is a space for dissenters of all kinds.

Mickenberg's research provides evidence to support Dusinberre's claims that at times of cultural change, children's literature becomes a place of visionary thinking and, Mickenberg would add, political engagement. For instance, she gives examples of books written during the depression 'designed not simply to enlighten children and set their spirits free, but to radicalize them' (50), while the increasing prosperity and industrialization of the post-war period inspired children's books that stressed the power of the imagination and creative thinking as an antidote to creeping mechanisation in most areas of work (40). In the same way, the Cold War years 'when the child became a focal point for national anxiety: anxiety about violence, social control, changing social norms, and "alien" – both extranational and extraterrestrial – influences' (132) stimulated children's book makers to create books that looked outside isolationist paranoia and featured narratives about social justice, freedom of thought and how technology could be used to solve the problems of the past. In other words, children's books encouraged young readers to think optimistically about the future and the pioneering roles they could play in improving society for all.

Avoiding the cultural spotlight is one reason why writers may find themselves drawn to write for children; especially if, consciously or not, they are exploring ideas that they feel may not sit comfortably within the literary establishment or other cultural institutions. There is a kind of liberation in writing for children that stems in part from what Philip Pullman calls their lack of sophistication (though it might be more accurate to relate this to their lack of experience of life and texts). This may be because writers assume children will be less judgemental than adults (and know that their views are unlikely to carry much critical weight). Even when writers consciously adhere to the various unwritten rules about what kind of material is suitable for children, there is abundant textual evidence suggesting that addressing a child audience removes some of the censors and filters that come into play when writing for adults. There are, for instance, many studies that identify Victorian and Edwardian children's fantasies and adventure stories as vehicles for a range of desires or unorthodox ideas that did not find expression so readily in adult fiction (see Brook, 1969; Carpenter, 1985; Kincaid, 1992; Reynolds, 2000; Rose, 1984).

Another appeal of children's literature for writers and illustrators comes from the oneiric dimension of childhood; the logic of dreams, fantasy, play, and the imaginary, all associated with the young, is seen to be more permeable and plastic than the rationality assigned to adulthood. This plasticity is reflected in children's literature's lack of generic rigidity; it not only tolerates but embraces generic mutation, and also takes in and nourishes kinds of literature that have temporarily fallen from favour in writing for adults, creative activities considered in more detail below.

For me, a crucial part of the explanation for why children's literature is so good at stimulating and nurturing innovation is that many children's texts operate two semiotic systems simultaneously: the visual and the textual, and the entire domain is bound up in interactions between formats and media that are beginning to change the nature and delivery of narrative fiction (see Chapter 8). The word-image dynamic is particularly adept at giving expression to meanings and concepts that reside at the edges of language – things for which the vocabulary and grammar that regulate verbal communication may currently be inadequate. As many examples in the following chapters will show (see, for instance, the discussion of David Weisner's *The Three Pigs* in Chapter 2 and contemporary French picturebooks in Chapter 3), those texts that combine visual and textual elements have been especially successful and active in preparing the way for new concepts to be called into language and introducing complex ideas to a juvenile readership.

The way children's literature and associated narrative playthings such as toy theatres and, more recently, book-related merchandise including multimedia products, lay down the foundations of aesthetic taste was well understood by the late-Victorians, as can be seen in the following quote from a review in the 12 December 1865 number of *The Bookseller*:

> There is no department of book-manufacture that requires more skill and conscientious art combined with good taste, than that of children's books; as a general rule, this has been overlooked; it is thought that any rubbish will do for a child. Cruel mistake! Were it possible, only the beautiful, the pure, and the good should be presented to the sensitive eye and ear of childhood. (in Masaki, 2006: 10)

Writing in the *Art Journal* in 1887, the drama critic and Ibsen translator, William Archer, claimed that without a foundation in childhood experience, adults were unable to develop an appreciation of art, and that childhood play (he was thinking specifically of playing with toy theatres, which included performing their accompanying play scripts) acted as a 'gymnasium for the imagination' (Farr: 84).[19] Many of the books I discuss in this volume provide similar intellectual workouts and aesthetic foundations, though I am equally concerned to identify the opposite trend: the areas in publishing for children which I suspect of impeding critical thinking and cultivating a taste for the narrative equivalent of junk food.

I am less concerned than Dusinberre about the way children's literature tends to be excluded from the high table of culture, not least because at least in Britain the situation has changed noticeably in recent years. For instance, since 2004 the National Theatre has staged works by Philip Pullman, Jamila Gavin, and Michael Morpurgo, reviews of children's books are frequently placed alongside those for adults in the broadsheet newspapers, and individual writers, notably Philip Pullman and Michael Morpurgo, regularly contribute to news and cultural affairs programmes. The creation of the Children's Laureate, who is mandated to speak on behalf of the children's book world, has added to the enhanced status and visibility of children's literature in British culture. Despite these improvements, cultural contributions made by children's literature continue to be largely invisible. One of the least recognised areas of creative enrichment and transformation takes place around the way children's literature both incubates genres that have ceased to be used in adult fiction and participates in generic innovation. In this way it functions both as restorative – receiving and returning in rejuvenated form genres originally associated with adult fiction – and as a wellspring from which adult writers can draw.

In and out of the nursery

This movement of genres between writing for children and adults is noted by Jacqueline Rose, who sees children's literature as being charged with the care of certain older forms of literary texts such as myths and legends as a means of preserving and eventually restoring values perceived as being 'on the point of collapse' in contemporary culture (1984: 44). In *Retelling Stories* (1998), John Stephens and Robyn McCallum draw attention to the way that the stories cultures choose to preserve and repeat serve a purpose. They disseminate values, pass on traditions, prop up what Stephens and McCallum call the Western metaethic, with its adherence to qualities such as loyalty, honour, courage, humility, duty, and responsibility. These are all characteristics shared by the majority of early heroes whose stories continue to be handed down from generation to generation; they are also attributes that make for good and governable subjects and citizens, which explains why so many retellings are directed at juvenile audiences.

Although traditional forms may be saved from extinction by being retold to the young, as Rose sees it, consignment to the nursery is ultimately damaging because in the process, the genres are infantilised and impoverished (50). She has a point. Largely to meet the needs of educationalists, many retellings of such cultural staples as myths, legends, and the plays of Shakespeare have been so vigorously adapted for children, so sanitised, flattened out, and restricted in their choice of vocabulary, that they have indeed lost their vigour and purpose. But the problem lies in the nature of the retelling; it is not a direct consequence of such materials being classified as 'children's literature'. Not only can the adjustment to a juvenile audience – which may involve no change to the text but, for instance, the inclusion of illustrations – result in high-quality and largely faithful retellings for new generations of readers such as those by Roger Lancelyn Green, Rosemary Sutcliff, Kevin Crossley-Holland, and Geraldine McCaughrean, but it can also lead to highly original new works that pay subtle homage to established genres and texts. For instance, a range of classic children's texts celebrates Arcadian pastoral literature, among them Kenneth Grahame's *The Wind in the*

Willows and A.A. Milne's Pooh books (see Carpenter, 1985). Both books may express a regressive desire to retreat from the demands associated with mature masculinity, but both equally offer original and enduring literary experiences. More recently, writers such as Allan Ahlberg, Christopher Bing, Anthony Browne, Kevin Crossley-Holland, Neil Gaiman, Jon Scieszka, and Diana Wynne Jones have produced outstanding fictions that are deeply indebted to traditional sources.

The intertextual richness of children's literature is part of the process by which children are inducted into culture. In the same way, there is a clear logic in giving genres that have fallen from favour in adult fiction space in the 'nursery' of children's literature. A nursery is both a place for the young and a place of development; far from necessarily languishing and becoming aesthetically inert when directed at a juvenile audience in the way Rose suggests, such genres are often refreshed and developed for use in new ways. Chapter 3 provides a detailed example of this process in relation to nonsense. It is also important to remember that children of nursery age are in the process of learning the primary narratives of culture as well as the more fugitive tales that will become part of the shared stock of cultural references for their particular generation. (Though the preponderance of the latter now come from television, film, and other media – just as for recent generations they were generated by radio and comics – many will still have their origins in books, not least because for Western children, education is an almost universal experience and learning to read print remains central to the curriculum.)

There is a certain affinity between acquiring traditional literacy skills and learning the tales that have helped pass on cultural knowledge for centuries, since such tales also contain basic information about genres, narrative conventions, and the styles associated with different kinds of narratives. Just as we never leave childhood behind, so the narratives ingested in childhood endure and shape adult thinking and behaviour at many levels. This has been discussed above with reference to writers, but it is true more generally as well; Mickenberg, for instance, sees a connection between the student-led radicalism of 1960s America and the children's literature of the 1950s, which actively urged the young to change the world (26).

Children's literature is not just capable of preserving and rejuvenating outdated or exhausted genres; it also contributes to the creation of new genres and kinds of writing, though to date this has gone unacknowledged because, as Dusinberre notes, there is a widespread assumption that children's literature is a second order of creativity that lags behind and imitates what happens in adult fiction. Until something is identified and named by the cultural establishment, which deals almost exclusively in art directed at mature audiences, it is culturally invisible. Magic(al) realism is a case in point and one that demonstrates well children's literature's role in aesthetic and social innovation and transformation as well as the tendency of children's literature towards generic hybridity.

Magical metamorphoses

> ... the marvellous begins to be unmistakably marvellous when it arises from an unexpected alteration of reality (the miracle), from a privileged revelation of reality, an unaccustomed insight that is singularly favored by the unexpected richness of reality or an amplification of the scale and categories of reality, perceived with particular intensity by virtue of an exaltation of the spirit that leads to a kind of extreme state [estado limite].
>
> (Alejo Carpentier, *The Marvelous Real*: 86)[20]

Studies of magic(al) realism as a literary form[21] trace its origins to a particular kind of writing that started to emerge from Latin American in the 1960s, typified by Gabriel García Márquez's *One Hundred Years of Solitude* (1967) (Hegerfeldt, 2004: 1). In fact, writers of children's literature were creating what can now be recognised as magic(al) realist texts long before. In her recent guide to *Magic(al) Realism*, Maggie Ann Bowers (2004) includes E. Nesbit's 'magic' books (1902–1913) as examples of the genre, and traces a strong tradition of magic(al) realist writing for children, including the Paddington Bear stories, *Charlotte's Web* and *Matilda*. While Bowers does not distinguish sufficiently between fantasy and magic(al) realism, her basic premise is sound: the roots of magic(al) realism lie in children's literature.[22]

That children's literature should have given rise to this curious literary hybrid is not surprising; the affinities between the two can quickly be established. At a primary level, magic(al) realism, with its emphasis on transformation, corresponds closely to the conditions of childhood and adolescence, which are intrinsically about change, metamorphosis, and growth of body and mind. Magic(al) realism's requirement that readers accept the improbable – even what is held to be impossible – also mirrors the constant mental adjustments the young make as they undergo new experiences and encounter new ideas.

In cultural and literary terms, magic(al) realism shares with children's literature links to ideas and values associated with the Romantic tradition. For instance, it values and is concerned with developing the relationship between humans and nature, and celebrates the power of the imagination. Just as the Romantics equated childhood innocence with spiritual and intellectual freedom and urged readers to break free from mental and social limitations imposed by self and society, so magic(al) realist texts attempt to transcend the restrictions of the mundane and commonsensical. They work on the willingness to believe that there is more to the world than we can comprehend with our senses and intellects, and so subvert and override epistemological certainties. Like the Romantics, magic(al) realist writers see the capacity for intellectual openness as being accessed by the imagination. As Margaret Mahy, the distinguished writer of many fine Young Adult (YA) magic(al) realist novels has one of her characters observe, the imagination 'makes magicians of us all' (*The Changeover*, 34).

Although its literary origins can be found in children's literature, until a critical vocabulary and definition for magic(al) realism came into being, its difference from traditional fantasy went unheeded, including by critics of children's literature. Even now, when it is well established as a literary mode, magic(al) realism has received little recognition in the field of children's literature. Writing in 1988 about New Zealand-born P.L. Travers's *Mary Poppins* (1934), for instance, Maria Nikolajeva can only see the text as an example of fantasy, and Mary as a guest 'from the implied secondary world' (86). This reading results in Nikolajeva's underplaying the extent to which the text, in true magic(al) realist fashion, offers a critique of the regimented, capitalist and patriarchal world view represented by Mr. Banks and the City, and sets up spontaneity, laughter, and the power of the imagination as superior to them. Where fantasy almost invariably initiates a return to reality for its protagonists, who by the point of closure are better able to conform to what is expected of them, magic(al) realism is driven by the urge for change. In these fictions, not only subjective perceptions but also the world itself are changed.

Mary Poppins is an example of a children's text working towards social transformation through the modes and impulses of magic(al) realism rather than traditional fantasy. It validates childhood and the socially marginalised (among them governesses and chimney sweeps) and is deeply committed to the idea that how we see and think about the world has implications for what the world is like. Travers uses the Mary Poppins series (1934–1988) to urge readers to keep their minds open and flexible however old they may become, and to resist the tendency to close off options with age.

The story of John and Barbara, the Bankses' infant twins, states this most explicitly. It begins with them able to understand and communicate with the whole natural world and possessing wisdom reminiscent of Wordsworth's 'clouds of glory', but by the end of the chapter, they have aged sufficiently to have lost their abilities. Travers makes it clear that what is special about Mary Poppins is that though a fully mature and, as she might say herself, supremely well-adjusted adult, she has never lost this capacity. This places her perpetually in the position of an observer whose viewpoint is off centre – she is Lyotard's monster-child in adult form, and a corrective to the rigidity and routine of modern bourgeois life. Through the figure of Mary Poppins, Travers makes the 'normal', with its dependence on rationality and scientific explanations (Mary Poppins defies both), seem both strange and inadequate.

A more recent YA novel that puts magic(al) realist devices to startling effect is Melvin Burgess's *Lady: My Life as a Bitch* (2001). The power of this text (discussed in more detail in Chapter 6) comes largely from its ending. Having turned its central character, sexually rambunctious teenager Sandra Francy, into a dog, the story seems to be heading for the predictable moment when she is restored to her human form. In fact, Sandra decides that she prefers the canine life and flees from her family and the possibility of regaining her girl's body and all the things (taking exams, getting a job, growing up) that that would entail: 'I want to be quick and fast and happy and then dead. I don't want to grow old. I don't want to go to work. I don't want to be responsible. I want to be a dog!' (199).

Lady is Burgess's only venture into magic(al) realism to date. David Almond, by contrast, has blended the idioms of magic(al) realism with other literary genres in all of his work that is classified as 'children's literature'. Almond's most recent book, *Clay* (2005), is magic(al) realist in its evocation of the supernatural-sublime in the form of a monster-figure created by two boys on the cusp of adolescence from clay they have dug out of a pond in a local quarry (Almond frequently uses mines, quarries, and other subterranean settings which place his characters in relation to the known present and the unknown past, between the rational now and the primitive then). In *Clay*, Almond makes full use of standard magic(al) realist devices and strategies, including calling attention to itself as a story in a way which allows the author simultaneously to assert and call into question the status of the events he has related. The final lines of the text, attributed to the focalising character, Davie, who claims to be recalling events of the past, read:

> So now I've written it all down, all of it. I don't care if there's craziness in it. I've learned that crazy things can be the truest things of all. You don't believe me? Doesn't matter. Tell yourself it's just a story, nothing more. (296)

Clay is a rite-of-passage novel, but significantly, and consistent with the tenets of magic(al) realism, the transition to maturity is not posited as the end of innocence or the loss of imagination and potential. Instead, in line with Almond's general aesthetic of experience as valuable, the events of the story are set out as a time of discovery that has permanently wedged open Davie's 'doors of perception'.

Margaret Mahy's *Alchemy* (2002) is the most recent in a long line of magic(al) realist novels that share Almond's optimism about what it means to grow up and acquire experience. It gives boy readers the same opportunity to embrace and enjoy the transformations that come with adolescence as her earlier, better known novel *The Changeover* (1984) offers girls. Mahy's protagonist, Roland, is a rather traditional boy. He cares about school and family, and experiences adolescence as a time of power, insight, and excitement. This is a magic(al) realist text in which the inexplicable elements function metonymically: the subjective reality of the thinking adolescent is that the world and the self are simultaneously bizarre and banal; known and unknowable; alluring and alienating. What is important, Roland discovers, is not to turn away from the possibilities growing up offers but to embrace them and to learn about yourself in relation to them. Among the opportunities on offer are sexual desire, which is shown as natural and pleasurable, and changes in the power dynamics in relationships with adults.

Mahy equates alchemy (defined in the text as 'a magical or mysterious power of transforming one thing into another' (101)) and adolescence. The book acknowledges the ambivalence associated with change, and the adolescent tendency to withdraw into the self, but ultimately it is the opposite of a nihilistic text. Roland is prepared to take risks and to change; he learns that the things he does make a difference (hugely important to political engagement), and as the book draws to a close, he is able to evaluate his strengths and weaknesses and decide that he is both strong enough and ready to act.

Mahy and Almond's optimistic insistence on the necessity for change is a good note on which to end this first chapter, for *Radical Children's Literature* is also a book about celebrating change. In particular, it is about changing the way children's literature is perceived in culture by recognising the way books – and increasingly other narrative forms – for children have fostered and embedded social, intellectual and aesthetic change, and about identifying the changes that are currently taking place – and those that are being resisted – in writing for the young.

2
Breaking the Frame: Picturebooks, Modernism, and New Media

> Radical experiments in the arts in the early modern period began in the books which Lewis Carroll and his successors wrote for children
> (Juliet Dusinberre, *Alice to the Lighthouse*, 5)

Juliet Dusinberre's identification of the indebtedness of modernism to children's literature is not reflected in studies of literary modernism, which pay no heed to writing for children. Indeed, accounts of modernism in the broadest sense generally ignore children's literature, a fact underlined by the major exhibition 'Modernism 1914–1939: Designing a new world' at the Victoria and Albert Museum in 2006, which failed to include any references to children's literature and surprisingly few to childhood. Even those working in the field of Children's Literature Studies have done little to advance knowledge in this area in the two decades since Dusinberre first articulated her thesis. This chapter begins to address this silence by demonstrating that far from turning its back on modernism in the way Jacqueline Rose claims, children's literature – and particularly in the form of the picturebook – has actively explored its concepts and styles, in the process providing precisely the kind of arena for radical experiments Dusinberre describes.

Several of the writers most closely associated with literary modernism tried their hands at writing for children. Though the short pieces I discuss briefly below have received little acclaim or had any obviously enduring influence, they are nevertheless useful indicators of how Virginia Woolf, James Joyce, and Gertrude Stein conceived and addressed the child reader. They were not the only writers of their generation to produce books for children, or even the most successful at addressing a juvenile audience: e.e. cummings, Walter de la Mare, Graham Greene, Aldous Huxley, D.H. Lawrence, and John Masefield, for instance, all wrote for children at some point in their careers. However, the three writers I have selected were leading figures in literary modernism and their work is often concerned with the sensibilities of childhood. They thus provide a useful base for comparing how modernist writers perceived children's literature and how writers and illustrators who concentrated on producing work for children responded to the modernist aesthetic and ethos. Additionally, their children's stories highlight distinctions between the aesthetic appropriation of childhood as theme, inspiration, or perspective, and writing for children.

Modernism for children

Virginia Woolf: *Nurse Lugton's Golden Thimble* (1923–1924)

Nurse Lugton's Golden Thimble with illustrations by Duncan Grant was published in 1966 by the Hogarth Press, having been discovered, as Leonard Woolf recounts in his foreword to the book, by Wallace Hildick in the manuscript pages of *Mrs. Dalloway* the previous year. Hildick, himself a writer for both adults and children, was attracted by a list of animal names on the back of one of the manuscript pages, and gradually realised, as he wrote to Leonard Woolf, that 'this 700–800-word passage … is actually a complete nursery story – and an absolutely delightful one at that'.[1] In 1991 the book was reissued as *Nurse Lugton's Curtain* with illustrations by the Australian artist, Julie Vivas.

Written for Woolf's niece, Anna Stephenson, who stayed with them while Virginia was writing *Mrs. Dalloway* (1923–1924), the piece was not intended for publication; however, as Wallace Hildick wrote to Leonard Woolf, together with 'one or two hints in Mrs. Woolf's essays' it shows that 'she had an uncommonly sympathetic grasp of the essentials of children's fiction (in her piece on Carroll, for instance)' (21 January 1965).

The story takes an everyday subject: Nurse Lugton is making a curtain out of fabric with an animal pattern. She falls asleep over her sewing, and as she dreams, the animals – who believe her to be an ogress who is imprisoning them through the act of stitching – temporarily escape from the material. The point of view shifts from omniscient narration to animal characters, inviting the reader to reinterpret the events and to see an alternative and vital world in what had previously been a mundane task. But the shift is less simple than it first appears since the animals' escape is entirely dependent on Nurse Lugton: they are only free while she dreams, and she dreams their freedom and autonomy.

Although a short piece, it contains traces of modernism in its setting, interests, and Woolf's characteristic phrasing and saturated use of language. Lines such as, 'Really it was a beautiful sight – and to think of it all, lying across old Nurse Lugton's knees, as she snored, on her Windsor chair in the lamplight. … ' could come straight from the pages of *Mrs. Dalloway*. The simple statement 'Nurse Lugton was asleep' (4) is redolent with significance for the animals who are released from their inert state by her dream, and for Nurse Lugton herself, whose interior reveals wild and active emotions concealed by her stolid exterior.

The dream motif reflects the modernist concern with the inner world of the self and the operation of the psyche, at the same time gesturing towards such typical interests of literary modernism as the potential of narrative to convey the subjective and shifting experience of time passing (how is dream time measured?), shifting and unexpected points of view, and the possibility of representing the random and simultaneous nature of events in writing. All of these concerns demand changes to traditional ways of telling stories, and they are considerably enhanced by the transformation of Woolf's text into a picturebook, with the opportunities this provides to accentuate and create gaps between word and image and to create ironic counterpoints between what is said and what is shown. For instance, Vivas, working at a time when modernist ideas had been widely assimilated, picks up on the modernist interest in extending the remit of realism to include the reality of the inner experience when she shows the animals breaking away from their fabric reality into the more real world of the fantasy, where they visit watering holes and speculate about the terrible Lugton's powers. In the same way, a succession of illustrators have done much to develop the modernist elements in James Joyce's contribution to children's literature.

James Joyce: *The Cat and the Devil* (1936)

> My dear Stevie,
>
> I sent you a little cat filled with sweets a few days ago but perhaps you do not know the story about the cat of Beaugency.
>
> (James Joyce, letter to his grandson,
> 10 August 1936 in Ellmann: 384–5)

The letter from James Joyce to his four-year-old grandson Stephen, the beginning of which is quoted on the endpapers of *The Cat and the Devil*, offers the first of several insights into the differences between work that is intensely informed by recollected childhood experience and something by the same writer addressed specifically to a child. Joyce and Stevie were close, and the fact that the letter is taken up with telling a story suggests that like many writers, and, indeed, his father before him, Joyce found telling stories a congenial way to interact with a beloved child (see Coghlan, 2005: 1). We can only speculate about this, however, since *The Cat and the Devil* is the only known example of a children's story by Joyce, although much of his most famous work includes a child's perspective and shows detailed knowledge of childhood games and culture (see, for instance, Eckley, 1985; Gmuca, 2005).

Since *The Cat and the Devil* was written near the end of Joyce's life and forms part of a letter rather than a work intended for publication, it is clearly not an example of the way children's literature provides a space in which a writer experiments at a formative stage with ideas and styles. Nonetheless, the way some characteristic elements of Joyce's best-known works are incorporated in the story make it relevant for a discussion of the relationship between children's literature and modernism. For instance, although set in

France, the story includes a thinly disguised version of Alfie Byrne, who had been Lord Mayor of Dublin for six of his record nine years in that office at the time the story was written. In this case, the devil, who has been reading about the difficulty the town of Beaugency has had in trying to build a bridge over the river Loire, 'came to call on the lord mayor of Beaugency, who was named Monsieur Alfred Byrne'. Byrne, who reputedly enjoyed appearing in his robes and chain of office, is also evoked in *Finnegans Wake* (alfi byrni), while Leopold Bloom imagines himself as decked out in the manner of Byrne, 'imposing in mayoral scarlet, gold chain and white silk tie' (Coghlan, 2005: 2).

Joyce's interest in traditional tales – the myths, legends, folktales, nursery rhymes, and ballads that help bind his most complex novels together – is evident in his decision to retell a tale using a 'long ago' setting as well as in his devil, whose character and behaviour are familiar from a number of similar tales. Perhaps most redolent of Joyce's adult style is the way the humour in this short piece arises from idiosyncrasies of language including in how it is spoken, the connections between sound and sense, and the potential for and consequences of semantic slippages. The opening passages of *A Portrait of the Artist as a Young Man*, where Stephen's thoughts come out as fragments of stories, songs, sounds, and sensations, testify to the fact that Joyce was a close observer of (and himself recalled) the young child's pleasure in responding to and playing with words, meanings, and rhythm.

The Cat and the Devil exhibits the same pleasure in and ability to derive humour and social observation from language. For instance, though the story ends conventionally enough with the reassurance that 'the bridge is there still and there are boys walking and riding and playing upon it', Joyce adds a PS which Roger Blachon, one of the many illustrators who have turned the letter into a picturebook (Coghlan lists five: Richard Erdoes (1964); Gerald Rose (1965); Jan de Tusch-Lec (1976); Roger Balchon (1978); Péter Vladimir (1997)), places on the final end papers where it balances the letter to Dear Stevie that appears on the inside front cover. The note explains that

> The devil mostly speaks a language of his own called Bellybabble [sic; in the original it is Bellsybabble] which he makes up himself as he goes along but when he is very angry he can speak bad French quite well, though some who have heard him, say that he has a strong Dublin accent.

The devil would seem to be one of Joyce's last self-portraits, and in this simple story he gestures discretely at his own work: like Alfie Byrne, the devil's private, apparently nonsensical language, Bellsybabble, is also mentioned in *Finnegans Wake*. In Stevie's story it takes the form of a light-hearted allusion to the way Joyce anticipated some critics would react to his own use of language in that text, rejecting it as a stream of personal nonsense that he made up as he went along. This joke in a children's book, then, conveys awareness of the challenges his version of modernism posed, and at the same time suggests Joyce's conviction that like the bridge, his work will be used for generations to come.

Gertrude Stein: *The World Is Round* (1939)

Gertrude Stein's *The World Is Round* differs from the examples of Woolf and Joyce in the way it deliberately incorporates a wide selection of the devices, ideas, and interests that drive and shape her work for adults. Indeed, Natov sees the story as embodying 'the aesthetic principles of the modernist hybrid form in an extended children's nursery rhyme and picture book' (2003: 5). Another important difference is that Stein always intended for the work to be published.

The World Is Round was written during the most active period in Gertrude Stein's career, and forms a recognised part of her oeuvre. Like Joyce, Stein employs elements associated with a traditional form, the accumulative tale (Natov: 104), but where he adopts the tone and style of the folktale for his young reader, rarely straying outside its conventions, she makes few concessions to children and employs many of the stylistic devices found in her writing for adults; indeed, at one level the text can be seen as an elaborate game based on what has become her best-known line, 'A rose is a rose. ...'

Stein's writing is informed by the modernists' concern with recovering the ability to see and experience the world with the freshness associated with childhood imagination: what Baudelaire described as 'all life in miniature, and much more vivid in colour, cleaner and shinier than real life' (in Warner, 2005: 4). This is no sweetly innocent vision of childhood, however; Stein's Rose inhabits a world of spontaneous but uncontrolled emotions and events. It can be overwhelming and disturbing, unruly and unsafe as well as delightful and vital.

In many ways Rose embodies the Surrealist concept of the child as 'the ideal alter ego of artists and poets, the medium of transgression, fantasy, sexuality, inspiration and the chief banner-carrier in the mortal struggle against the bourgeoisie' (Warner, 2005: 13), a symbol with which Stein would have been thoroughly familiar. It is not surprising, therefore, that in her energetic engagement with what she saw as the necessary revivification of the arts, Gertrude Stein recognised the importance of addressing the future generation as well as those currently responsible for culture. Doing so was not a simple investment in the future, but a recognition that children are not outside culture, and that through their interactions with adults and institutions, and in their roles as sons and daughters, pupils and consumers, they regard, respond to, and affect the world around them more than is often acknowledged in the fine arts.

Like many of the most active and influential modernist writers and artists, many of whom she knew well and worked with in various capacities, Stein focused on the child's relationship with language, which she saw as enviably spontaneous and free from the deadening accretions of meaning that contaminate adult speech and writing. A central tenet of the literary modernist sensibility held that language is a clumsy way of representing reality which, especially in classic realist novels, often seduces readers into sharing the world view of the writer. In *The World Is Round*, Stein mobilises some of the characteristics of writing for children and children's experiments with language to suggest ways in which over-familiar, over-burdened language and literary forms can be renewed and replenished. Her strategies include unconventional phrasing, syntax, and structure. (Rather ironically, Stein's entirely modernist view is very much in accordance with Rose's argument that the child in children's literature stands for a time when language was pure.)

The story is not obviously orchestrated by an omniscient author or narrating persona; the events often seem dreamlike and random, controlled almost entirely by increasing patterns of sound, achieving an effect Stein strove for in all her writing: 'shattering … the notion of an "organic" or "natural" or "necessary" connection between signifier and signified' (DeKoven in Natov, 104). While her linguistic experimentation in itself was not new to this work, *The World Is Round* shows clearly the modernist interest in the 'primitive', unschooled and playful aspects of childhood, and Stein enters new territory here by exploiting the potential of format and medium through conceiving it as a visual text – a text in which illustrations and design are part of the overall conception.

Reading *The World Is Round* is a synaesthetic experience: sounds and colours contain and evoke each other and make up character ('Rose knew that in Rose there was an o and an o is round', 106). The 'round' in the title is repeated in the typography, design and phrasing, and the very structure of the narrative is circular as it begins with a statement of what Rose knows and then follows her on a journey to discover what she knows. She achieves this understanding over time and seemingly in response to her initial series of questions about why she is a girl called Rose, when and where she is Rose, ending with a 'line' in which question is followed by answer and answer by question so that it turns back on itself: 'And which little girl am I am I I the little girl named Rose which little girl named Rose' (6).

Before she can recognise herself as Rose, she must struggle through a period of confusion, when the understanding that language is arbitrary throws her sense of self-identity into jeopardy (see the discussion of nonsense in Chapter 3). Emerging from this chaos, she finally declares herself 'Rose'. Her stable identity, achieved through considerable effort and at a cost, the text implies, though it also acknowledges that not to achieve it is intolerable, is given form when she carves a circle made up of the words, 'Rose is a Rose is a Rose is a Rose is a Rose' on a tree.[2] The endless circle signifies wholeness, so mentally it is a small step to 'the top of everything' where Rose chants the lines that stake her claim to self-knowledge and her challenge to others to make this rite of passage: 'I am Rose my eyes are blue/I am Rose and who are you/I am Rose and when I sing/I am Rose like anything' (136).

Natov makes a satisfying reading of the story as an exploration of the movement from the inarticulacy of infancy through the acquisition of identity and subjectivity via language through gendered socialisation (Rose's story is complemented by the adventures of the boy, Willie). I am more concerned with the modernist characteristics of the prose, and the contribution of the illustrators, Clement Hurd (1939) and Roberta Arenson (1993). The extent to which *The World Is Round* was conceived as a visual text is evident in the way the words, images, and design echo and extend each other. Roberta Arenson's updating of the book makes use of simple images that look as if they have been printed with blocks, while the book's tiny format gives it an attractive, toy-like quality that sits well with the modernist interest in the objects of childhood – an interest that was fully explored in Marina Warner's 'Only make believe' exhibition and accompanying catalogue (2005).

Stein's illustrated story is a fully fledged example of modernist children's literature written nearly half a century before Rose proclaimed that children's literature rejected modernism. Since Stein and Woolf both briefly taught illustrator and editor Margaret Wise Brown, one of the most loved and influential figures in the history of publishing for children in the United States and who commissioned Stein to write *The World is Round*, the book can be regarded as the beginning of a strong modernist vein in twentieth-century children's publishing in that country. Outside the United States even greater modernist activity was taking place in the creation of books for children; especially among some of the most progressive artists and writers, collectively known as the 'avant-garde'.

Avant-Garde influences

> The avant-garde harps on the theme of the child. It has created a kind of religion for his sensibilities and imaginative powers, into which it reads its own better moods. It believes that the dreamlike state of mind in which it specializes and which it interprets with primitive graphic signs, is part and parcel of the child's daily routine. In creating for the child it has trusted in his being all prehistoric art plasma, and nothing of a bloodthirsty young savage.
>
> (Averill, 1930: 89)

The centrality of the child to the modernist sensibility has been discussed at some length; the work of avant-garde artists stands apart because it was not merely interested in childhood but also in creating work specifically for the young. The result is what Esther Averill, writing about French avant-garde illustrations for children in 1930, recognised as 'a blending of fine literature and fine art' resulting in 'milestones in aesthetics' (90).

Averill had in mind the one-off productions by artists such as Joan Miro, whose illustrations in the Surrealist style for *Il était une Petite Pie* (1928) 'are springboards into a dream state, where the private imagination, supposed to be functioning at top speed with the child, weaves in whatever anecdote the individual may require' (89). While much of the most important work in this area was done by European writers and artists, the circulation of artists in the first four decades of that century – particularly in the years leading up to and during the Second World War – was such that many eventually ended up working in the United States and publishing in English.

Among the most dynamic centres of avant-garde activity for children was post-Revolutionary Russia. Under Lenin, Soviet avant-garde artists participated with enthusiasm in projects which promoted the goals and aspirations of what they hoped would be a new world order. This activity reached its peak in the *Okna Rosta*, a huge publicity campaign which used posters to educate the public by disseminating and winning approval for the ideas emanating from the government and its institutions. The *Okna Rosta* combined striking graphic images and very short pieces of text so that they could be understood by every member of society, including those who were effectively illiterate or preliterate. A related area of publishing activity was the creation of picturebooks for the children of the USSR.

Both the *Okna Rosta* and the children's picturebooks of this period share the characteristics of being mass-produced yet exemplifying some of the best in contemporary art and design. Their success owed much to the contributions of the artists, but the production process itself was also instrumental in generating books that had popular appeal as well as artistic merit. As Averill observed at the time 'the fitful brilliance' of French avant-garde artists might have made a greater impression if it had been subject to the Soviet production regime in which

the most modern of artists are working out the problems of the children's book, but before projects are worked up for actual publication, they are submitted to groups of ten children – sometimes as many as thirty such groups – for criticism. (90)

Early Soviet children's books clearly show how comfortably modernist styles and ideas could be directed at the young. Because the books were produced in huge numbers, they were highly affordable, and many survive in private and institutional collections making it relatively easy to find striking examples of books that applaud the new Soviet philosophy and aspirations: workers are celebrated as are everyday activities and organised groups (rather than heroic individuals). The splendour of machines, industrialisation, the military, and urban life are captured in images and text that variously draw on styles and theories derived from Futurism, Cubism, Suprematism, and Expressionism to evoke impressions of the sounds, patterns, and rhythms of modern life – all in an energetic and approving manner. Dockyards and theatres, marching armies and factory floors, women builders and mighty cranes are juxtaposed to create a sense of vision, purpose, and collective enterprise.

What is perhaps most striking is the complementary – even symbiotic – relationship between people, animals and technology. In Alexander Deineka's *Parad Krasnoi Armii* [The Parade of the Red Army, 1931], for instance, women are shown striding out on a sunny day in their gas masks (the sun itself looks as if it has been lifted from a child's drawing, while the women resemble both television aliens and elephants) on one page; on others, men and tanks are placed together in images designed to underscore the impressiveness of each. Speeding motorcyclists and cheering crowds convey energy and movement on the ground, while overhead, messenger pigeons and an airplane circle. Because birds and plane are shown as much the same size, with wings nearly touching, the intended message of harmonious symbiosis between nature and machine is unmistakable.

The cover of Boris Pokrovskii's 1928 *Dikovinki* [Wonderful Things] is characteristic of illustrations of the period with it buildings in bright colours that look as if they could have been assembled using a Meccano or other child's construction set. Despite their modernist credentials and their references to toys, little play or playfulness is evident in most of these post-Revolutionary works. They may be dynamic visually, but overall these books are earnest in tone and committed to showing the collective engagement by all members of society in creating the new Union.

When disillusionment about the Soviet project began to set in among those artists who continued to live and work in the USSR, their use of objects and styles associated with children became highly political. At this point the writers and artists associated with the avant-garde set out to expose the illogic and excesses of contemporary society not least by exploiting the opportunities for humour and social critique provided by picturebooks. In her doctoral thesis '*in fant non sens*: The Infantilist Aesthetic of the Russian Avant-Garde, 1909–39', Sarah Pankenier argues that the avant-garde and childhood are linked through their interest in play and exploration (2004: 1) and that this led some writers, among them Daniil Kharms and other members of the avant-garde group known as OBERIU (Union of Real Art), to write 'almost exclusively for children for the final period of their activity' (1).

Significantly, while equally committed to the principles of contemporary art as those involved in the mass-produced, officially approved books for children published in the decade after the Revolution,[3] Kharms and his set seem to have used the implied audience of children as a shield behind which to voice their most severe criticisms. Pankenier suggests that their interest in play was a response to increasing levels of repression in Soviet Russia, though this interpretation does not take into account the extent to which other branches of modernism also embraced play and childhood.

The members of OBERIU wrote and performed for adults as well as for children, but their living came from the children's books they produced – when openly addressing adults they were accused of 'counter revolutionary activities' by those who saw 'The illogic of their work ... as a deliberate attempt to confuse the proletariat' (Ostashevsky, 3). Whether or not this was their political aim, as avant-garde artists the group certainly set out, if not to confuse, at least to confound those who relied on well-trodden paths for interpreting the arts.[4] The avant-garde as a movement deliberately refused connections between the elements in their work and tried to eliminate obvious themes and meaning, even (or particularly) at the level of language. Words are not always attached to the things they are normally agreed to represent: the signifier and the signified are set loose in what can seem like meaningless creations providing a glimpse into a communication void (these practices have much in common with the work of nonsense makers discussed in the next chapter).

Jean-François Lyotard, by contrast, suggests that the focus on avant-garde activity as anarchic obscures the fact that avant-garde artists were not merely iconoclasts attempting to dismantle the habits of tradition and alerting other artists and spectators to the false promises of 'truth' made in the name of realism; they also uncovered and put in place new rules. Precisely because the avant-garde by definition pushes back the boundaries of the known and understood, however, these rules tend not to be recognised at the time, so that it is only with hindsight that their influence on subsequent generations becomes clear.[5]

Perhaps the Soviet authorities of the time objected to the aesthetic vision implicit in the first phase of avant-garde activity and which they could not fathom; perhaps it was the irreverent attitude to established institutions and their representatives that grated, or perhaps they objected to the lifestyle associated with the avant-garde. Whatever the reason, eventually Kharms and all the other members of the group died prematurely in ways that seem connected to official disapproval.[6] Before this happened, however, Kharms in particular had produced a number of picturebooks that exhibit modernist concerns. For instance, through their nonsense games, which involve repeating and recombining words, and their privileging of rhythm over obvious sense, his books eschew linearity and test ideas of consequence and sequence. Kharms also destabilises perspective and credibility when, for instance, he shows young children being accepted as adults through the ludicrous 'disguise' of wearing a false beard, though in every other sense they are clearly recognisable as children. His books present a Gogol-like world of self-interested, self-deluding characters who have little grasp on any of the key events taking place around them.

Importantly for child readers, Kharms's work displays respect for and enjoyment of the modes of childhood interaction and understanding, and a determination to provoke readers of all ages to think about what it means to use language (as opposed to, say, mime, puppets, dance, or illustrations) to tell a story. The uses and abuses of language are very clear in Kharms's tales, and in this way he alerts child readers to 'the autonomy and artificiality of the artistic text' (7), and beyond that, to the way language can be manipulated by those in positions of power and authority.

Daniil Kharms was one of those literary figures whose work was published in the United States in the 1960s. Another writer associated with the avant-garde beyond the USSR, who shares Kharms's focus on language and whose work was transformed into wonderfully inventive picturebooks at that time is Eugene Ionesco.[7] While his stories are discussed in detail in Chapter 3, it is worth noting here that he had a life-time interest in the condition of childhood and this directly fed his later, more celebrated writing for adults. Ionesco's first published work was a collection of poetry for children, *Elegii pentru finite mici* [Elegies for small beings], written in 1931 when he was just 19, and his little-known paintings and lithographs depict 'little crooked manikins – vividly coloured, or simply reduced to dark silhouettes – who dance and play, take a walk with their family, fight (purposelessly), go to school, engage in sports, run' in an obviously child-like style (Debattista, 2005: 20–21).[8]

Elegii pentru finite mici shows Ionesco working out themes and ideas that are fully realised in his later work including 'man as marionette, death, nostalgia for the lost paradise of childhood, and language' (19). Here is an excellent example of an artist who finds his voice through writing for children and for whom the domain of children's literature acts as both a reservoir into which he can dip for material, and a crucible in which ideas, jokes, images, and formal ideas about style and structure can be mingled so that they take on new properties and react differently when set on the page. Dipping into the reservoir of children's literature often takes the form of drawing inspiration from the objects and culture of childhood in which children's books have traditionally held a central position.

Children's books and childhood culture

The role and nature of the book in the culture of childhood took on new significance in the hands of those whose interest in modernist ideas were primarily directed to creating books for children rather than with drawing on childhood as part of an evolving modernist aesthetic. A book is not a toy, yet there are many ways in which books function as toys. Major historical collections of children's books recognise this fact when they include toys, cards, paper dolls, and theatres and games; often the boundaries between books and such items are very unclear. With this in mind it is worth thinking about the accusations levelled against toys by Roland Barthes in his essay on the subject before moving on to look at some examples of picturebooks that fuse the interests and needs of modernism and children's literature.

Although 'Toys' was written more than thirty years ago and much has changed in Western toy industries since then, nevertheless certain of the charges it contains continue to have force. I am thinking specifically of Barthes's claim that toys which faithfully reproduce the adult world reduce the child to a mere owner-user who can never take up the position of creator-inventor (1984: 55). There are untold numbers of children's books that function like the toys Barthes condemns; even an active, experienced reader is likely to accept the premises, settle into the conventions, and develop empathic relationships with characters in those books that make up the mainstream of writing for children – indeed doing so may be a source of pleasure and satisfaction for readers of any age, though doing so makes the reader highly susceptible to a book's world view. Positioning young readers in ways that encourage acceptance of generally approved ways of thinking about how society is organised and operates contributes to the process of acculturation. But this reading position is not inevitable, and there are many outstanding examples of picturebooks in particular that not only invite but require readers to join forces with the author and illustrator (or author-illustrator) to make meaning; in other words, readers of such books are not mere users of the kind Barthes deplores but creators, interpreters and innovators. A particularly good example of such a book is *The Book about Moomin, Mymble and Little My* (1952).

The Book about Moomin, Mymble and Little My was Finnish author-illustrator Tove Jansson's first picturebook, but by the time it appeared, she was already well established as the author of the Moomin books. It is regarded as a significant contribution to children's literature in all the Nordic countries, and has recently been reissued in the United Kingdom as a 'children's classic'. While Joyce, Woolf, and Stein were instrumental in shaping literary modernism, Jansson was working at a time when its precepts were well established, some even to the point of being popularised and parodied. Nevertheless, in 1952 the modernist aesthetic was still firmly associated with an intellectual elite, and perhaps because many of its proponents were associated with bohemian lifestyles – characterised as immoderate and unstable in their relationships, sexualities, political opinions, and affiliations; erratic in their parenting and unconventional in their fashions, tastes, and attitudes to domestic life – they tended to be kept apart from the world of childhood. In fact, the best-known association between modernism and childhood was the charge frequently levelled at extreme examples of modernist art and letters, that 'any child could do it'.

Jansson's book is an unapologetic – indeed a playful and celebratory – response to modernism for children. This is evident in such things as the emphasis on the act of telling the story through the medium of the book – how it is told is much more important than what actually happens. Jansson calls attention to the fabric of the text and its status as fiction through witty use of peritetxtual elements and by exploring the natures of paper and handheld books as media. For example, the endpaper (recto) carries a drawing of a publisher with a large pair of scissors in one hand, pointing at an actual hole cut into the paper under the announcement 'The holes are cut at Schildts!' There is no attempt here to disguise the fact that the book is a mechanically reproduced product: the work normally hidden behind the publisher's imprint and the information in minute type about where it was printed and by whom becomes part of the text itself. At the same time, the status of its characters is subtly called into question: if the publisher is now a character in the book, does this mean that he is in some sense no longer Real? Or that the characters too have a life outside its pages?[9]

Another way in which the book calls attention to itself is through the use of cut-out sections, beginning with the hole to which the publisher directs the reader. All of the pages in this text (most of which are organised as double-page spreads) include some kind of cut-away section – these are of different sizes and shapes and found in different places on the pages – that physically leads the eye both back to the previous page and forward to the next. Where pictures normally represent a moment of frozen time, this device allows more than one time to exist simultaneously on a single spread resulting in a visual rendering of past, present, and future: memory, now, and speculative daydream. Modernist writers had to resort to complexly layered prose to achieve this effect; Jansson's use of the picturebook format is devastatingly simple and effective.

The cut-outs serve a textual purpose as well as engaging with intellectual and aesthetic puzzles about the representation of time and memory. Mymble's little sister, Little My, has gone missing, and Moomintroll is helping Mymble to look for her. At one level the gaps provide places to hide and in which to look, at another, they explore the spatial relationships on the page and between pages, adding to the feelings of anxiety about what has happened to Little My. As Elina Drucker (2004) observes:

> The complexity of the form and the changing mode of spatial and temporal relations express a strong feeling of disorder, a disorder that is gradually revealed as we enter this distinctive narrative space. The shifting visual experiences of the landscape, and of space as such, can be compared to the fantasy worlds created by Lewis Carroll ... or to Dante's *The Divine Comedy*, where the changes of the nightmarish environment express the underlying themes of searching and identity. (2)

Just as the cut-outs break down temporal and spatial linearity, so Jansson's use of typography breaks down the conventional division between text and image. The text changes size and style to reflect character, mood and action: Little My's name is shown in little text, for instance; the word 'TALL' is made taller than the other words, while the word 'F L A T' is printed to convey flatness. In the same way, when the text reads, 'They search and search but find no trace' the words move up and down to mimic the activity of searching high and low. Although this book is not a toy, a significant part of its intention is to activate the child's propensity to play, including playing with the nature of books.

When learning to read, children become familiar with the conventions of the book: the cover, title page, index, blurb, information about the author, and so on. They quickly learn that in most books the 'real' story begins on the first page. Jansson here introduces an aspect of picturebook making that has become central to the work of many contemporary illustrators, a number of whom were children when *The Book about Moomin, Mymble and Little My* first appeared, which is the inclusion of peritextual features (covers, endpapers, dedication, title page – even the page containing such details as the publisher's information, Library of Congress catalogue number, ISBN) in the body of the text.

At every level then, the book calls attention to itself as a book in the same way that those associated with modernism called attention to the conventions of their art forms. Jansson plays with time and space, questions the divisions between fiction and reality, and uses colour, images, typography, and design to create a sense in the reader of how the character feels without resorting to authorial pronouncements. The reader has to activate these qualities by examining the pages, looking through holes, turning pages backwards and forwards, responding to tones and shapes; in other words, Jansson invites readers of all ages to join in the activity of textual creation and experimentation.

The Book about Moomin, Mymble and Little My was innovative in its day, and its aesthetic vision for the picturebook continues to seem contemporary half a century later. Another picturebook maker whose work embraces modernism is Swiss artist Warja Lavater. Lavater trained and studied at the École des Arts et Métiers in Zurich and acknowledges her roots in modernist movements such as the Bauhaus (Beckett, 55). Her interpretations of well-known tales take the form of friezes of the kind often used to decorate the walls of nurseries and young children's classrooms – they consist of long accordion pleats rather than bound pages. She plays not only with the physical properties of books, but also with the language of storytelling – each of her 'books' retells the story in images alone; only the key or legend at the beginning of each text incorporates words (in several languages, sometimes shown together, sometimes individually, depending on the edition) to establish what the symbols represent. In *Snow White* (1974), for instance, Snow White is shown as a circle 'as red as blood' surrounded by one 'as white as snow' outlined by a ring 'as black as ebony'. The seven dwarves are represented by seven red diamond shapes; the wicked Queen by a black circle surrounded by a golden circle or 'crown', and the mirror is a golden frame around a blank white centre. Although the stories are rendered pictorially, Lavater regards herself as an author rather than an illustrator.[10]

Like Jansson, Lavater shares the modernist interest in the physical characteristics of books and the way these contribute to – but also conventionalise – how narrative works. In these tales she alters the rhythm and expectations associated with the page turn to create continuous text. Her decision not to bind the books encourages readers to look at several images simultaneously, moving back and forward between them as part of the reading/decoding process. The effect of this alters both the temporal and spatial relations that would have been created by bound pages, though these can be experienced by turning over the folds in the hand in the manner of a conventionally bound book rather than opening out the complete text. When spread out on a table or mounted as a frieze, the images also invite reader-viewers to ignore the sequence and focus on smaller sections of the tale, depending on where they are standing in relation to it.

The modernist aesthetic, with its interests in expressionism, abstraction, form and play, clearly shapes Lavater's picturebooks and gives them an appeal that crosses the barriers of age, class, sex, and language. In many ways, Lavater's series of fairy tales can be seen as the apotheosis of the modernist project; however, her work not only encapsulates key principles and characteristics of modernist thinking about the visual arts, but also anticipates ideas about narrative structure and organisation that have come to fruition in electronic texts – such things as interactivity, fusions of visual and verbal narrative modes, and disruptions to sequencing. This kind of anticipation shaped the context in which contemporary picturebooks and digital technologies began to come together and is now resulting in a new generation of picturebooks. With this in mind, the final section of this discussion looks at the legacy of modernism manifest in the way picturebooks are interacting with digital/electronic media to re-envisage the possibilities of the picturebook as a narrative medium. As part of this development, some of those who are currently creating picturebooks are introducing ideas that many adults find challenging, and doing so in ways which I believe are preparing readers to advance thinking about self and society in philosophically and aesthetically exciting ways. These range from purpose-free, ludic creativity to radical questioning of how new technologies and changing environments affect the human psyche. Where much fiction about cyberspace and new technologies currently falls short of positive engagement with new technologies (see Chapter 8), picturebook makers are referencing and drawing on characteristics of new media at the levels of narration, design and the text–reader dynamic in ways that recall the modernists' excitement about machines, new technology, and the future of culture.

Picturebook responses to new media

Contemporary picturebooks are responding to new media and technologies through experiments in form and format in ways that are significantly affecting the aesthetics of visual narratives. British author-illustrator Sara Fanelli's *Dear Diary* (2000) encapsulates these changes and also shows the influences of modernism and postmodernism in its use of collage, found objects, and bricolage.

The story is primarily concerned with the effects of shifting point of view on narrative; it is told from a variety of perspectives through the diaries of eight characters: the little girl Lucy, a chair in her classroom, a spider on the ceiling, a firefly, a fork and knife, Lucy's dog Bubu, and a ladybird. In many ways, Fanelli evokes the familiar worlds of home and school that have been the staple fare of children's books since they began, and there are no overt references to new technologies or media – indeed, there is an almost old-fashioned feel to the world shown, partly arising from the pages of the 1921 diary that feature on the endpapers and some of the background pages. Nevertheless, Fanelli's work assimilates many attributes of new media. This can be seen in the way she organises her pages and merges text and image.

Traditionally picturebooks have reflected the cultural priority given to language – and to the fact that young readers are in the process of acquiring linguistic competency – in their design. They have tended to be organised like a page of text, read from top to bottom, left to right, with images organised to make up a usually chronological sequence. *Dear Diary*, however, incorporates many of the principles associated with the screen-based media that now dominate popular culture – especially the computer screen. Screens are not organised by the logic of print, but the logic of icons and principles of visualisation (Kress, 2003: 138). What you 'read' first is what is visually prominent, and young people conversant with the narrative structures and hermeneutics of computer games intuitively know that information will be organised spatially rather than in chains. This means that instead of assuming that a page or double page spread should be decoded from top left to bottom right, with the printed text treated as the primary source of information, they know to move around the page, assembling information including subplots and clues that may only be activated later in the text. Just as in a computer game, when this happens it is necessary to track back to join up the subsidiary storylines or add crucial information. This is a roundabout, back and forth process rather than a linear, front to back one.

A benefit of breaking the hegemony of linearity is that it opens up new ways to render time and action on the page. Where once children's texts tended to provide very clear information about time and to measure it by external symbols such as clocks and meals, as Fanelli's text shows, time on the page can be depicted in terms of experience and emotion: how events feel as they happen, whether this reflects pace, duration, awareness of simultaneity or parallel events, inner states or reactions to others. In *Dear Diary*, this aspect of the text is emphasised through the use of multiple viewpoints and page design, though the text also provides a standard chronological dimension in that it starts in the morning and ends in the evening.

A good example is found on the second double page spread which forms part of Lucy's diary. The eye is immediately drawn to the large, exuberant figure of

Figure 2.1   From Sara Fanelli's *Dear Diary*

Lucy that fills much of the right-hand page (Figure 2.1). It shows her running and waving her arms. Then the image of Bubu, her dog, registers. Bubu is placed in the top left-hand corner, just below some text (handwritten as if by Lucy) including his name in large letters. Having arrived at some text, it's time to read, 'It was getting late but I still took BUBU out to the park to PLAY'. The words are very much a part of the overall design and image, but at the same time they provide and confirm information that is absent from the various drawings that make up this spread. Indeed, additional words label and comment on some of the drawings: Bubu's friends, clouds, the pond, and Lucy's friend Amy. The emotional importance of each to the events being shown is suggested by the size and proximity to Lucy; at the same time, there are many small, unidentified characters and unexplained objects that seem incidental until they reappear on other pages, setting off one of the backwards and forwards comparisons of pages that develops a discrete subplot.

The organisation of the page not only provides information about how Lucy feels about the place and the other characters in it, but also conveys a sense of simultaneous action: Lucy's friend Amy is playing by the pond with her father at the same time that Bubu is playing with his friends, some people are sheltering under umbrellas from an isolated rain storm, and Lucy is running past some flowers. Two tiny vignettes create a separate time frame around the image: in the lower-middle of the left-hand page we see Lucy and Bubu arriving at the park. She is on her bicycle and he is running behind her on his lead. They move in a left-to-right direction, which Western readers recognise as indicating entry and the initiation of action. The top of the right-hand page shows this image in reverse, with Lucy and Bubu riding into the gutter, so leaving the action and retracing their journey. This one image, then, uses spatial organisation familiar from screens and icons to establish multiple times, set up several interconnected plots, convey emotion and experience, and adds information about the plot.

Another contemporary illustrator whose work shows clear evidence that picturebooks are using elements of electronic media to devise new forms of storytelling on the page is Lauren Child. Like Fanelli, Child works with mixed media, incorporating real objects and materials (through collage and digital images) as well as hand-drawn and computer-generated illustrations in the pages of her books. The effect is to raise questions about what is real, and also to challenge the conventions or thresholds of what Gerard Genette termed the 'paratext', referring to the extratextual elements of books such as the author's name, the title, endpapers, and illustrations (Genette, 2001).

I would say that the most radical experiments with paratextual elements are taking place in children's books, and especially picturebooks, and Child's work demonstrates this well. A good example is her use of the narrating persona's voice on the covers, in what would normally belong to the domain of the epitext, generated outside the text itself, and in the way she plays with the status of the official threshold to the narrative, the title page. In *What Planet Are You from, Clarice Bean* (2002), for instance, there is a page that looks like a title page followed by what looks like the beginning of the text. But just as with films and television dramas such as *ER*, where the credits often follow an introductory episode, so the page turn reveals that the book has not actually begun because what it discloses are the acknowledgements (not the usual, formal, essentially invisible bits of information but made up of personal comments, photographs and other ways of making them more prominent and meaningful to readers) and a second, more detailed 'title page' which also contains the beginning of the story. The effect of each of these disruptions to the way books normally operate is, curiously, to enhance the interpellation effect by establishing a collusive relationship with Clarice Bean. This, we are asked to believe, is the world as it is experienced by Clarice.

While Child and Fanelli are experimenting with ways of storytelling and exploring the aesthetic potential of combining elements from electronic media and picturebooks, at the level of plot and content their work is essentially conventional. There are, however, a small number of contemporary picturebook makers who are using the form to raise some extremely interesting philosophical questions and introduce some challenging concepts. American author-illustrator David Wiesner is one of these. *The Three Pigs'* (2001) can be seen as a typical example of Wiesner's inventive use of fantasy, but it also strikes me as providing a way of thinking about the domain that Lacan calls the 'Real', or that which exists but is 'undefined, unaccountable, perhaps, within the frameworks of our knowledge' (Belsey, 2005: 5).

Imaging the Real

Wiesner's picturebook is based on the familiar tale of the three pigs who defeat the wolf who huffs and puffs to blow their houses down; this use of a pretext is central to the games the text plays with meaning, most of which depend on readers knowing what 'should' happen. Familiarity with the original works on several levels, from knowing the traditional tale to knowing the genre in which it fits and even knowing the medium – what a book is and how it works.

It begins in the usual way: 'Once upon a time there were three pigs who went out into the world to seek their fortune', and the initial illustration too feels familiar, being a pastiche of 1950s/1960s picturebook art. But with the first page turn everything changes; the pig is blown out of the story (not eaten up as the text insists to the perplexity of the hungry wolf), raising the first question which is 'where does he go?' His eyes are fixed on a point (or person?) in the distance, and he seems to be telling someone what has happened. Meanwhile, as parts of his body reach the edge of the page, they disappear.

This trick of breaking the fourth wall, either by introducing elements from outside (including the addressee who is evoked in several of the illustrations), allowing characters to migrate from their pages or, as here, seeming to release characters from their texts, in itself isn't new – not even in children's literature. Picturebooks have played with the possibilities it affords for more than a century, animated cartoons employed it very early on, and increasing numbers of films, probably the best known of which is Woody Allen's *The Purple Rose of Cairo* (1985), have found it an effective way to reflect on the conventions of the medium. The originality of Wiesner's text begins to emerge with the next page turn: the pigs find themselves in the space 'behind' the two images. As they start to explore, it gradually becomes clear that they are in a new kind of space altogether. One way of reading what happens here involves drawing on knowledge of new technologies: what is being represented can be compared to the way layers of windows are built up on a computer screen. Although each window gives the appearance of being complete, and we know intellectually that the screen is flat so that there can be no actual depth to what is shown, nevertheless windows can be laid on top of each other and the knowledge that there are levels behind the screen being read that can be accessed and even incorporated in the focus screen subtly affects how it is read.

This way of thinking about Wiesner's image of the pigs in the gap between images is a good example of the way one medium presents and plays with the characteristics of another (see Chapter 8 for a discussion of 'remediation'). But the image, and those which follow, is more than just a playful imitation of digital media. When the image of the page is pushed aside and then folded up to make a paper airplane – the vehicle that allows the pigs to explore this new place in which they find themselves – the text becomes a realisation through visualisation of an idea that can only partially be expressed in language. The elements of the page represent a space outside the physical text: the pigs, though still clearly on the page at one level, at another are inhabiting a metaphysical space – the gap between images and behind narrative.

By using the pigs' story in new ways, by literally reshaping it and mastering its material existence, Wiesner takes the pigs into a space that I see as analogous to the Real. There is no way of saying where they are or what it means for them to be there, and Wiesner has not represented it (that would be impossible), but *The Three Pigs* points towards the Real and attempts to imagine how it could be experienced. Because the Real has been given form of a kind, readers are required to think about it, even if they do not know that this is what they are doing. According to Lacan,

> One can only think of language as a network, a net over the entirety of things, over the totality of the real. It inscribes on the plane of the real this other plane, which we here call the plane of the symbolic. (in Belsey, 4)

Through the combination of word and image characteristic of picturebooks, Wiesner's text shows what language cannot say: the pigs' paper plane is made of the plane of the Symbolic; beneath it is the vast, unknowable space of the Real.

In the Real, silence prevails, so when a few pages later the pigs land and begin to speak, it is clear that they have returned from the Real to a kind of reality – in this case the reality of nursery fiction. Their escape has broken down the boundaries between stories, so characters, visual styles, and languages morph as they move from text to text in a space that seems to consist of chains of pages, none of which is now able to contain its characters. The text has become an intertextual carnival at this stage, and as all revellers know, the return to reality is an essential part of the process and pleasure. The pigs discover that there is no place like home, so they return with their band of fellow escapee-characters to remake the ending. In the process, the very letters – the basic element of the narrative – are shown for what they are: bits of print that are in themselves meaningless and could as easily be used in soup as in text. As text, however, they make words of power; in this case, the power to exclude the wolf from the story and alter the expected ending. Indeed, the final page of the book starts a sentence that is not finished, raising a series of questions about what happens next, and in the process breaking one of the conventions that Rose associates with children's literature, its adherence to the tenets of the classic realist text, among them firmly resolved closure.

If, as Dusinberre argues, the first generations to grow up on *Alice* and the new kinds of children's literature it inspired gave birth to modernism, those whose understanding of fiction and culture has been shaped by picturebooks such as those by Fanelli, Child, and Wiesner, can be expected to reach similarly radical conclusions about the nature of narrative when they become the authors and writers of the future.

3
And None of It Was Nonsense

I can swim just like the others. Only I have a better memory than the others. I haven't forgotten the former inability to swim. But since I have not forgotten it, being able to swim is of no help to me; and so, after all, I cannot swim.

(aphorism from Franz Kafka's *Wedding Preparations in the Country and other Prose Writing*: 326–7)

Somehow it seems to fill my head with ideas – only I don't exactly know what they are!

(Jabberwocky, *Through the Looking-Glass*, Chapter 1)

Like myths, legends, and fairy tales, nonsense is a mode of writing that has come to be associated with children's literature. Chapter 1 discusses the broadly conservative nature of traditional tales and the way they attempt to transmit long-held values and ideologies. Nonsense, by contrast, sets out to question received wisdom and in the process it stimulates new ways of thinking. This makes it a highly effective mode both for writers who want to comment on and so affect society, and those who propose new ways of representing culture. As Susan Vigeurs observes, nonsense – which ranges from quite simple examples of word play through highly complex novels – can make an important contribution to creative development (1983: 148–9). This makes nonsense particularly appropriate for writing that is intended to be read while the intellect is in formation. In a discussion of Edward Lear's nonsense verse, Vigeurs suggests that the way Lear encourages children to play with rational order enables them 'to use nonsense as a route to meaning ... to develop a fully creative mind' (148–9). Dusinberre too credits nonsense with stimulating new forms of creativity when she points to Lewis Carroll – one of the best-known writers of nonsense – as inspiring the first generation of modernist writers. If Vigeurs and Dusinberre are right, the importance of nonsense for nurturing aesthetic development and releasing creative energies in successive generations should not be underestimated.

The history and nature of nonsense

In general usage, the word 'nonsense' implies that something is meaning-less, foolish, unimportant, and sometimes impudent. By contrast, literary nonsense, though it may appear to be similarly frivolous and pointless, is a complex form of writing with a distinguished intellectual pedigree and a long literary heritage.

The modes of nonsense were clearly established by the sixteenth century; they are found in a number of dramatic texts of this period including John Redford's *Wit and Science* (written in the 1530s). Although this play was not written for an audience of children, it was intended to be performed by schoolboys – probably the choir school at St. Paul's to which Redford was attached. While not a sustained piece of nonsense, it includes one scene in particular which bears most of the hallmarks of later literary nonsense. This occurs when a character called Ignorance deliberately fails to learn to read his own name despite the increasingly frustrated antics of his temporary schoolmaster, Idleness.[1]

Such literary antecedents for nonsense have tended to be overlooked, while oral sources such as nursery rhymes and folk tales are usually held up as the sources of nonsense. However, in his study of seventeenth-century nonsense, Noel Malcolm demonstrates that the popular belief that non-sense grew from folk traditions is erroneous; in fact, literary nonsense derives from highly specialised discourses in high culture. For instance, many of the early examples of nonsense were created to be performed at the Inns of Court and consist of parodies of the kinds of rhetorical and courtly skills on which the legal profession depended and in which its practitioners needed to excel. The pleasures of this kind of nonsense derive from know-ing languages, arguments, rhetorical styles, and professional information available only to an educated elite. It is not, then, a carnivalised folk-based literature in which all readers can participate, but a self-conscious, insider humour.

Literary nonsense makes much use of the mechanisms of logic and puzzle-making. One of its underlying logic-puzzles is the question of whether it is possible to use grammatically correct language or other signifying systems that readers will recognise to write something which is entirely without meaning – something that has no sense. Some of the earliest and most extreme examples of such an attempt are found in the work of John Taylor (1578–1653), the so-called Water-Poet, writing in the late sixteenth and early seventeenth centuries. Taylor devised special languages to try to subvert meaning as in 'Epitaph in the Bermuda Tongue', the rubric for which explains that it is to be 'pronounced with the accent of the grunting hog'. It begins 'Hough gruntough wough Thornough/Coratough, Odcough robun-quogh', and carries on in this vein until the end. Because this ingenious device depends on readers understanding the rules of pronunciation which require them to make words sound in particular ways, it soon begins to seem likely that there is meaning concealed in even this initially baffling text (is it an epitaph – and how is this term being used? – for someone named Thornough (Thomas?) Coratough (Cormas?)). Alerting readers to the possibility of hidden meanings and so suggesting that in written documents all may not be as it seems is a subversive strategy. Given that this was the period in which many of the systems of modern government and legislation as we know them today originated as well as one of great political intrigue involving coded letters and Machiavellian strategies, such a warning seems replete with social and political commentary.

Probably the best-known effort to create a sustained piece of meaningless text in English is Samuel Foote's (1720–1777) *The Great Panjandrum*,[2] devised, it is said, to test the ability of an actor-friend to learn lines. It consists of a series of separate sentences linked by false cohesive ties: 'So she went into the garden to cut a cabbage leaf to make an apple pie, and at the same time a great she-bear, coming down the street, pops its head into the shop. What! No soap? So she died.' Despite the deliberately random nature of the lines, the ties suggest narrative progression so the events seem to make a story despite Foote's best efforts – particularly when illustrated, as the text famously was by Randolph Caldecott in 1885. With the smallest encouragement, then, resourceful readers subvert the effort to deny meaning, showing how difficult it is to create something that can genuinely be said to lack or deny the possibility of sense.[3]

Edward Lear revived the term 'nonsense' after it had been out of use for more than a century. He used it to describe the humorous verses and drawings he did alongside his more serious paintings, suggesting that they were of little value and lacked meaning. In one of the earliest studies of the genre, Elizabeth Sewell observes that nonsense is equated with 'Inconsequence, pointlessness, senselessness, incongruity – all negatives which lead us to equate Nonsense with disorder' (1980: 39). With the exception of 'incongruity', these are not terms of disorder but of dismissal. The label 'nonsense' invites readers to assume that something is trivial, even if it is entertaining. However, far from being the inconsequential products of a fatigued brain in the way Lear's use of the term suggests, literary nonsense requires a high degree of technical knowledge and intellectual sophistication for its effects. When applied to literary tradition, then, the term 'nonsense' is something of a misnomer.

Several critics have analysed the linguistic and stylistic features of nonsense in great detail, and their conclusions have been explicated, harmonised, and synthesised by Wim Tigges in his *An Anatomy of Literary Nonsense* to form an authoritative summary of its characteristics. I quote this in full since it clearly sets out the elements and parameters of literary nonsense and shows well the highly determined nature of literary nonsense. It is, Tigges says,

A genre of narrative literature which balances a multiplicity of meaning with a simultaneous absence of meaning. This balance is effected by playing with the rules of language, logic, prosody and representation, or a combination of these. In order to be successful, nonsense must at the same time invite the reader to interpretation and avoid suggesting that there is a deeper meaning which can be obtained by considering connotations or associations, because these lead to nothing. The elements of word and image that may be used in this play are primarily those of negativity or mirroring, imprecision or mixture, infinite repetition, simultaneity, and arbitrariness. A dichotomy between reality and the words and images which are used to describe it must be suggested. The greater the distance or tension between what is presented, the expectations that are evoked, and the frustration of these expectations, the more nonsensical the effect will be. The material may come from the unconscious (indeed, it is very likely in many instances to do so), but this may not be suggested in the presentation. (27–28)

Literary nonsense, then, combines disguise, masquerade, and imposture. It simultaneously purports to say nothing and points to meanings that may or may not be there. In this way it sets up hermeneutic challenges to readers that force them to think of unexpected ways in which texts might make meanings (Box 3.1 sets out the most frequently used nonsense devices). As the following discussion of Victorian nonsense illustrates, it also offers writers ways of expressing ideas and feelings that might otherwise be prohibited.

Box 3.1   Nonsense devices

Additive narratives
Alliteration (to imply connection)
Arbitrariness
Borrowing
Exaggeration
Incongruity/mixing unrelated or contradictory elements
Inversion/reversal/mirroring
Negating
Neologisms
Non sequiturs
Omission/silence
Parallelism
Paralipsis
Parody
Portmanteau words
Puzzles/codes
Repetition
Simultaneity
Silence

Nonsense and the Victorian male

According to Tigges, literary nonsense depends on a dichotomy between reality and the words and images which are used to describe it. By simultaneously inviting and denying meaning, literary nonsense creates a tension between what is presented and the feelings of expectation it arouses. A similar, and I believe related, phenomenon occurs in canonical Victorian literature. Putting the two together offers some clues as to why literary nonsense flourished in the Victorian era and adds credence to Dusinberre's claim that Carroll's nonsense nurtured the modernists' rejection of Victorian values and literary conventions.

As I have discussed elsewhere (Reynolds and Humble, Chapter 3), there is a paradox in Victorian arts and letters which is how, at a time which is widely characterised as sexually repressive, images that to post-Freudian eyes seem unmistakeably erotic could regularly be shared in public and domestic spaces. Visually such images include the languorous paintings of Alma Tadema, or Lord Leighton's 'Flaming June', in which the sleeping subject's gossamer dress reveals as much as it conceals. Similarly striking is the way young women would read to their parents, companions, and suitors from popular works of the day, including such voluptuous verse as Tennyson's love lyrics in *The Princess* (1847), with their images and lexical evocations of penetrating and unfolding. An analogy with the phenomenon known as the 'ambiguous figure' helps to explain this paradox and also points to ways in which nonsense offered similar spaces where nineteenth-century writers could express private or controversial material.

'Ambiguous figure' is the term used to refer to the well-known visual phenomenon in which one set of lines contains two images; for example, a pair of vases and a couple kissing or an old crone and an attractive young woman. Semiotically, these are very interesting: one sign in one situation offers two meanings, one of which, in these cases, is sexually suggestive. When thinking about Victorian nonsense, another useful aspect of the ambiguous figure is the fact that though it is possible to know that both ways of seeing the image exist, and most viewers can learn to make both images emerge, only one can be seen at a time: seeing one cancels out the other. Moreover, it is not inevitable or even likely that without prompting, viewers will recognise the double nature of the image; even when coached, some viewers are never able to see both though they know intellectually each is there.

The ambiguous figure makes it possible to understand how readers and listeners could respond to the textual equivalent of an ambiguous figure and be oblivious to double meanings which to post-Freudian eyes seem so dominant in an image or text. This can be understood as an unconscious process, in which the audience hears or sees what it expects in that context from a particular artist or writer. At the same time, historians and critics have shown that sexual knowledge was not as far below the surface during this period as has sometimes been suggested. Recognition of the fact that significant aspects of the self were veiled or denied in public art forms but nonetheless found expression underpins Steven Marcus's argument in *The Other Victorians* (1977) and usefully sheds light on the context from which nonsense grew.

According to Marcus, Victorian art and letters had its shadow side in an extensive body of pornographic representations, and the two were in a knowing, dialectical relationship. He shows how, on the one hand, pornographic writers made use of official literature through borrowings, inversions, and parodies, while on the other, Victorian novelists and artists evoked the forbidden worlds and images of pornography through devices such as omission, silence, and paralipsis, and also by employing a way of signalling to the reader that is very familiar to those who study children's literature. This is what Barbara Wall has termed double address, the textual device of addressing a more knowing audience over the heads (or behind the backs) of the young people who are the implied readers of a text.

Although exegeses of novels have made us alert to the strategies identified by Marcus, little attention has been paid to the way this kind of bifocal interpellation works in other kinds of texts. It seems to me that the writing labelled 'nonsense' by its Victorian practitioners is making use of precisely the same techniques – fusing official and unofficial images and discourses, slipping between fantasy and reality, deploying parody and paralipsis, and hailing a knowing reader – which characterise much nineteenth-century fiction, and that this was, at least to some degree, a conscious and intentional process.[4]

The strategy by which nonsense-writers exploit the potential of texts to conceal meaning was an established part of the repertoire of nonsense conventions by the time Carroll started writing. Renaissance nonsense, for instance, delighted in the knowledge and use of codes such as those from the cabbalistic tradition, among them anagrams, acrostics, transposition of letters and words, and highly evolved numerical patterns. For the most part, in earlier nonsense the emphasis is on burlesque, and there remains a strong tradition in literary nonsense which continues to mock over-elaborate scholarship or the kind of obscurantist verbiage which characterises legal documents, political double-speak, bureaucratisation, and computer manuals (Malcolm, 14–15). But the focus on puzzling which underpins literary nonsense suggests that it is used for more than humorous or satirical effect – the devices associated with puzzling have their roots in the desire to disguise and secrete meaning.

Lewis Carroll certainly enjoyed the challenges of every kind of puzzle and frequently used them when writing to his young friends. Invitations would be issued in, for example, a rebus form, and once the obvious message had been decoded (perhaps an invitation to tea), there were often other pieces of concealed information to locate, such as the recipient's birth date.[5] That the inscription of hidden meaning could not be based on purely personal rules or information is part of the nonsense-maker's challenge: there would be no game if the rules were not followed and could not be identified. Carroll makes this clear in his Preface to *Through the Looking-Glass*, which explains that despite a few liberties with sequence, every move in the text is 'strictly in accordance with the laws of the game [of chess]'. Like chess, literary nonsense has its own conventions and logic: as well as obeying the rules of grammar, it employs inversion and wordplay, mixes unrelated or contradictory items (usually suggesting an affinity between them through rhyme or parallelism), and tends to present things in terms of extremes. Literary nonsense also tends to be highly intertextual, frequently, though not invariably, through parodic relationships such as Carroll's use of Isaac Watts's *Divine Songs* (1715).[6]

Despite the need to adhere to the rules and minimise the purely personal, dependence on logic, adherence to conventions, and use of intertextuality mean that literary nonsense tends to be what Freud called 'overdetermined'. That is, as in dream-work, its images, motifs, and structures become condensed, displaced, and disguised so that at times it is only by finding correspondences with other texts – especially those by the same writer or writer-illustrator – that meaningful readings are possible. But it has to be asked, if literary nonsense is overdetermined and/or functions like an ambiguous figure – if it is offering more than one meaning – what does the reader who responds to the nonsense-writer's wink discover after decoding the text?

In the case of Edward Lear, the answer seems to be more personal than cultural. His verses contain psychologically revealing self-portraits: there are clearly correspondences between the stout, bespectacled, lonely man with the unfortunate nose and many of the characters who feature in his non-sense verse and drawings, perhaps most movingly, the Yonghy-Bonghy-Bo. Tigges's reading of the sonnet 'Cold are the crabs that crawl on yonder hills' also identifies the presence of personal content: at one level this consists of complaints about digestive problems, at another of a sense of isolation and loneliness (28–31).

The shadow side of Dodgson/Carroll's nonsense is more complex and wide-ranging, again helping to explain its attraction and value to genera-tions of writers and thinkers, including the early modernists. Where Lear's nonsense depends primarily on neologisms, portmanteau words, and *non sequiturs*, Carroll's involves high levels of logic and problem-solving skills. These feature elsewhere in his writing, and in his mathematical work; in his private life, however, puzzling tended to be particularly associated with his child friends and his bedtime hours. Such was his activity that eventually (1893) he published a collection of his *Pillow Problems*: the intellectual tasks he set himself in an attempt to keep unwelcome thoughts at bay.[7] It seems reasonable to suggest that at least in part Dodgson/Carroll was attempting to use mental activity to overcome sexual desire. Given his predilection for little girls, it is conceivable that he was resisting recognising that he found them sexually attractive, but there are other possible explanations. For instance, some interesting work has been done on the sexual orientation of Victorian middle and upper-class men which suggests that the way they were raised made it difficult for some to relate sexually to women of their age and class (see, for instance, Davidoff, 1983; Reynolds, 1993).

The fact that it was normally working-class women (servants) who looked after such boys' basic physical and emotional needs, while they were taught to regard their mothers and sisters as 'angels in the house', may go some way towards explaining why a striking number of Victorian men are known to have been attracted to working women and impoverished girls. (Amongst the costumes in the dressing up box Carroll used when photographing his young friends were clothes like those of the beggar-girls he observed on the streets.) The fact that these boys tended to be moved from one all-male environment to another (prep school to boarding school to the military or civil service and the men's club) could make women seem hugely strange and other.[8] Added to this were voluble warnings about sexual impurity, disease, and waste; together these experiences and warnings could turn sexual relations between men and women into something rather fearful.

Perhaps in response to these patterns for caring and organising males socially, it was not uncommon in the nineteenth century for grown men to be attracted to young girls – girls too young to be sexually demanding or threatening.[9] For example, E.W. Benson (who became Archbishop of Canterbury) fell in love with an eleven-year-old to whom he proposed when she was twelve. Swinburne allegedly proposed to Jane Faulkner when she was ten or eleven; Ruskin became obsessed by Rose La Touche when she was eleven; Queen Victoria's daughter, Princess Beatrice, was engaged at thirteen; Dodgson's own brother, Wilfred, became attached to his future wife when she was fourteen, and Captain Mayne Reid (a well-known children's author) even wrote an entire autobiographical novel about his 'child wife' (1869).[10] Under the circumstances, it seems quite possible that men like Dodgson/ Carroll were attracted to young girls at least in part because they were *not* sexually mature and demanding. Like nonsense, the relationship with the girl child concealed unresolved areas of desire and tension, which may have had their roots not in the paedophile's wish to violate the young, but in a fear of sex, particularly with mature women. That the beloved was female could be seen as adding an additional layer to the relationship: since the girl is mother to the woman she will become, she also stands in for that which frightens in a way that no same-sex relationship could.

Men in Wonderland: nonsense as regressive fantasy

Such readings do not require knowledge of the modes of literary nonsense however; indeed, on their own they suggest that the nonsense-maker's energies are directed towards letting unconscious desires loose rather than deliberately working out ways of covertly articulating (and so gaining relief from) an area of anxiety. The two do not have to be seen as mutually exclusive: while nonsense can be a conscious and purposeful way of giving expression to frustrations arising from the need to manage ideas and desires known to be problematic in society, it also shares many characteristics with fantasy, the genre most closely associated with psychoanalytic criticism.[11]

Fantasy operates through the substitution of something permitted for something forbidden – a process that again replicates the workings of the dual images that make up ambiguous figures and which mirrors the relationship between the conscious and the unconscious. Lacan has argued that fantasy is largely driven by the desire to return to the condition of pure symbiosis which preceded entrance into the linguistic order: the preoedipal realm of the Imaginary, which is for him characterised by connection (specifically to the mother) rather than difference – it knows no divisions on the basis of sex, gender, time or power.

The attractions of overwhelming connection to Victorian men raised in systems which monitored and exercised difference and separation vigorously are not surprising, but they were potentially risky. Once it has been left, return to the Imaginary can only be achieved through total regression (taken as insanity), or death.[12] Linguistically, the two are very close, for if we accept that meaning is based on a system of differences, then a condition which denies difference also denies meaning and so existence.[13] Returning to the Imaginary is not about discovering a more authentic, untraumatised self, but about embracing absence of meaning and becoming nothing – precisely the threat that hangs over Alice's head each time she eats something in Wonderland. Humphrey Carpenter sees this opportunity to annihilate the self through language as one of the attractions of nonsense for Edward Lear. According to Carpenter, Lear realised that 'Nonsense is inextricably associated with violence, destruction, annihilation, and that any Nonsensical proposition, if pursued logically to its conclusion, must end in Nothing' (1985: 60).

Also thinking about language and the construction/deconstruction of the self, though taking her cue from Lacan, Karen Coats suggests that one reason why nonsense has historically been directed at children and in the United States is now a genre particularly associated with those who are learning to read is because preliterate children are not fully secured in the Symbolic. She models entry into the Symbolic as a two-part process: learning to speak and understand language, and becoming literate. Written language exposes the arbitrary and idiosyncratic nature of the rules of grammar, spelling and syntax which children are supposed to accept (not master) on the way to becoming fully paid up members of the Symbolic club. Membership of this club is costly: it entails learning to read 'correctly' (according to the rules and decoding meanings that can be recognised by and communicated to others) rather than creatively (fed by energies outside language) (2004: 64), and each 'correct' reading constitutes a denial of the Imaginary and so the mother. Nonsense, however, is a creative rather than a correct mode and so generates a wild zone between the Symbolic and the Imaginary meaning that

> in learning to read nonsense, [the child] manages to hold on to that bit of outlaw *jouissance* – as it appears in the humor, music and anarchy of the nonsense text – that has broken off from the mother and winds up circulating in language itself. (65)

Though it is unlikely that Carroll was consciously 'holding open a place for [the mother]' (65) through his nonsense-making, that he was fully aware of the relationship between language and identity is evident by the number of times that Alice intimates that the semantic confusion of Wonderland makes her uncertain of her own status, prompting her to ask repeatedly, 'Who am I?' and 'How am I' (how am I here; how am I this size; how will I behave?). Although Carroll has a girl-child ask these questions, they are at least as germane to men who were uneasy in the presence of sexually mature females and with more aggressive forms of masculinity being promoted in the second half of the nineteenth century (see Reynolds, 1990; Robson, 2001). That these pressures might provoke a desire to return to the maternal, feminised domain of Lacan's Imaginary, to unmake the self which fits uncomfortably into the niche in the world it has been assigned, is understandable.

However understandable, regression of this kind needs to be resisted. Returning to the analogy with the ambiguous figure, nonsense, which on the one hand recognises the arbitrary nature of language and on the other displays high levels of intellectual effort expended in attempts to master it, simultaneously represents both capitulating to and triumphing over language. Lecercle (1994) sums up this phenomenon:

> The grandeur of nonsense, as a literary genre, is that it foregrounds the predicament of every speaker of language [do I speak it or does it speak me?]: we are torn apart between the two opposite poles of the paradox and yet we must, somehow, hold them together. (25)

What Lecercle overlooks is that for most people, most of the time, this paradox is unfelt and unrecognised; for the makers of literary nonsense, however, it is key. Carroll captures this difference exactly in the famous exchange between Alice and Humpty Dumpty in Chapter 6 of *Through the Looking-Glass*:

> 'When I use a word', Humpty Dumpty said, in a rather scornful tone, 'it means just what I choose it to mean – neither more nor less'.
> 'The question is', said Alice, 'whether you *can* make words mean so many different things'.
> 'The question is', said Humpty Dumpty, 'which is to be master – that's all'.

Nonsense has always been a peculiarly male-dominated genre, and it seems likely that at some level its interest in exploring the gap between word and meaning, which opens up the possibility of substituting another word for the self, is about the desire for an alternative self, in this case a self denied by hegemonic forms of masculinity. Often this takes the form of a modified regression; not back to actual preoedipal experience (if this were possible), but to an idealised, metaphoric version of it – Romantic childhood.[14] Longing for such a return is clearly expressed by Hilaire Belloc in his *Cautionary Tales* (1907), the opening poem of which ends:

> And when your prayers complete the day,
> Darling, your little tiny hands
> Were also made, I think, to pray
> For *men* that lose their fairylands. (My emphasis)

Although it is possible to identify a regressive component to nonsense, it is more concerned with changing the present than restoring the past. I have pointed to the way it seeks to find a space for male sexual behaviour that does not conform to prevailing definitions of what is 'normal', but nonsense is equally capable of poking fun at religion, politics, education, topical issues, and the adults and organisations that control them. In the case of Dodgson/Carroll, religion and education are both potentially subverted in the *Alice* books in, for instance, their apparent allusions to the act of Communion through the commands that Alice encounters to 'Eat Me' and 'Drink Me' and their nonsense-jokes about the curriculum (the teacher called 'Tortoise' because he 'taught us', and lessons in Reeling, Writhing, Laughing, and Greek which lessen from day to day (*Alice in Wonderland*, Chapter 9)).

Another source of transformative activity that may lurk beneath the surface of nonsense and nurture a desire to subvert the status quo is scrutiny of the relationship between ways of knowing and ways of being. Nineteenth-century nonsense, for instance, can be seen as a response to the overconfident, highly rigid systems of education and morality, and the obsession with collecting, classifying and so spuriously claiming possession over information about the world, past and present, which dominated much of the nineteenth century. It was precisely this rejection of the 'certainties' on which earlier thinking had depended, including the certainty that the world could be rendered on the page, that Dusinberre says Virginia Woolf and her fellow literary modernists were rebelling against.

For Carroll, a similar area of conflict arose between the discoveries and new thinking of the natural sciences and religious orthodoxy. As the son of a clergyman and with his own professional involvement in the church, it was not always prudent to enter too forcibly into teleological arguments, but the *Alice* books provide ample evidence of Carroll's interest in and knowledge of Darwin's theories and the Natural Sciences generally. In this instance, nonsense offers a good-natured and discretely concealed response to topical and potentially contentious issues. Although concealed, close reading shows that Carroll's message accepts and even celebrates the fact that scientific discoveries and the new ideas they were generating would require change. Carroll's Alice book epitomises the way literary nonsense allowed nineteenth-century writers to negotiate the warring needs for discretion and expression at a time when long-standing ways of thinking about and organising society were under pressure. In other words, its modes, attitudes, and eclecticism helped prepare the way for the social and aesthetic changes associated with modernism.

Nonsense and the modernist aesthetic

> The meadow isn't ready for this yet.
>
> (Russell Hoban, *The Mouse and his Child*)

The discussion of Gertrude Stein's *The World is Round* in Chapter 2 focuses on the interaction between modernism and the picturebook, but Stein's children's book also owes much to the tradition of literary nonsense. This is evident in her use of repetition, the disjointed nature of the text, the way she stretches the rules of grammar and syntax, her interest in sound-play, and its intratextual references. She was not alone in using children's literature to explore the possibilities arising from putting nonsense into the service of modernism; indeed, Richard Hughes's *The Spider's Palace* (1931) anticipated it by several years and, as briefly mentioned in Chapter 2, Eugene Ionesco's first work, with its anticipations of the Absurdist plays for which he is known, appeared in the same year.

One of the most important periods in the development of literary nonsense in children's literature occurred in the 1960s, when affluence, vision, and optimism combined to set in motion a co-ordinated campaign to eliminate poverty and spread social benefits in the United States. Lyndon Johnson's plans for the 'Great Society' saw education as a lever for social reform and this led to increased spending on and interest in children's books in schools and libraries. The flourishing of literary nonsense was one manifestation of a related determination to produce children's literature of the highest literary and artistic merit (see note 6, Chapter 2). Nonsense, with its emphasis on language, literary knowledge and intellectual play, matched the aims and mood of the period well. The atmosphere in which the new wave of nonsense flourished was very different from that in which Victorian nonsense makers worked, not least because it was a time of greater openness with energies being directed at including and respecting those who had traditionally been marginalised in culture. This changed context resulted in a changed register for literary nonsense which became more optimistic in tone and playful in its workings. Puzzles, for instance, began to be less concerned with concealing personal content than with encouraging readers to enjoy playing with words – devices such as puns, double meanings, and parodies were designed to be recognised and decoded.

Key works from this period include Norton Juster's *The Phantom Tollbooth* (1961), with its inventive literal-mindedness (the hero, Milo, encounters a spelling bee, is accompanied by a watchdog whose body is actually a clock, and eventually has to eat his own words), and Russell Hoban's *tour de force*, *The Mouse and his Child* (1967). Of these, Hoban's is the book that most explicitly brings together children's literature, modernism, and literary nonsense in ways that confound Jacqueline Rose's pronouncements about children's literature's conservative rejection of modernism.

In *The Mouse and his Child*, Hoban explicitly refers to modernist writers, groups, and movements including the Theatre of the Absurd, represented by Mr. and Mrs. Crow's theatre company, 'The Caws of Art'. He also shows his concern with language as a signifying system – a hallmark of his writing, arguably reaching its apotheosis in *Riddley Walker* (1980), with its invented language of the future created to suggest how society might degenerate after a nuclear-holocaust. *The Mouse and his Child* anticipates many of the themes and issues that later emerged in Hoban's adult novels (and already familiar in modernist work such as the poems of T.S. Eliot, also alluded to in the text), including parallels between human existence and the increasingly hazardous, haphazard, urban, and disposable society we inhabit (represented by the dump overseen by the villainous Manny Rat), with its over-dependence on intrusive, simplistic mass media.

While there is an elegiac tone to sections of *The Mouse and his Child*, it ends with an optimistic vision of a new, more tolerant, and equal society. The writing is characterised by wordplay and a jocular juxtaposing of abstruse philosophical thinking with the mundane: the turtle philosopher C. Serpentina's great idea ('the last visible dog') comes from looking at the disintegrating label of a dog food tin in the muddy water of the pond where he lives (significantly, this motif's focus on infinity threatens the possibility of nothingness/annihilation in the same way as does the food Alice eats). Just as Norton Juster's Milo is ultimately successful in his quest to rescue Rhyme and Reason and so restore the balance between words and numbers in the Kingdom of Wisdom, so Hoban allows his child hero to prevail.

The Mouse and his Child employs many of the modes of literary nonsense – not least its determination to use humour and logic to discredit repressive social systems. The story is a quest for three things: family, territory, and autonomy (to become self-winding), and ultimately all three are achieved. This strongly affirmative use of nonsense is a significant and sustained adjustment to the mode, which also migrates from poetry to the novel in the second half of the twentieth century.

The years 1970–1971 saw the publication of three tales by Eugene Ionesco, originally written to form part of his memoirs. Where Hoban's combination of modes – from nonsense to allegory – has led many critics to conclude that

The Mouse and his Child is too complicated for its intended readers (see, for instance, Rustin and Rustin, 182–3), no such charge can be laid against Ionesco's work. His short stories use simple language, are based in the child's familiar domestic world, and incorporate the voice of the child and the child's facility and manner of making both nonsense and stories through the character of Josette, who is thirty-three months old when we first meet her.

Although Josette's father is officially the storyteller (and alter-ego for Ionesco?), Josette increasingly participates in and controls the telling. *Story Number 1* ends with her repeating elements of the tale her exhausted and debilitated father has told her while only half awake in bed that morning (in what seems to be a child's vision of parental excess, the text explains that Josette's parents have spent the night carousing in restaurants, bars, and theatres). The story featured a world in which everyone, including the dogs, was named Jacqueline, like the family's maid. When Josette meets a real little girl called Jacqueline while out shopping with Jacqueline the maid, she disconcerts the adults around her by saying:

> I know. ... Your papa is named Jacqueline, your mama is named Jacqueline, your little brother is named Jacqueline, your doll is named Jacqueline, your grandpa is named Jacqueline, your wooden horse is named Jacqueline, your house is named Jacqueline, your little chamber pot is named Jacqueline ...

The list itself demonstrates characteristics shared by children's nonsense play and literary nonsense including repetition, connection through alliteration, removing words from their contexts, additive narrative, incongruous juxtapositions (parents and chamber pots), and excess.

This story shows that like Carroll, Ionesco sees correspondences between nonsense and dream, and just as Alice's adventures turn out to be dreams, so Josette's father always tells his stories while still in bed and struggling with the after effects of too little sleep and too much to drink.[15] The dream state was of considerable interest to the Surrealists, with whom Ionesco was associated, and it seems likely that the phrasing of the stories, with their run-on sentences, shifting terrains, and the maid's accusation that her father will make Josette mad, is intended to place these stories in the domain of nonsense that had been aesthetically charted by Dadaists, Surrealists, and others of the more extreme modernist groups. The illustrators of the stories frequently point in this direction by, for instance, including designs on wallpaper that float off to form new shapes, melting cars, and in one of Philippe Corentin's illustrations for *Story Number 3*, an obvious tribute to Magritte in the form of a man's head, the top half of which is an open window showing blue sky and little Josette hanging from a branch by her underpants.

Whether or not the links to artistic groups and activities is intentional, the Jacqueline list puts Josette in the position of storyteller. While here she is simply retelling her father's tale, by *Story Number 3*, she is actively involved in crafting the new story. Sometimes this takes the form of correcting her father's version of events, as when he says Josette puts on her pink jumper and she changes it to her white one. At other points she adds details of her own and acts them out, as if the story were a game. When they have flown to the moon and are hungry, Josette announces, 'I eat a piece of the moon. It's good, it's good! ...' The text adds in parentheses, '(And Josette gives a piece of the moon to her papa, and both of them eat the moon.)'.

Ionesco shows Josette as co-creator in other ways too. *Story Number 3* is set out as if it were a dramatic text, and Josette's share of the dialogue affects the shape of the story being told, sometimes reasserting reality when it becomes too real or overwhelming:

> *Papa:* You see the lion, you hear him? He goes browrrr! browrr! ... (And papa shows how the lion goes with his claws and he makes a terrible face.) Browrrr! browrrr! ...
> *Josette:* No, no, don't do that! ... You're not a lion, are you? You're a papa; you're not a lion!
> *Papa:* No, I am not a lion; I'm a papa. I was just pretending to be a lion.
> *Josette:* No, don't do that any more.

Passages such as this, which presumably reflect interactions with Ionesco's daughter, to whom the stories were originally told, are also interesting for the way the voices of child, father, and narrator merge; particularly in the text shown in brackets. When, for instance, the text states 'papa shows how the lion goes with his claws and makes a terrible face', it is unclear whether this is a kind of stage direction, an observation on the part of the narrator, or a moment of free indirect discourse associated with Josette. As this example shows, writing about childhood for a child using the idioms of play has resulted in a complex form of narration that is nevertheless easily comprehended by young readers. In fact, whatever the age of the reader, the Josette stories create textual and imaginative pathways through which to understand Ionesco's extended adult writing.

A comparable merging of creative voices takes place in the illustrations. For instance, in *Story Number 3*, as part of an exaggeratedly detailed description of Papa and Josette's progress from their flat to the airport (at which point the level of functional relevance is adjusted and their passage from town to moon to sun and back to bed is virtually unremarked), they pass a butcher's shop and Papa observes 'If the butcher kills any more calves, I am going to kill the butcher. ...' The full-page illustration facing it shows the butcher – now a bull, standing at the door of the shop in an apron hung with knives. A human head is displayed on a platter surrounded by lettuce, a chart of the human body showing the best cuts of meat hangs from the wall, and a cow is doing the accounts. Such reversals are characteristic of nonsense, but in this case the image is the addition of the artist since the text does not say that cattle will kill humans but that Papa will kill the butcher.

These stories have been removed from their original context and purpose – as conclusions to chapters in Ionesco's memoir – and represented for a child audience, they nevertheless display the originality and vitality that Ionesco found when writing for a child audience. As Debattista argues, children's literature is not a nostalgic forum where Ionesco seeks to be reconnected with the sensory and perceptual experiences of childhood, but serves an important role in his artistic development. Children's literature, she claims, provides,

> a genre in which he can put forth the literary nonsense inaugurated by the proto-Surrealists ... under the appearance of children's tales, Ionesco playfully, but deliberately, illustrates such favourite Surrealist devices as the absurd and language games. (16)

There are aesthetic and practical reasons why the kind of nonsense that interests Ionesco works particularly well as writing for children. For children, the world often seems bewildering and its rules illogical. Children move more readily than adults between the modes of reality and fantasy, particularly when involved in play and storying. They are also relatively new to language, which intensifies the potential for wordplay, and they are still in the process of internalising concepts to do with time, distance, and spatial relationships. All of these factors, together with children's lack of formal awareness of genres and conventions, lessen the hold of reality on narrative, so an implied audience of children eases the degree to which some of the more extreme ideas and positions associated with modernism, the avant-garde, and the absurd need to be asserted. At the same time, adults who might be inclined to be sceptical about enterprises such as the Theatre of the Absurd, are likely to enjoy the playfulness, wit, and observation in stories such as these. For instance, those familiar with Ionesco's work will spot the intertextual reference to and joke on his own play, *The Bald Soprano*, in which all the characters are called Bobby Watson (Debattista: 17), and having been confronted, verbally and visually, with a world of Jacquelines, will better understand the threat posed to identity by this multiplication of a self. Although the register of the story told to Josette is comic, it shares the dark tones of Ionesco's work for adults; the world of Jacquelines is both a world in which identity is problematic and one in which signification has collapsed, making it impossible to distinguish between people and things.

The shift in audience for Ionesco is accompanied by shifts in register and tone. As in the nonsense works of Juster and Hoban, the melancholy and regressive tone of nineteenth-century nonsense, with its fears of isolation and the loss of childhood, are replaced by pleasure in play and confidence in the child's ability to cope. Ionesco does not send Josette into an existential void by questioning the possibility of language to make sense, and though disjointed, his stories have clear structures and reflect a knowable and purposeful world in which regular meals mark the domestic routine. Nevertheless, writing for children served an aesthetic purpose for him, and child readers who encounter these three stories are gently introduced to some challenging and sophisticated ideas.

As these examples show, during the time when it was regarded as a mode suited only for the nursery, nonsense, with its focus on questioning the relationship between language, self and reality and its rejection of grand narratives and the conventions and subjects of 'serious' realist fiction, anticipated and was called into the service of modernist movements in literature and art such as Futurism, Dadaism, Surrealism, and the Theatre of the Absurd. But modernism is not the literary mode best suited to nonsense: in its playful testing of boundaries, evocations of false histories, experimentation with identities and subjectivities, and its iconoclastic mixing of styles and forms, nonsense finds its natural place in literary postmodernism.

The politics of nonsense

Resistance and transformation – two key impulses of literary nonsense – are at the heart of Salman Rushdie's *Haroun and the Sea of Stories* (1991), a children's book that owes a strong debt to earlier nonsense writers, ranging from the Beatles to Norton Juster's *The Phantom Tollbooth*. In *Haroun*, Rushdie employs a vast array of nonsense conventions: literal mindedness, lexical exhibitionism, inversion, parody, juxtapositioning of literary styles, incongruity, blending the ordinary and the extraordinary, and an intertextual patchwork which stitches together ancient oral tales and examples from the post-war culture industries. Carroll's *Alice* books contribute substantially to the text's intertextual dynamic; for instance, in the dream framework, the talking beasts and the army of pages who closely resemble Carroll's playing-card gardeners.

The text begins with an acrostic puzzle spelling out the name of his son, Zafar, from whom Rushdie was separated as a consequence of the fatwa against him. In *Haroun*, Rushdie rejects the conventions of realism as being a false way of making sense of the world; nonsense is presented as the more meaningful and truthful idiom. Where nonsense verse tends to leave out or provide ambiguous clues about context, which makes it hard to distinguish between the literal and the figurative – what happens or is observed and what is metaphoric (McHale, 1992: 11) – nonsense novels such as *Haroun* (and those discussed above) have recognisable plots, settings, and authorial voices that are supported by the nonsense elements rather than disrupted by them. The plots do not reduce the richly metaphoric nature of nonsense writing, however, which leaves the texts open to multiple interpretations, some of which relate closely to the authors' personal contexts. Rushdie, for instance, uses the strategies of nonsense to give expression to frustrations during the first years of the fatwa. Through the nonsense devices in *Haroun*, he weaves together thoughts on individual liberty, censorship, linguistic diversification, and the need for fantasy in a technological world, and does so without complaining about his circumstances or capitulating to a nihilistic world view.

As with the Alice books, the diversity of styles and activities which characterise *Haroun* enable it to work in different ways for different readers. Experienced/adult readers tend to find the way it refuses to foreground the child's point of view and its incorporation of texts and ideas satisfying; however, these practices do not necessarily deter inexperienced/young readers. As in the case of the ambiguous figure, adult and child readers discover two different but equal texts in *Haroun*. For me this makes Rushdie's novel a fine example of how a text can stimulate what Peter Hollindale has called 'childness', by which he means the ability to be 'dynamic, imaginative, experimental, interactive and unstable', in its readers (1997: 46). As in Carroll's work, adult and child readers alike are hailed by Rushdie, though at different points and in different ways. For both, however, the text's rejection of sensible, conventional, apparently coherent, and stable realism as a false way of making sense of the world predominates. Nonsense is presented as the more meaningful literary mode.

In her discussion of '*Haroun* and the Politics of Children's Literature' (1995), Judith Plotz suggests that Rushdie was drawn to writing for a child audience in part because after the imposition of the fatwa he found himself constrained and marginalised in ways that replicated some of the aspects of childhood. As a text which is characterised by its use of the conventions and strategies of literary nonsense, *Haroun and the Sea of Stories* offers a paradigm of the dichotomous nature of children's literature itself. On the one hand, it is dependent on and respectful of the education system and the didactic tradition; on the other, it is subversive and liberating, mocking and critiquing the values and practices of these same systems and the institutions and individuals responsible for upholding and disseminating them. It is associated with popular culture and held in low esteem by some, but many of its practitioners have been major literary figures. It is simple and often directed at an inexperienced audience, yet it can deal in philosophy, psychology, and linguistic theories beyond the levels of most young readers. As Rushdie's experience shows, there are still risks in dealing in what might be regarded as an irreverent way with serious issues, but nonsense has the power to be a courageous mode, offering opportunities for giving expression to opinions, and experiences that might otherwise be silenced.

Cognitive maps: nonsense and the contemporary picturebook

The use of nonsense by contemporary children's writers shows how successive generations have found it useful for expressing and interacting with the shifting ontological, epistemological, and political landscapes of modernity. In many ways, however, as has been true in other areas (see Chapters 2 and 8), the most radical use of nonsense is to be found in picturebooks. This comes in part from the opportunities for more elaborate sense-play provided by the visual element of the text, but equally important is the way some picture-book makers are using the physical properties of books as part of the narrative. These two kinds of nonsense – nonsense that relies on a combination of visual and verbal wordplay, and that which uses the book form itself – can be observed in some recent French picturebooks, resulting in what Fredric Jameson has called 'material thought' (McHale, 28).

The first kind of nonsense predominates in the work of Paul Cox, though he also plays with form. For instance, in *Le livre le plus court du monde* [The shortest book in the world][16] (2002), he begins by dismantling the order of the text by erasing the concept of front and back covers, and changing the nature of the spine. The book is spiral-bound; each page is of the same thickness (it is printed on a heavy cardboard), each has the same layout and text – the single word 'Cependant' [meanwhile/ however] – and running up the bound edge, each page contains the formal information about author and publisher legally required of published works. For those who do not pass over this element, the information reveals that 'Cependant' is not the title; it is in fact called *Le livre le plus court du monde*.

The spiral means that the pages can be read in any order, so effectively the pages become the kind of additive list familiar from nonsense, displaying characteristics of repetition ('Cependant', the publishing details – even the design – are repeated throughout) and apparently meaningless juxtapositions of images. The usually enforced order of the bound book is disordered by the form, raising any number of questions: What comes first? What is the title? Is there a text? Why these images? How do you read it?

Other nonsense-based elements of the book surface as it is scrutinised, beginning with the title: although the printed text may consist of a single word, far from being the shortest book in the world, it is quite long: 58 pages printed on both sides so offering 116 images. Moreover, at a variety of levels, each of these pages exhibits nonsense's interest in infinity and duality. As Marie Derrien observes (2004: 45), it is possible to read each image as a picture of something that is happening at the same moment in many parts of the world (a diver dives while some people watch a football match while someone makes a telephone call ...), in which case it *is* an extremely short story (a single moment in time). But it is also enormous in that *Le livre le plus court du monde* tells a global story (indeed, the spiral of the text can be compared to the axis of the earth, and when fanned out, the pages resemble the spherical shape of a globe) and a story of globalisation. The images are made of dots which bring to mind the pixels associated with screen-based media, and given that the text implies all of these events are happening simultaneously (simultaneity being another preoccupation of nonsense), it alludes to instant communication (47).

Beyond these broad-brush themes and connections, there are many intra-textual links to be found between the images as well as a variety of points of view; recognising the connections involves the same kind of problem-solving required by literary nonsense in the tradition of Carroll, though in this case depending almost entirely on interpreting visual clues. By contrast, Cox's *Ce nains portent quoi???????* [These dwarves carry what???????] (2001) employs visual, verbal, and aural elements equally to create its puzzles and encode meanings, again, beginning with the title. Derrien notes that the sound of the title is likely to be heard (without reference to the printed text or by a non-reader) as '*C'est n'importe quoi*' meaning 'It's nonsense' (65). And so it is. For instance there are seven question marks in the title and it refers to dwarves: an intertextual link is established. Incongruity is the next feature to emerge: the hardcover book with its dust jacket evokes high-quality literature, but the neon palette and images that are deliberately made to look as if a child has drawn them are from the realms of mass and childhood cultures (66). This is an additive narrative since the dwarves carry an ever-increasing number of unrelated items, including a door, a fish, some shoes, a saw, a lamp, and some orange peels, to their beloved Snow White.

Cox's is nonsense of the most complicated kind:

> ... he demonstrates that homonyms, the names of colours, pictorial rep-resentations, the use of a book as well as the alphabetic system – an invented alphabet is available to be tested in the book itself – are exclu-sively built upon accepted and shared conventions. Some ... are more institutionalised than others. ... The viewer is required to know these fluctuating conventions to understand the sign – whether pictorial or verbal. (69)[17]

Cox uses nonsense strategies to make readers of whatever age aware of the extent to which people interpret the world through codes of which we are seldom aware. This is precisely the purpose of nonsense: 'to expose common sense as ideology, as a cultural product and alibi rather than what it pretends to be' (Susan Stewart in McHale, 25).

Paul Cox is one contemporary picturebook maker whose books employ the codes and conventions of nonsense to create texts that encourage read-ers to think about books, narrative, and culture in new ways. Other examples include two works by Czech author-illustrator, Kveta Pacoviska – *Ponctuation* [Punctuation] (2004) and *Un Livre Pour Toi* [A book for you][18] (2004) – which seem to me to constitute interesting examples of Jameson's 'material thought'.

Jameson formulated this term to refer to his sense of what we who are living in the complex economic phase he terms late/multinational capitalism need if we are to be able to grasp it imaginatively and so become capable of resisting or changing it (McHale, 27). Jameson's concern is that we cannot cognitively map the current system because our existing models function only at the level of language, dealing in content and theme, and these are inadequate tools for representing the webs, currents, forces, patterns, and scale of late capitalism. Without new ways of thinking that can provide an overview of the system and a way of comprehending how it works, he warns, it is not possible to locate ourselves within this economic phase nor understand how we are being manipulated by it.

Jameson contends that change can only come about through an intellectual leap, and for this we need new conceptual platforms: content and theme have to be extended by other analytical and classificatory modes. He believes these will take shape outside language in plastic form (2000: 287), thus 'material thought'. The logic behind this is that though we cannot yet think thoughts for which we have no language, we live the experience and can symbolise it in other ways. The example he gives is drawn from one of the most exclusive, most elite areas of the arts: the family home built by architect Frank Gehry in California at the end of the 1970s. According to Jameson, the way Gehry wraps a new building around a traditional core creates an unsettling space that allegorises postmodern life in America (McHale, 28).

Inevitably, in the nearly twenty years that have passed since Jameson first articulated his concern, there has been activity at all levels in culture to help move on thinking about what it means to live in what can now be termed our post-postmodern era, but as I have suggested, some contemporary picturebooks, working in the nonsense tradition, seem to be fulfilling the function of material thought – and not for an elite few. They use the modes of nonsense and appeal to cognitive characteristics of childhood in ways that are both playful and profound.

Ponctuation is large in size: 16″ x 11.5″ (41 x 29 cm), and though it has many physical and textual features derived from the conventional children's picturebook (covers, page turns, characters, didactic address) none is exactly as it seems. Thematically it is another example of the ambiguous figure: ostensibly it is a lesson in punctuation, introducing the most commonly used punctuation marks and explaining their functions, but by exaggerating their size, anthropomorphising them and giving them their own world (Punctuation City), what are usually regarded as servants of language are suddenly seen as its masters. This inversion of the child's view of punctuation (learned long after language) is both instructive and subversive, suggesting as it does the latent power of small and marginalised beings and authorising topsy-turveydom in the name of education. It also appeals to the young child's propensity, observed by Freud, to treat 'words' (in this case the punctuation signs) as things, that underpins many kinds of nonsense (Dusinberre, 61). But this is standard nonsense fare. The true aesthetic radicality of the book is seen in its design and production.

The front cover begins the interrogation of form. It is not solid and informative but full of large cut-outs in the shape of punctuation marks. The reader can see and reach through to the next layer, a reoccurring pattern of colours. The front and back covers do not simply open, but unfold to make three-gated openings that break out of the expected confines of the binding and allow the cut-out section to be laid over other pages, creating new patterns, textures (the amounts of gloss and ink on the pages varies creating different textures), and ideas.

Like the Gehry house, then, the book refers to and displays traditional elements and materials but does so in new ways, and far from creating a harmonious effect, the different elements are exciting but unsettling. Like Cox's work, it foregrounds formal characteristics of written sign systems (music, traffic signs, and mathematics are also shown to use similar shapes and codes) and exposes ways in which they control us. A particularly powerful effect comes from juxtaposing different registers: the tone is simultaneously didactic and a parody of teacherly children's books, and this is mirrored in print that does not conform to the rules of top to bottom, left to right, or capitalisation. The handwriting too challenges the didactic content: it is not neat, properly formed, and consistent, but spiky, marred by blotches, and difficult to read. Page design and layout confound the commonsense of books for new readers: black print is printed on a black page; in a book about punctuation, punctuation is used decoratively rather than for its stated purpose; pages incorporating cut-outs bring several pages together into the same space, creating fragments of images and text analogous to digital bits of information. At many levels, then, the book is a physical response to both the book-as-medium and modernity, and in trying to make sense of it, the reader is encouraged to think in terms of images and forms as well as language.

Un livre pour toi takes these ideas further and incorporates other nonsense devices. On removing the book from its shrink wrapping, the reader quickly discovers that the beautiful dust jacket is the only cover in a formal sense and must be removed if the book is to be read because this is a book that is not a book (negation): its 'covers' are two unhinged boards, and the pages a chain of accordion pleats that are inclined to spill onto the floor in a very disorderly way if not read on a flat surface. Trying to return them to their original order both introduces readers to sections in the middle before those at the beginning, and reveals that this is not a frieze because it is printed on both sides. Which is front and which is back? Should one be read first?

Reversals and mirror images abound – there are even reflective sections and pages where readers see a hazy (as if far away) self-image in the book, an appropriate metaphor for the way the task of trying to make meaning both absorbs readers and keeps them at an intellectual distance. Like nonsense, the book is unconcerned with stirring up the emotions: it is interested in ideas about shape, form, texture, and sequence. This book has moved beyond theme and content, but it contains the potential for multiple narratives, activated by the reader.

In this unbound format, cut-out sections function in more complicated ways than they do in *Ponctuation*, bringing through material from the 'back' of the text as well as that on surrounding pages to intriguing and puzzling effect. The reader folds and unfolds, reads backwards and forwards, trying to see how the sections relate. In the same way, incomplete sequences initiate determined searches for hidden material: the numbers 7, 9, and 0 are not pictured – are they concealed? There is no sustained narrative, but a series of fragments that seem to shift between the literal and the figurative in precisely the way required for material thinking.

These are new ways of playing with books, language, and concepts for children growing up in the twenty-first century. Cox and Pacoviska have employed nonsense strategies to serve their purpose of calling attention to (not necessarily dismantling) conventions so that their effects on our lives are more visible. They refer to multiple sign systems, reminding readers both that other systems too have rules and codes that determine how we think and behave, and that language is not the only medium of thought and expression. They make aesthetic and intellectual demands on readers, and reassess the nature of narrative. Nonsense is supremely good at making such demands, which is why, no matter how it is utilised in fiction for adults, it needs to be retained in the domain of children's literature where it can move on the thinking of future generations.

4
Useful Idiots: Interactions Between Youth Culture and Children's Literature

> Once upon a time in the traditional, pre-1950s society, being mature was what mattered; being young was no more than an unfortunate period through which one had to proceed, best left behind as soon as possible. Not until one attained man- or womanhood, and even then not really until one reached middle and even better old age, could one really be said to have come to grips with life. Those who lived longest had to be the wisest, since they had worked out the various ways of best surviving in a world which was, in its essentials, pretty immutable. 'Authority had authority, and one of its tasks was naturally to repress, educate and control the feckless and expansive instincts of anyone younger than oneself.'
>
> (Green, 1998: 1, quoting Malcolm Bradbury's 1961 essay, 'The Pubertoids')

Mainstream children's literature of the kind produced in the United Kingdom and the United States until the final decades of the twentieth century, exemplified by the writing of Enid Blyton, Arthur Ransome, E.B. White, and Laura Ingalls Wilder, stands for almost everything that youth culture has rejected since it came to prominence in the 1950s. This is evident in the way that, with very few exceptions, children's books and reading are embraced by the establishment, while youth culture strives to operate outside it. In the twentieth century, the majority of British and American young people construct and perform their cultural identities through predominantly non-literary forms including fashion, popular music, television, clubbing, the Internet, and mobile telephones. However, there are writers and readers for whom Young Adult (YA) fiction plays a significant role, and adolescents who value reading for its ability to entertain and/or empower. Looking at what is being produced for the current generation of adolescent readers reveals a great deal about changes in the way they are being constructed in social terms. Many of these changes do not flatter the young; more than that, as many of the examples discussed in the following pages show, they suggest that the period of adolescence has little value.

My focus in this chapter is not on YA/teenage fiction *per se* but with identifying ways in which writing for this age group represents and addresses adolescents as a group in culture, and how far YA fiction acknowledges and interacts with the areas in culture in which the young are the primary makers and consumers. Most of the chapters in this study look at both the aesthetic and the cultural influences of children's literature, but here the emphasis is on the way contemporary YA fiction is participating in shaping thinking about what adolescents are and do and the roles that are being constructed for them in society.

Considerable attention is given to the economics of today's youth culture: the extent to which it has been commodified and entangles young people in costly and time-consuming habits of consumption – especially of music, television, radio, fashion, films, and more and less legal substances (see, for instance, Brooks in Mallan and Pearce). This is a significant departure from the youth culture of the 1960s and 1970s which 'chose to stand against the consumption of the era, offering a parallel and quite contrary nirvana to the "white heat" of Prime Minister Wilson's technological revolution' (Green: xi). Nevertheless, it is also important to remember that the young are not just consumers, but also active creators of culture in the form of poetry, fan sites, lyrics, fashion, music, and, increasingly, filmed material using web cams, mobile phones, and other new technological gadgets. Their bodies, too, are sites for creative activity, from hair cuts and colours through tattoos and piercings, at the more comfortable end of an aesthetic that incorporates acts of self-mutilation (see Chapter 5 for a discussion of new trends in self-harm).

Much adolescent creativity has traditionally been rejected by adult/official culture on the grounds that it is variously puerile, offensive, self-indulgent, and/or bathetic. The accuracy of these descriptions could be contested (though many adults have evidence from their own pasts to support such charges), but the act of dismissing young people's efforts is important in itself to the us–them dynamic of youth culture. One of the issues that will be raised in the course of this chapter is the extent to which this oppositional relationship has been undermined as previously distinct areas of culture become blurred, contributing at various levels to the disenfranchisement of the young. Symptomatic of this change is the way significant categories of YA fiction focus on characters who are rendered impotent either as a consequence of the terrible things that happen to them or because they are encouraged to see themselves as frivolous and peripheral.

Before looking at the way current writing for young people responds to youth culture, it is helpful to trace the historical relationship between the two. Since we are dealing with a specific subgenre, this means beginning with the construction of its implied reader (Weinreich, 2000). The case of YA/teenage fiction has a relatively brief formal history, since before there was a clear social image of adolescence and teenagers – and so a possible implied readership – there could not be a literature for, about or to this group.

Born in the United States: inventing adolescence

In his influential study, *Centuries of Childhood* (1962), the French historian and critic, Philippe Ariès, suggests that: 'to every period of history, there corresponded a privileged age and a particular division of human life' and goes on to identify adolescence as the privileged and favourite age of the twentieth century (1996: 29). While it is easy to argue with many of Ariès's claims, he is surely right in recognising that the first stages in human development are not just biological – not just about getting bigger and learning to function in society – they are also cultural inventions and shaped according to society's needs and sense of itself at any given moment. Ariès proposes that the twentieth century is the age of adolescence because it created adolescence in its own image.

The ground was prepared in 1904, when the first full-length study of the subject was produced by the American psychologist, G. Stanley Hall, and the creative process was largely completed in 1950, when the psychoanalytic theorist, Erik Erikson, published *Childhood and Society*. In this early study, Erikson characterised adolescence as heroic; at this stage in human development, he said, young people find themselves struggling to achieve an identity and so undergo what he called an 'adolescent identity crisis' which plays a crucial role in personal development (in Appleyard, 1994: 96).

Images of youth and youth culture in adolescent fiction testify to the widespread influence of Erikson's ideas. At the front of what is recognisably a canon of adolescent fiction are J.D. Salinger's *The Catcher in the Rye* (1951), S.E. Hinton's *The Outsiders* (1967) and *Rumble Fish* (1975), and Robert Cormier's *The Chocolate War* (1974). Whether or not the authors themselves had read Erikson's work, they all present adolescent protagonists who are both heroic and in the throes of an identity crisis, suggesting that Erikson had both caught and was influencing the mood of the times in his recognition of the central role adolescence was beginning to play in the twentieth-century cultural psyche.

It was in the postwar period in the United States that both the teenager and the YA novel first came to public attention. At this time the transitional period between childhood and adulthood came to be regarded as important, interesting, and volatile. Previously, becoming a teenager was notable because it signalled that a young person was approaching the moment when s/he would 'come of age' and take up a position as a full member of society. Usually this meant leaving school, entering paid employment, and more or less reproducing their parents' lifestyles and attitudes (Green: x).

In the postwar years, this pattern started to break down in response to a changing economy. Increasingly industrialised methods of production reduced the demand for unskilled workers; at the same time, the United States was unprecedentedly wealthy, meaning families could support dependent children longer while they carried on in education to gain the skills needed for the new job market. The young people who would once have joined the workforce and been absorbed into adult culture were legislated into schools until their mid-teens (school leaving age varied by State but was normally between 16 and 18), and put in charge of modest but entirely disposable incomes in the form of allowances and money earned through summer and after-school jobs. Simultaneously frustrated by this extension of childhood and liberated from the demands of work, they had the time, the inclination, and the money to explore themselves and to discover that there were ways of having fun and responding to the changes in size, shape, and the desires of their bodies which were outside the familiar world of family. Youth culture had arrived, and quickly became a counter-culture in that it neither sought nor wanted adult approval. A new force for social change was emerging and with it new ideas about how society should function.

Youth culture is not monolithic. Class, sex, sexuality, race, ethnicity, intellectual/athletic ability, tastes in music, fashion and illegal substances, and geographical location affect the forms it takes. It also responds to the wider culture so that, for instance, the disparate strands of Anglo-American 1960s and 1970s youth culture were largely united in their opposition to the Vietnam war, though they were engaged in their own culture wars at other levels. This formative period in youth culture's history confirmed many public institutions – from the family through the government and its official bodies (together referred to as 'the establishment') – in the sense that teenagers comprise a disruptive force that needs to be controlled. Over time, some areas of YA fiction, which, like children's literature generally is almost without exception produced by adults for the young, have begun to serve a wider cultural project concerned with subduing the perceived teenage threat by re-presenting youth and youth culture not as disruptive and powerful but as impotent and puerile to readers who are anticipating and undergoing adolescence. Novels about and directed at teenagers have contributed to reconfiguring adolescence – and so transforming culture – in two key ways: by adjusting the stereotype of the teenager they disseminate, and by revising and reinflecting the conventions of the genre.

Descriptions of YA/teenage fiction found in standard reference works and academic studies (see, for instance, Carpenter and Prichard, 1984; Cullinan and Person (eds), 2001; McCallum, 1999; Watson (ed), 2001; Trites, 2000; Eccleshare in Hunt (ed.), 2004) identify a set of characteristics associated with writing about and for adolescents and teenagers. Critics agree that it tends to be concerned with real life, including social issues, school, romance, and other relationships – not least those reflecting the difficulties of family life.

YA fiction, they say, features characters caught up in the turbulent and complex emotions associated with the teenage years, and is addressed to readers in this state of turmoil. It deals with teenage identity and concerns, as distinct from those associated with adulthood and childhood, and often as part of this concern, identifies (and is preoccupied by) a division between an 'authentic' but hidden inner self and a 'false' public self.

Studies of adolescent fiction also present the trajectory of adolescence as a movement from feelings of isolation/alienation accompanied by distaste for the status quo to a sense of acceptance and willingness to invest in the very social structures that gave rise to the original sense of critical detachment. Characters in YA fiction may be prepared to enter and validate the adult world, but as Roberta Seelinger Trites notes, YA novels stop short of following their protagonists into adulthood, meaning that they are about growth and development (*entwicklungsroman*) rather than coming of age (*bildungsroman*) (2000: 10–20). Trites also, and importantly, emphasises the extent to which YA fiction instructs characters and readers in cultural power dynamics; for instance, showing young people where they currently fit in established chains of domination and repression, giving an indication of how much power they are likely to acquire, and conveying the need to accept limits on power as part of acquiring an adult identity.

Despite its concern with the stresses and strains of the adolescent years, writing for this age group also frequently adopts a humorous tone (even if the humour is black). In many cases humour is derived from confessional elements, often arising from first-person narratives in the form of diaries, letters, or journals. Perhaps because of these characteristics, many adult critics regard YA fiction as reflecting and appealing to adolescent narcissism, qualities that are increasingly reflected in paratextual features, from titles to marketing strategies. Series such as those by Louise Rennison, Meg Cabot, Rosie Rushton, Kathryn Lamb, and Sue Limb are typical, with their obsessive teen's eye views signalled by pastel and glittery covers studded with shiny teenage accessories such as phones, lipsticks, hearts, and guitars, and titles such as *Brothers, Boyfriends and Babe Magnets* (2006) and ' ... *and that's when it fell off in my hand.' Further fabbitty-fab confessions of Georgia Nicolson* (2005).

Are you a girl, or are you a boy? Gender and adolescent fiction

A comparison of what is currently stocked in the teenage section of bookshops and the critics' view of what constitutes YA fiction suggests that in some important respects, the critical model summarised above is out of date. The critics are harking back to the formative years of adolescent fiction (the 1950s to the 1980s) and ignoring a number of prominent trends, including the dominance of novels clearly directed at girls. This shift offers insights into changes in youth culture as well as publishing for this age group and suggests that attitudes to the young have been steadily moving away from Erikson's heroic image and the juvenocentricism of the middle decades of the last century. The extent of the change becomes apparent when looking back at some of the earliest and most influential examples of YA fiction – the kind of books the critics had in mind when defining adolescent fiction – and focusing specifically on their images of and attitudes to adolescence and youth culture.

The first books for teenage readers provide evidence of the deeply rooted connection between terms such as 'youth', 'adolescence', and 'youth culture', and masculinity. It is not difficult to explain why this association came about. At the time when adolescence was being identified and examined, society was unashamedly patriarchal. For the young, as in most other social spheres, femininity was defined in opposition to masculinity, and constructed in terms of dependency, passivity, weakness, and purity. In other words, femininity was equated with childhood. In the same way, adolescence and the fiction of adolescence were and are largely defined by their difference from childhood and children's literature: adolescence emphasises attributes traditionally associated with hegemonic masculinity, such as independence and public displays of power, to distinguish it from childhood.

A brief look at the central characters of early adolescent fiction will show how radically they depart from traditional behaviour associated with the feminine. S.E. Hinton's Motorcycle Boy, the hero-figure in *Rumble Fish*, is typical. He has fashioned a unique persona by performing a role on the streets – a traditionally masculine forum (McRobbie, 1991: 24). In his first appearance in the novel, Motorcycle Boy breaks up a street fight between two gangs of adolescent boys, some armed with knives, with an apparently effortless, understated but undeniable display of machismo:

> The Motorcycle Boy stepped out, grabbed Biff's wrist and snapped it backwards. You could hear it crack like a matchstick. It was broke, sure enough … 'I think', he said thoughtfully, 'that the show is over'. (31)

As well as being shaped and masculinised by its rejection of childhood and femininity, in the early days of YA fiction, its heroes, like Motorcycle Boy, embodied the characteristics of Erkison's adolescent hero. They were inevitably in conflict with authority, radiated a rather romantic sense of alienation tinged with superiority, and had to make difficult decisions. Although not confined to male experience, Erikson's account of the phase has many features in common with the traditional trial and testing of the manly literary hero, perhaps another reason why classic YA fiction focussed on male protagonists.

YA fiction's focus on teenage boys and their struggles to achieve identity and independence masks the fact that at least since the nineteenth century, fiction had identified the liminal space now occupied by teenagers as territory belonging to girls and young women. While the heroes of Ballantyne, Henty, Hughes and Stevenson's novels leave school and/or home and are instantly absorbed into the male worlds of work or the military, once their formal education has finished, girls in nineteenth-century fiction tend to suffer the tedium of domestic tasks and languish in drawing rooms until marriage releases them into activity and responsibility. (Not all girls were released by marriage, but with age many found other ways to take up positions of responsibility, not least in the roles of spinster aunts running siblings' households and daughters looking after widowed fathers.) The situation was different for the poor, whose daughters generally followed the male path of entering the workforce early and so avoiding a period of enforced dependency, but middle-class girls in nineteenth-century novels are often introduced at a fretful and rebellious stage. In the course of their stories they learn to cease to think of their inactivity as oppressive and to accept the curbs on their behaviour that make them acceptable and, paradoxically, effective women.

One of the paradigms of this fiction of female adolescence is Ethel May, the central character in Charlotte M. Yonge's *The Daisy Chain* (1856), who can be seen as the prototype for Jo March (*Little Women*, 1868) and Katy Carr (*What Katy Did*, 1872). Yonge's Preface describes the book as an early form of crossover fiction, 'neither that "tale" for the young nor the novel for their elders'; it addresses the needs of real girls – as distinct from those they read about – who were caught between the nursery and the drawing room. In other words, early critics of children's literature recognised the need for a body of writing for the constituency we would now see as implied readers of YA fiction (neither adults nor children, physically mature but not yet integrated into adult society), and saw this as comprised entirely of females.[1]

In many ways the situation has come full circle; at all stages in life girls and women now read more fiction than do boys and men, and this is reflected in the preponderance of female characters in contemporary YA fiction, an implied reader who is female, and aggressive marketing aimed at adolescent girls. These factors in themselves need not be a reason for concern, but this area of juvenile fiction has been subject to other pressures that have worked together to make the critical definition of YA fiction outlined above obsolete, and could lead to the whole are of YA fiction being perceived as trivial, banal, and even enervating. Of particular concern is the way these changes both mirror and reinforce changes to the nature and impact of youth culture, which in turn suggest that in some western countries – notably America and Britain – many young people have not only been de-radicalised, but also effectively encouraged to collude in their own marginalisation.

Rebels without a cause?

There are many ways in which the visible social and political power attained by the young during the 1960s and 1970s has been eroded – not least by those who were themselves teenagers during those decades – and these changes can clearly be seen in writing for teenagers. The work of Aidan Chambers usefully encapsulates such changes at the domestic level. His most powerful novels are those, like *Breaktime* (1978) and *Dance on My Grave* (1982), which capture the us–them dynamic of a time when the worlds of adults, teenagers, and children were clearly demarcated, a time when young people's energy was directed towards attaining the necessary exit velocity that would take them out of the home and into new territory, symbolised in Chambers's work by sex, education, and youth culture.

Hal, in *Dance on My Grave*, is a mystery to his parents, not primarily because he is gay (they do not realise this), but because he is clever, creative (his teacher wants him to stay on to study English in the sixth form), and young. His world revolves around the beach, bikers, and Barry, the first boy with whom he becomes sexually and emotionally involved. Hal's parents want him to model himself on their lives – leave school, get a job, get married – which is as undesirable and incomprehensible to him as his life is to them. The tension at home helps propel him into action, and it is clear that eventually, like many of the generation in Britain about whom Chambers is writing, he will move beyond his parents' world. He belongs firmly to the male, motivated, rather superior model of the original YA hero.

Chambers's last, and to my mind least successful novel, *This is All: The Pillow Book of Cordelia Kenn* (2005), has a female central character living in the early twenty-first century. Cordelia Kenn lives with her father, her mother having died when Cordelia was five. Like many contemporary children, she not only has a single parent, but moves between households since her aunt Doris has taken on the role of surrogate mother to her and looks after her for parts of every week. Eventually Doris also becomes Cordelia's father's lover.

In a departure from the young versus old tensions that drive his earlier teenage novels, *This is All* gets mired in the liberal attitudes of the adults – who belong to the generation that worked so hard to escape the straight-jacket of 1950s' respectability and 'change the world'. Far from harking back to a golden age, however, Chambers writes dismissively of the 1960s and its legacy. He has Cordelia's father observe:

> Revolution my bum! Load of old bull ... Nothing revolutionary about it. We were self-indulgent, self-righteous prigs ... look around you at the people of my generation who are in power. The politicians. The remnants that were the Beatles. Jagger and his gang. To name but a few. Pitiful. (126)

Although he dismisses the efforts of the 'Sixties generation, Cordelia's father typifies their more relaxed attitudes to parenting and more open relationships with their children. For instance, where *Breaktime*'s Ditto and *Dance on My Grave*'s Hal have to keep their sexual lives private,[2] Cordelia makes no secret of the fact that she is determined to lose her virginity before she is 16. Her aunt even encourages her to 'get on with it' (108) and suggests Cordelia organises a 'sex saga' (148) to get her boyfriend, Will, in the mood. When she finally manages to become sexually active, she and Will take it for granted that they may have sex at her house.

This shift in boundaries and lack of tension between the generations means that Cordelia and Will generate no exit velocity. There is also no sense of an alternative world as represented by youth culture in this book: Cordelia and Will like the same things as the adults with whom they live and aspire to live similar lives (Cordelia's other influences include her English teacher, who becomes her closest female friend). They are approved of by the older generation, while their interactions with people their own age are minimal and occasionally damaging, in one case leading to Cordelia's being abducted by a boy they have befriended. The couple give up plans to study at university to live in a caravan with the baby they are expecting and run a small business with the help of their parents. The only obstacle in the steady progress of these young people as they move towards becoming clones of their parents' generation is Cordelia's death in childbirth – but even in this she is following in her mother's footsteps by dying young and leaving behind a daughter.

As these examples show, in his career as a children's writer, Aidan Chambers has charted one of the fundamental changes in the domestic relationships between the young and the old – a change that is working against radical elements in youth culture – the liberal attitudes of a generation of parents who want to have closer relationships with their children than many had with their own parents. While in itself this is not undesirable or damaging, as one of several simultaneously experienced factors, the narrowing of the generation gap it effects contributes to the social and emotional quagmire of comfort and acceptance that is inimical to creativity; particularly since young people as a group also remain economically dependent on their parents longer than did previous generations.

Related to parents' more liberal views on sex, sexuality, and children's experiments with alcohol and drugs is the fact that many of these same parents have a proprietary attitude to youth culture, believing themselves to have participated in the originary moment of popular music and so dismissing the contemporary youth scene as derivative as evidenced by its retro fashions, remixed music, and a seemingly endless recycling/remaking of American television programmes of forty years ago on television and film.[3] The same aging group protests against cruelty to animals and environmental issues, and monopolises the range of campaigning activities that once would have been the provenance of youth. If the generations cease to leave youth culture behind, the spaces for youthful creativity become overcrowded.

Creative congestion in the sphere of youth culture is compounded by the fact that hot on the heels of adolescents are 'tweenagers' or 'tweenies' – children who are taking on the fashions and interests of teenagers – while encamped before them is the current middle generation (mid-twenties to thirty-somethings) who are not prepared to give up the things that interested them in youth, giving rise to terms like 'kidult' and 'adultesence'. Like the generation of aging rockers before them, this set manifests what has been termed 'cultural necrophilia' (Peretti in Brooks, 2003: 4), 'consuming and validating the hip and fashionable and spouting ideologies that are irrelevant to the position and economic power they now hold' (4). Cultural necrophiliacs effectively prey on and feed off young people, surrounding themselves with the paraphernalia of youth at least in part because it gives the illusion that they are still young. To capitalise on this strategy of youth-by-association, corporate culture has harnessed youth culture for commercial purposes, and even industries traditionally associated with radicalism and rebellion (for instance, music and fashion) now commodify and sell youth to older, more affluent generations.

For all of these reasons, it can be difficult for contemporary adolescents to take control of youth culture in the very visible and dynamic ways employed by the young in the 1960s and 1970s. This is not to suggest that there is currently no youth culture or no subversively energised, politically and aesthetically sophisticated creativity by the young, but that the public space in which it has traditionally operated is being colonised by those who, on the basis of age and social position, belong outside youth culture. Alternatives exist: cyberspace, for instance, has become an important forum for youth culture, but its relative invisibility and tendency to operate outside the mainstream economic nexus means that its cultural impact is considerably narrower than was the case for its post-1950s antecedents. (The grassroots power of the medium is, however, beginning to be demonstrated; for instance, by the success of the indie rock band the Arctic Monkeys, who built up their fan base almost entirely via the internet, but this is still an emerging force for youth culture and as yet it has little impact on wider culture.)

Youth culture in cyberspace may seem a long way from YA fiction, but this background is important for understanding both how much recent writing aimed at teenage readers functions as a strand in the web of containment and ways in which some YA writers are rediscovering its potential to be a transformative medium, offering radical responses to culture. To see how these strands manifest themselves and the strategies they employ, it is helpful to think of YA fiction as participating in three spheres of activity: (1) books that trivialise adolescents, (2) nihilistic fiction, and (3) books that celebrate adolescent creativity and agency.

Canon fodder: YA fiction as a literature of containment

Books for adolescents are part of a much larger repositioning of youth in culture. Just as much 'authentic' (as opposed to mainstream and globalised) youth culture seems to be being hived off into a designated cultural space and so made safe, youth, which for a long time was almost a synonym for disturbance or agitation, is being encouraged to become quiescent, and the young seduced into handing over responsibility for the way they look and behave to consumer culture (see the discussion of M.T. Anderson's *Feed* in Chapter 8 for a dystopian projection of this phenomenon). The American cultural commentator, Henry Giroux, puts it this way:

> Denied any political agency, youth are narrated in social and cultural spheres by voices that turn youth itself into an 'empty category inhabited by the desires, fantasies, and interests of the adult world'. (in Brooks, 2003: 2)

Some forms of YA fiction are implicated in the narrating of youth into an 'empty category'. One reason for this has been identified by Julia Eccleshare:

> Impelled by the widespread anxiety that teenagers may abandon reading in favour of entertainment from other, easier-to-access media, teenage fiction has evolved as the most narcissistic of all fictions as, in its current form at least, it seems primarily directed towards mirroring society rather than asking questions of it. (2004: 542)

Initially, the adolescent critique of social organisation and interaction as dramatised in adolescent fiction was invested with meaning. Holden Caulfield and his successors pointed a finger at the world and cried 'phoney', and the world appeared to listen. Somewhat ironically for those involved professionally with children's literature, one reason for this seems to be that many young people were reading outside the domain of children's literature, which had yet to develop the ample and wide-ranging body of YA fiction available today. Instead of specially targeted teen novels, young people read works such as Herman Hesse's *Siddhartha*, the books of Carlos Casteneda, and *Zen and the Art of Motorcycle Maintenance*, all of which encouraged them to take on board philosophical, political, spiritual, and intellectual ideas so that, as the German critic, Winfred Kaminski, noted when writing about youth culture as late as the 1980s, young people were 'linguistically competent and, therefore, able to attack adult abuses of language' (1986: 202). Those in the vanguard of youth culture not only used and deconstructed language to expose what, with the healthy arrogance of youth, they identified as the hypocrisy of adolescent society, but also created alternative, often highly developed and sophisticated, forms of speech and art with which to contest and replace them. It is precisely these abilities that Roberta Seelinger Trites claims has given rise to the shape and nature of YA fiction:

> If adolescents did not have social and biological power so great that it is defined by authority as *needing institutional regulation*, the entire genre of

the postmodern *Entwicklungsroman* would not have emerged in the form that it has. ... (141; my emphasis)

Trites identifies why those in positions of authority would be interested in seeing YA fiction become a fiction of regulation and in the process reveals the antinomy at the heart of YA fiction: on the one hand it is understood to be a literature of breaking away and becoming, on the other, it is a literature of control and conformity, preparing the way for successive generations of teenagers to take up established roles in the existing social order.

Writing the present

This antinomy has resulted in YA fiction's breaking down into the three categories named above, reflecting the dominant constructions of adolescence in contemporary western culture. By far the largest and most fashionable groups in British bookshops today are those books that depict and address teenagers as superficial, hedonistic, and narcissistic. Books such as Louise Rennison's highly popular 'confessions of Georgia Nicolson' (beginning with *Angus, thongs and full-frontal snogging*, 1999) ignore the established wisdom that teenagers want realistic books about social issues and difficult decisions. Belonging more to the domain of popular than youth culture, books of this type justify Theodore Adorno's concerns about mass culture. They are readily available in bookshops, newsagents and supermarkets as well as online. They are highly readable, reassuring in the sense that they present a familiar world in a conventional way and, the crux of Adorno's thesis, all these elements make them invisible and effective carriers of ruling-class ideology. For Adorno, the problem with mass/popular culture is that it enslaves its consumers by naturalising the dominant ideology, and this is precisely the effect of reading these bestselling teen novels.

These books eschew political debate, topical issues, and significant areas of conflict, assuming that their readers (who from their 'chic-lit' covers to the sex of the central characters are clearly female) are only interested in friends, fashion, and fun. They not only encourage readers to accept the way the world is run but also to assume that they have no responsibility for it. Their characters' most challenging decisions are about what to wear and how to catch a partner. They unashamedly and openly attempt to manipulate their parents, make no effort to do more than appease teachers, and have no qualms about exposing their ignorance on everything from geography and history to travel, time zones, vocabulary, and basic logic.

Despite their books' impoverished levels of plot and banal preoccupations, Rennison and others like her do capture some of the linguistic creativity of youth culture, with its insider-outsider codes, idiosyncratic pronunciation and emphasis, enjoyment in extravagant adjectives skewed towards the risqué, the disparaging and the adoring, and magpie-like collecting of the bizarre. Rennison's books even provide a glossary with entries such as:

> **red-bottomosity.** Having the big red bottom. This is vair vair interesting *vis à vis* nature. When a lady baboon is 'in the mood' for luuurve, she displays her big red bottom to the male baboon. (Apparently he wouldn't have a clue otherwise, but that's boys for you!) Anyway, if you hear the call of the Horn, you are said to be displaying red-bottomosity.

Humour is often subversive – a way of dismissing what is held up as admirable. Sadly, the comedy in these books tends to be turned against its subjects, so that the overall effect is to trivialise young people and what passes for youth culture. The joke is from an adult perspective: we were once like you and (ho, ho, ho) you will soon be like us. Such books offer no encouragement to their readers to contest and replace the adult world of whose body and fashion sense the characters are endlessly critical, but encourage a sense of complacency about everything but appearance. Global warming, famine, war, disease – any sense of political engagement – feature not at all amid the chatter about snogging and exfoliating.

Trites's thesis that adolescent fiction is primarily concerned with how its characters (and vicariously its readers) learn to balance conflicting areas of power and repression cannot accommodate this kind of writing since no lessons are learned: failure to persuade parents to subsidise a shopping trip one day may fail, but on another the same tactics succeed; the current 'luuurve god' may be charmed after school but indifferent in the evening – there are no patterns and very little in the way of discernible cause and effect to events. These young people don't rebel, though they frequently fall foul of the authorities through their silliness. The narratives' direct address, collusive mode, and insider language (which the reader must learn to decode the text) align readers with the characters and so, by drawing them into positions of vacuity, temporarily disarming this potentially disruptive group. Significantly, while much tends to be made of young people's power as consumers, these books provide a portrait of economically useless youth: all of the characters know how to spend; none of them has learned how to earn.

As recreational reading books of this kind can be entertaining, and for those young people who read widely and so bring to bear a range of reading strategies, they may even invite readerly resistance which would counteract the tendencies I have identified. I have yet to find any evidence that this is how these books are being read. They disseminate an image of young people as dependent, parasitical, and powerless, a group transfixed by their own narcissistic natures.

Blinded by the light

The second group of teenage books has much in common with the early examples in the genre and so the definitions offered by critical studies, but books of this kind are now usually considerably darker, featuring protagonists who are damaged products of damaging societies. Robert Cormier was one of the first writers to adopt a nihilistic tone in writing for this age group, and though his scenarios continue to be among the most pessimistic, he has been joined by many fine writers whose often profound work ultimately implies that things will only get worse and that there is little point in striving to change or understand how the world works. A recent addition to this area of YA is Anne Fine's *The Road of Bones* (2006), notable because Fine is on record as believing in the importance of hope in writing for young people (Tucker, 2006: 199–209).

Yuri, Fine's protagonist, is growing up under a totalitarian regime reminiscent of the worst days under Stalin. After falling foul of the authorities, he survives beatings, deprivation, and years of incarceration under the harshest conditions. He loathes the system and observes closely its degrading and corrupting effects on people at all levels in the society. When he finally escapes, however, Yuri does not work for reform but becomes the leader of an equally tyrannous and ruthless movement intent on achieving power for personal gain. The closing pages, in which Fine reveals that Yuri's efforts to survive have perverted his instinct to be generous and to value free speech and thought, may encourage readers to question how they themselves would behave under similar circumstances; the book certainly avoids unrealistically sentimental optimism. Fine's unflinching and uncompromising portrait of Yuri-the-leader may be designed to provoke readers to try to find ways to counter the brutalising effects of totalitarian regimes, but in fact their effect is likely to be enervating. No suggestions about how things could be different are mooted; the cycle seems unbreakable, and the setting too remote to encourage most readers to think about situations closer to home and the need to nurture and protect the values missing from Yuri's world.

The kind of dark, intelligent, and often extremely well-written books produced by a few writers such as Robert Cormier and Gudrun Pausewang (see Chapter 5) encourage readers to think about issues and behaviours that are ignored by the engaging but disingenuous YA fiction currently dominating the market. As analytical responses to the economics of power/repression that Trites sees as central to writing for this age group, however, they too risk encouraging conformity and disillusionment. They illuminate problems, but offer only restricted ways forward. As Trites argues, starting with Cormier's *The Chocolate War*, books of this kind have warned against 'disturbing the universe'. Jerry Renault, Cormier's protagonist in that novel, actually has a poster in his school locker asking J. Alfred Prufrock's question, 'Do I dare/ Disturb the universe?' By the end of the book, the advice many readers would give him is not to try.

The nihilism of novels such as Cormier's can make it hard for readers to think why they should struggle for change when the consequence is unwelcome attention and recognition of impotence in the face of complex, entrenched, and inert social and political systems. Interestingly, books of this kind rarely acknowledge the existence of youth culture, or see it only as a scaled down version of the forms of repression and coercion taking place in society more generally (this is the model Cormier repeatedly presents to his readers). In failing to acknowledge the creative dimension of youth culture, these books overlook its potential for subversion and resistance, and its function as a forum for new ways of thinking. A failure of adult vision for how the world could be changed for the better leads to an overemphasis on the negative and destructive sides of youth culture.

We can change the world

By contrast, the third category of contemporary YA fiction celebrates the coming to creativity and power that takes place in adolescence and shows young people as ethical, engaged, and effective. When confronted by disappointments and challenges, the characters in this group of books prove to be resilient, and the texts hold out a belief that change is necessary and, crucially, possible. This makes purposeful action – whether rebellious or reformative and no matter how unlikely to succeed – meaningful. In celebratory adolescent fiction, participating in planned, goal-orientated action provides an aesthetic of transformation that, in contemporary culture, substitutes for the kinds of culturally agreed rites of passage that formerly signalled maturity. It is often accompanied by changes in lifestyle – from how and where characters live to how they dress and with whom they associate. For Trites, achieving maturity in YA fiction is synonymous with the characters becoming reconciled 'to the power entailed in the social institutions with which they must interact to survive' (20). Books that focus on young people's creativity, however, are in fact concerned with how the protagonists will move on from sites of confrontation and resistance to explore and test the self against new opportunities. In other words, they are still coming into their power and have not yet found its limits or experienced the need for institutional regulation.

Books in this category may be stylistically innovative, but there are many, and especially those primarily concerned with social injustice and the need for change, that focus primarily on content: this is the kind of book Dresang describes as radical change type 3 (books that deal with previously forbidden subjects and/or previously overlooked settings and/or that include new and complex depictions of characters and/or that represent new types of communities and that may have unresolved endings, 1999: 26). Books of this kind that are worth mentioning before turning to more stylistically innovative examples (Dresang's type four) are Terri Paddock's *Come Clean* (2004) and Jonathan Kebbe's *Noodle Head* (2005). Both are about the systematic and abusive repression of young people who are unjustly deemed to be out of control. For me, they function as metaphors for how some sections of society would like to disable those young people who challenge orthodoxy.

Paddock's novel is set in the United States and features a family dominated by highly conservative and actively religious parents. Their son has recently committed suicide after being incarcerated in a Christian rehabilitation unit where they placed him when, on the basis of his adolescent behaviour, taste in music, and the clothes he wore, they decided that he was a drug addict. Despite his death, they turn his twin sister over to the same centre the one time she experiments with alcohol. Justine experiences institutionalised abuse – physical, sexual, emotional, and mental – under the guises of religion, therapy, and self-help regimes. Eventually she escapes with a male friend, and they spend many weeks in hiding, recovering from the experience and terrified that they will be captured and readmitted. Paddock's indictment of American institutions (including the family) that seek to silence and repress the young is mirrored in *Noodle Head*, set in the United Kingdom.

Fifteen-year-old Marcus King looks older than he is, and with his red dreadlocks (Jamaican musician father, red-headed mother from the East End of London), claustrophobia, and fear of control he seems to typify the aspects of youth culture that many institutions find threatening. He is in fact an intelligent, loving, and good-natured teenager, who is phobic rather than deliberately troublesome. Marcus has good relationships with his parents, friends, and social worker, but after running away from school for the umpteenth time, he is sent to a juvenile detention centre. There, instead of educating or helping the teenagers in their charge, the staff medicate them heavily on highly addictive drugs.

The book follows Marcus's struggle to resist losing himself in the medication and to escape from the institution. As in *Come Clean*, the powerlessness of the young people incarcerated in the institution, where they are physically subordinated by guards, mentally and emotionally controlled by drugs, and have no advocates, mirrors the way dictatorial regimes have always treated dissidents. It is worth pointing out that the books being discussed in this section are not isolated examples of juvenile fiction that highlight ways in which the young have been constructed as inconvenient to authorities seeking to impose their visions for society. For instance, towards the end of the Thatcher/Reagan era, children's writers began to produce lively, dystopic scenarios about what society would look like if the very similar ideological agendas and programmes being instituted in the United Kingdom and the United States were followed to their logical conclusions. Disruptive youths – usually depicted in these books as the brightest and least easily quashed young people – are shown to be particular targets as typified in Malcolm Rose's (1993) *The Obtuse Experiment*, in which large numbers of such young people are put on an ocean liner under the pretence that they are going to be given extra tuition. In fact, the government intends to sink the ship and rid itself of their troubling behaviour.

The desire to remove challenging young people from society arises from the perception of youth as a disruptive category, and institutional associations between youth culture (linked to sex, drugs, and popular music) and counter culture. Both *Come Clean* and *Noodle Head* suggest that the problems lie not with the young or youth culture, but with those who misuse positions of trust and power and begrudge those who are capable of independent thought and action. Unlike *The Road of Bones* and other examples of nihilistic fiction, however, these books seek to energise their readers and galvanise them into action by exposing harmful and hypocritical regimes specifically affecting their peers while validating the young, whose friendships, determination, and strategic planning allow them to escape and expose what had been going on. They reinstate the image of the adolescent as hero.

The transformative energy of this third – and crucial – area of recent adolescent fiction can be seen in the variety of formats, issues, and characters it embraces. For instance, Judd Winick's *Pedro and Me: Friendship, Loss and What I Learned* (2000) is a graphic novel based on a relationship formed during an American reality TV series in which it was revealed that Pedro, one of the participants, was HIV positive. Winick relates the events leading up to Pedro's death from AIDS, from his journey to the United States from Cuba through his participation in the gay scene that ended up in his contracting AIDS. Although the book culminates in Pedro's death, it is nevertheless intentionally presented as uplifting since it focuses on his effective campaign to inform young people about HIV/AIDS. Pedro is not bitter; neither is he an outcast. He operates both within a close circle of friends and as a national figure, talking publicly about his situation.

Winick exploits the similarities between graphic novels and television/film in some very effective ways. For those familiar with the original television programme and who might be reluctant to read a conventional novel, the emphasis on images rather than text is reassuring. The use of close-up and reaction 'shots' enabled by the graphic style similarly draws on the conventions of television, as does its reliance on dialogue over description and analysis. Much of the content of the book is comparable to the kinds of scenes frequently included on DVDs of films and television programmes: footage that was never broadcast, behind the scenes conversations, personal interviews with the personalities, and insights into what happened next. The interactions between visual and textual material ensure that the content functions on several levels, conveying information about relationships, states of mind, behaviour, and characteristics despite the relatively small amount of text.

The graphic format is associated with the kind of popular, mass-media publications that have traditionally been regarded with suspicion by educationalists, suggesting to readers that *Pedro and Me* stands apart from official instructions about the needs for safe sex and acceptance of those who have contracted HIV/AIDS. There is also an association with tales of superheroes – the figures most associated with graphic fictions. Most superheroes have been transformed by contact with contaminated or unearthly substances, and this association gives a slightly different gloss to Pedro's illness and the powers of speech and persuasion it unlocks.

As a homosexual Latino youth, Pedro could easily have taken up the role of alienated outsider in conflict with authority so familiar from traditional YA fiction. Instead, *Pedro and Me* shows him participating in what has become one of the staples of mainstream culture – reality television – and gives him a voice within the institutions most associated with preparing young people to take up places in society: schools. Significantly, the scenes that show him in schools also contain dialogue that takes it as fact that young people are sexually curious, sexually active, and sometimes sexually abused.

The rise of the Religious Right, particularly in the United States, and programmes promoting sexual abstinence are making it increasingly difficult to speak about teenage sexual activity as normal, expected, and enjoyable. *Pedro and Me* does precisely this, urging not abstinence but responsibility – responsibility to oneself and one's partners. Judd Winick's book is an interesting hybrid. It combines formats (graphic fiction and television) from popular/youth culture and a central character who represents those usually associated with the marginal and disruptive areas of society (young, male, Latino, and gay) to teach values about friendship, responsibility, ethical behaviour, and rites of passage that uphold longstanding official values but also validate more inclusive and safer relationships.

Pedro and Me takes youth culture for granted and references it casually through such things as viewing, settings, allusions to fashion, and socialising; two innovative books that actively incorporate elements of youth culture at the levels of plot and presentation are Ellen Wittlinger's *Hard Love* (1999) and Janet Tashjian's *The Gospel According to Larry* (2003). Pleasingly, both also include and address the kind of adolescent males who are given little attention and credence in modern British society (notably, neither of the books is British and both are by women): boys who are intelligent, able, ambitious, and engaged.

John, the central character in *Hard Love*, uses writing to help him understand his feelings about sex, sexuality, his parents' divorce, his mother's new partner – and many other aspects of his life. The narrative progresses through first-person summary of events, told directly to the reader, and pieces of creative writing. John discovers the world of fanzines, extracts from several of which are included in the text. Through them he enters a new world of slightly older, more sophisticated young people who use language, texts, and writing to explore themselves and to act on those around them. Marisol, the high school student who introduces him to fanzines, is very publicly and politically lesbian, and much of the text involves John's coming to terms with his feelings for her and learning to recognise his own heterosexuality.

As an artistic teenager who communicates primarily with girls, John initially seems to exemplify what Sharyn Pearce calls the 'wussy boy' in new millennium fiction (2001: 61), but in fact, John's intellect, integrity, and maturity are tested in his relationships with parents, friends, and prospective lovers, and through his writing. Robyn McCallum points to the way much adolescent fiction iterates a liberal humanist model of self-identity as something to be struggled for, but if recognised, achieved, and properly cared for, this 'true' self lasts a lifetime. *Hard Love* offers a different model, as John gradually realises that identity is the product of self-fashioning; it is permanently plastic and a lifelong project.

Wittlinger shows adolescence as a dynamic phase in this process, a time when realisations and decisions are most visibly affecting the public persona as young people sample from the menu of lifestyles around them. Where earlier adolescent fiction was preoccupied with the sense that there was a true and authentic self waiting to be revealed in the way McCallum suggests, *Hard Love* shows identity, including sexual identity, as complex, flexible, and permanently in process.

Significantly, this novel celebrates the value and creativity of inventing a self, making it an encouraging and empowering work. Through its emphasis on writing, *Hard Love* reminds readers that language is fundamental to subjectivity and identity (see Butler, 1997). The way John and his friends constantly exercise and experiment with their linguistic skills and styles makes them more effective in managing themselves, better able to understand their circumstances, and capable of adjusting the way they are placed in relational and institutional hierarchies of power. It also gives them pleasure and helps generate the exit velocity needed to leave home to make lives of their own. However, one of the key differences between this book and many works of adolescent fiction is that while it validates youth culture and shows it as promoting growth and encouraging individuation, it does not assume that the only way for the young to become independent is through rejecting and despising the previous generation – especially as represented by their parents. Through his writing and the discussions about it that he has with Marisol and his new friends, John realises that he has misrepresented and misunderstood things about his parents and their needs. He opens up what had become nogo areas in their relationships in ways that make it possible for them to grow together at the same time that he is preparing to leave home.

Janet Tashjian's *The Gospel According to Larry* also features a teenage boy who explores relationships and ethical issues through writing; in this case, in the form of a website. Unexpectedly, the site, which he has created to woo a girl who thinks of him only as a friend, becomes a cult phenomenon. Tashjian explores the power of the Internet as a form of instant mass media, the rampant nature of consumerism, the lack of self-awareness of current educational curricula, and infatuation with the media and its celebrities. This is a self-reflexive text, which regularly comments on and adjusts its narrative through footnotes, photographs, and additional remarks. It foregrounds the subjectivity of truth, the manipulative dimension to love, and the ethical complications of even the most day-to-day relationships and events.

The Gospel According to Larry and *Hard Love* do not presuppose that young people have stopped being creative because the Internet, computer games, satellite television, and the whole panoply of electronic gadgetry now available to them occupy their time and attention. Rather, they show the possibility for fusion and invention between old and new forms of expression, and in doing so, they offer much-needed ways forward through narrative for their readers. New ways forward are central to the work of radical, transformative texts. Although fictions that feature creative and participatory young people represent a small percentage of the YA market, those readers who have the chance to find and read them will have internalised stories that can help them interact with culture – including the part of culture represented by YA fiction – in dynamic ways. As the following chapter shows, at a time when the young are exhibiting many symptoms of distress, the need for such positively transformative texts has never been greater.

5
Self-harm, Silence, and Survival: Despair and Trauma in Children's Literature

> What a thrill –
> My thumb instead of an onion.
> The top quite gone
> Except for a soft hinge.
> > (from Sylvia Plath's 'Cut')

Children's literature that deals with hopelessness and specifically with the response to it known as self-harming is a relatively recent trend; to the best of my knowledge, this chapter comprises the first exploration of the relationship between what young people read and attitudes to self-harming. The role reading can play in transforming the lives of young people who are caught in cycles of despair and anger directed against themselves is suggested by reformed self-harmer turned journalist Nick Johnstone. In an article about the rising numbers of young people in Britain who are self-harmers, he explains how reading helped him, concluding, 'A good place to start breaking the habit is in a library: find out why you are doing it, how you can stop, learn new ways to cope' (*The Guardian*, 8 June 2004: 9). Even better than learning how to break the habit would be a prophylactic approach in which children's literature provided opportunities for readers to recognise and understand their hostile feelings, and offered them new ways of storying their lives.

The paucity of children's books about depression, despair, and self-loathing is not surprising. One of the oldest and most active debates among those involved in bringing children and books together concerns what kind of material it is appropriate for children to read. Nicholas Tucker's *Suitable for Children?* (1976) traces the argument back to the beginning of the nineteenth century, when concern tended to focus on the way what many educationalists and critics regarded as the wrong kind of stories (such things as fantasies, fairy tales, and ghost stories) could prevent children from growing up to be rational, capable adults. In recent years, concern has shifted from the kind of material that is published to how potentially disturbing material is handled. Many writers, editors, publishers, and critics argue strongly that whatever happens in the course of books, and no matter how realistically it is presented, if they are intended to be read by children, books should end on a note of optimism, or at least hope.[1] Natov (2003), for instance, argues that a book for children 'must not leave the child-reader in despair. And although what evokes hopelessness varies from child to child. ... A poetics for children requires a delicate rendering of hope and honesty' (220). Such a pronouncement overlooks the fact that children's literature caters for readers from birth to sixteen, from different backgrounds and with different needs, sometimes including the need to acknowledge disturbing experiences and overwhelming feelings of despair, anger, and frustration.

Despite efforts to protect children from books and other kinds of reading that could leave them feeling hopeless, the young have always encountered frightening, nihilistic, and depressive 'stories' in a variety of contexts – from the news through popular soap operas and even such 'family favourite' films as Walt Disney's version of *Bambi*. Chapter 7 looks at the appeal and need for frightening fiction among juvenile readers; here I want to concentrate on books that are transforming long-held views about what is suitable for children through their explorations of some of the damaging and traumatic aspects of growing up in contemporary Western culture. The changing attitudes reflect adjustments both to how childhood is understood and to what children's literature is and does, and have become sufficiently established for Kenneth Kidd to observe in a forum on 'Trauma and Children's Literature' that there 'seems to be a consensus now that children's literature is the most rather than the least appropriate forum for trauma work' (2005: 120). Kidd is referring primarily to children's books dealing with the Holocaust and other traumatic conflicts, but he alludes to a more general willingness to explore, even in books for very young readers, dark emotions, damaged lives, disturbed behaviours, and characters whose distress is not relieved by the arrival of a fairy godmother or a fortunate twist of fate. By making it possible for children to encounter such emotions and situations on the page, these works are not only reshaping children's literature, but also creating opportunities for young people to gain insights into themselves and those around them that may have positive long-term social and emotional benefits.[2]

Contextualising depressive fiction

Adults do not have the monopoly on powerful negative emotions or suffering. Indeed, often the things that lead to destructive and overwhelming feelings in maturity have their roots in childhood experience. As well as having their own difficult experiences, children also witness and are affected by adults whose anger, frustration, and despair lead them to behave irrationally and sometimes dangerously, whether at home, as part of more general disputes or disasters, or in the media. In the United Kingdom, one in four people will suffer from a form of mental illness in the course of their lifetimes,[3] but even as some boundaries around children's literature are shifting, until recently, in Britain and America, writing for the young has rarely acknowledged this fact, preferring instead to shield children from even such a widespread form of illness as depression. This protective rationale has withheld one means by which even very young children could learn to recognise and articulate destructive feelings and behaviours, and in doing so may have increased their susceptibility to powerful negative emotions. Recent research in the United Kingdom and the United States suggests that record numbers of young people are on the verge of mental breakdown as a result of family break-up, exam pressures, and growing inability to cope with the pressures of modern life (see Thompson and Goodchild, 2005; Hill, 2006; Honigsbaum, 2005), so it behoves us to look at ways of reversing this trend including by addressing such topics in the fictions they read.

Since emotions are often captured better in abstract forms such as images and music than in words alone, the picturebook, with its combination of words and images and its tendency to be read aloud, encouraging writers to explore rhythm and sound-sense as well as literal sense, can be a particularly effective medium for representing a range of emotional states, including depression and despair. There is an implicit demand on picturebook makers, who know that their work is likely to be shared with young children, to produce something that is an accurate, powerful, and complex representation of a state of mind in a way that is fully comprehensible to a young reader. This often means honing and condensing material and language to a point where it functions poetically, signifying at many levels and feeding back on itself to generate multiple meanings. Again, the counterpoint made possible through the visual elements – including the inventive use of peritextual features – can be aesthetically enriching.

Culturally there is a more abstract reason why picturebooks, normally associated with very young readers and so unaffected by ambiguities about audience that surround much YA fiction, can be so important for exploring emotions such as despair. Despair and depression constitute mental wounds: they may be both responses to and forms of trauma. Trauma theorists often point to the importance of the figure of the dead or wounded child in psychoanalytic theory, frequently citing Lacan's rereading of Freud's story of the burning child in *The Interpretation of Dreams* (see, for instance, Caruth, 1996; Felman, 1985; and Ragland, 1993). The wounded child may symbolise a damaged self, but it may equally stand for a damaged culture; this means that if the image of the self as a child can be kept intact and unviolated, the myth of innocent childhood that Rose maintains is central to the well-being of adults and the work of children's literature remains in place individually and socially. Just as the child in Lacan's mirror stage needs to accept that its seemingly coherent reflection represents the self in order to effect the transition to the Symbolic, so it seems that in Western culture at least, entry into adulthood involves subscribing to the cultural myth of childhood.

Despite the demand that the myth of ideal childhood be passed on and accepted, it eventually needs to be understood as an invention, distinct from the lived experience of individuals and the collective experience of childhood. The Symbolic does not cancel out the Imaginary any more than the myth of childhood erases actual childhood; rather, the Symbolic represses and reshapes the Imaginary just as the myth of childhood reshapes individual lived childhood, and both falsify, delimit, and ignore significant aspects of self. Many fictions that deal with self-harming explore the way mistaking an ideal of childhood for reality can lead to a sense of crisis, for believing that one has been or should have been the ideal is likely to make unhappiness, anxiety, and other less-than ideal emotions seem illegitimate (How can I, who have had such a happy life, feel unhappy? Who am I – well fed, loved, educated – to feel anxious when others endure real deprivation and suffering?).

As the second part of this chapter shows, in adolescent fictional accounts of despair and distress as well as in memoirs and other personal accounts of living through such periods, characters frequently blame themselves both for what happens to them and for the way they feel. Fictional opportunities to explore the fact that even early childhood is not always and for all children a carefree and happy period could help young people recognise emotions, symptoms, and patterns of behaviour before they become acute. As Perry Nodelman observes,

> To deprive children of the opportunity to read about confusing or painful matters like those they might actually be experiencing will either make literature irrelevant to them or else leave them feeling they are alone in their thoughts or experience. (1996: 86)

That some powerful explorations of hopelessness and depression can now be encountered in picturebooks is further evidence of the participation of children's literature in the reshaping of childhood in culture that Kenneth Kidd points to in his discussion of trauma literature for children. It is, he says, 'part of [the] complex history of childhood's revaluation, of its merger with the idea of interiority ... childhood is now imagined as a psychic-developmental space at once sacrosanct and violated' (2006: 133–4). The picturebooks discussed below reflect current efforts to rethink, revalue, and refashion what childhood is and how it is experienced in some of the books that young people encounter.

Pictures of darkness: the child in the book

Although there is a growing body of critical work about picturebooks concerned with the Holocaust and atrocities committed in the course of other conflicts (see, for instance, Bosmajian, 1989 and 2002; Walter and March, 1993; Russell, 1996; Baer, 2000; O'Sullivan, 2005; Kidd, 2006), there are still relatively few picturebooks that directly tackle some of these darker issues. I am specifically interested in picturebooks that explore how previously happy children may be affected by strong and lasting feelings of despair, sometimes leading to self-loathing and causing young people to harm or even kill themselves.

Tomi Ungerer's *Le Nuage Bleu* [*The Blue Cloud*] (2000) falls between the categories of conflict literature and books depicting self-harm and suicide, making it an interesting point of comparison with books in which these behaviours are associated exclusively with the feelings and behaviours of a child character's everyday life. It tells the story of a joyful little blue cloud. The cloud is so happy that it never cries rain or joins the other clouds making tempestuous weather. Because it never rains, it steadily increases in size, casting a beautiful blue shadow wherever it goes. Life is good until one day the blue cloud encounters an enormous black cloud. The cloud is made of smoke from fires caused by a battle between the different groups of people who live in the town: '*Les blancs tuaient les noirs, les noirs assassinaient les jaunes, les jaunes trucidaient les rouges at les rouges exécutaient les blancs.*' [The whites kill the blacks, the blacks assassinate the yellows, the yellows overpower the reds, and the reds murder the whites.] (All translations from this text are mine.) Ungerer's illustrations zoom in on women and children of all colours huddled together while their men chase each other in a never-ending circle amid the bodies of the fallen.

The blue cloud is unprepared for what he witnesses. Horrified by the violence, he decides to act – but his action takes the form of self-immolation. He rains on the town: '*Ce fut un deluge bleu*' [It was a blue flood]. Every drop of his being pours down on the town, bathing it in his happy blueness. The fighting stops, a celebration begins, and from then on the people live together in harmony. They rebuild the town and, in memory of the cloud who sacrificed himself for them, they paint all its buildings blue and rename the town Nuagebleuville.

There are many ways to read this story, including as a religious allegory and as Ungerer's attempt to instil in his young readers a sense of the horrors and futility of war and the need to see beyond cultural differences. Himself a child in German-occupied Alsace during the rise of the Third Reich and World War II, Tomi Ungerer has written powerfully about the way he adapted to – even enjoyed – the war years, including the extent to which he was affected by Nazification (see Lathey, 1999: 192–6). Much of his work reflects a concern to counter the kinds of hatreds that fuel ethnic conflicts in particular and war in general. For the purposes of this discussion, however, I am interested in the way the cloud functions as a child character and how he reaches the conclusion that his death is the necessary price for change.

That the cloud is a child is clearly signalled: the picture of him on the first page looks exactly like a beaming naked blue baby; he begins small, and though he grows, he has no responsibilities and retains his unfinished features and youthful exuberance until he comes upon the battle. The decision to give up his life for others is not debated; it is what he feels compelled to do, and his action is never subsequently questioned. (In the six years since this book was published, suicide has become strongly associated with bombers and other kinds of terrorists who are promised spiritual rewards for their actions, and some may feel that the association between suicide and utopia in this story is therefore problematic. However, since the cloud hurts no one but himself and his self-sacrifice brings about peace and reconciliation, the cloud's action stands apart from contemporary suicide bombings.)

There is an established tradition of stories ending in redemptive child death including Andersen's *The Little Match Girl* (1848), Sendak's *Dear Mili* (1988) (based on a tale told by Wilhelm Grimm in a letter to a motherless little girl), and Innocenti and Gallaz's *Rose Blanche* (1985). The power of these stories often stems from the sense that the child protagonist's death was preventable, unnecessary, and involuntary; it is thus an indictment of the societies that permit it to happen. Andersen and Grimm offer the Christian consolation that the Match Girl and Mili have gone to heaven and have been reunited with their loved ones, but neither pretends that the girls' deaths are anything but premature and wasteful. None of these books suggests that the deaths will bring about change.

Ungerer offers not the slightest hint that the blue cloud is able to observe the outcome of his action from some form of afterlife. Neither is there a sense that because he was a cloud, he will be reformed in the fullness of time and able to act again, elsewhere. The blue cloud was unique and is gone, but its death was meaningful.

The lack of an afterlife works against reading the book as a religious allegory, emphasising instead that what we do with the lives we have is what is important. The impact of children's lives – no matter how short – can be profound; heroism is not the prerogative of adults. *Le Nuage Bleu*, then, can be seen to fit into the category of humanist children's literature that credits children with ethical thought and agency, and in many ways can be read as having a happy ending since the people are changed in the way the cloud hopes they will be. Read in one way, Ungerer's is a political tale designed to encourage readers to recognise that in war all lose while life in a community benefits all. Written in the wake of *glasnost*, the end of the Cold War and after the fall of the Berlin Wall, this book can nevertheless be seen as warning against complacency about the future; it works to implant a distaste for intolerance and violence in the rising generation.

Politically vigilant children's texts such as Ungerer's are rare. In a sometimes searing article about the current state of American political health and the 'banalization of trauma' arising from responses to the September 11, 2001 attacks on the United States, Kenneth Kidd (2005) calls for children's books and criticism about them to detach from an overdependence on psychologically driven models and their preoccupations with the self in favour of work that is more politically aware, as in the case of *Le Nuage Bleu*.

Even though Ungerer's picturebook has a strong political message, readers conditioned to finding psychological meanings in texts may read it as a story that focuses on and legitimises the sense that 'the world will be a better place without me'. This is precisely how many young people suffering from depression and other more and less temporary forms of mental illness often feel, and so it is a state of mind that writers dealing with characters who self-harm or contemplate suicide have to try to create on the page.

The most explicit picturebook on the subject that I have encountered is Serge Kozlov's *Petit-Âne* (1995), illustrated by Vitaly Statzynsky, which begins, '*Il était une fois un petit âne qui désirait se pendre, mais ne savait comment faire*'. [Once upon a time there was a little donkey who wanted to hang himself, but he did not know how to do it.[4]] Petit-Âne asks several of his friends to help him, but all say they cannot, and the pictures, which are in a cheerful style reminiscent of folk art (bright colours, extensive use of decoration), show several of them weeping as they listen to Petit-Âne's request. The little donkey's original despair is compounded by their refusal. His bright colours fade to grey, with only some vestigial pink details. At last, as night falls, he meets his best friend, Ourson, and asks if he will help. Ourson is ready with a rope and a nail, and the deed is done by hammering the nail in the sky, where '*il se mit à briller comme une étoile*' [it shines as brilliantly as a star], and securing the rope over it. The final double page spread shows Petit-Âne hanging from the rope, watched from the ground by Ourson (Figure 5.1).

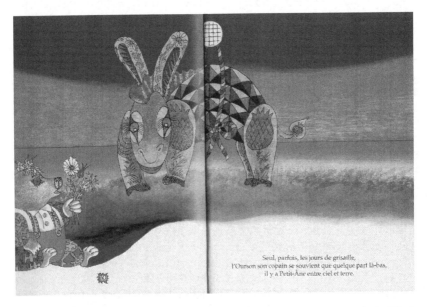

Figure 5.1 The final double-page illustration from Serge Kozlov and de Vitaly Statzynsky's *Petit-Âne*

Petit-Âne received a hostile critical reception when it appeared in France, after which the publishers withdrew the book from their catalogue (Derrien, 2003: 2). *La Revue des Livres pour Enfants* carried a typical review by the critic Claude-Anne Parmegiani, for whom its depiction of suicide was a 'scandalous seduction [of the] perverse message [that induced] a dangerous amalgam in the child reader's mind' (in Derrien: 4, Derrien's translation). The vocabulary used by critics to denounce the book (including 'perverse', 'obscene', 'scandalous seduction') 'might be borrowed from the lexical register of child abuse' (5). Its depiction of suicide as something inexplicably longed for and accomplished in a book for children clearly makes adults very anxious, despite the fact that Petit-Âne is shown as a stuffed toy and there are familiar fictional tags ('Once upon a time') to make it clear that this is a story and to distance it from real life.

The author and illustrator also include intertextual links to Saint-Exupéry's much-loved *The Little Prince* (1943), another book which ends in the death of the main character. The Little Prince is a child who, from the outset, is filled with great sadness and who, it transpires, has been preparing for death in the course of the book. These links begin on the front cover, which shows Petit-Âne and Ourson standing on a curved surface that is reminiscent of the Little Prince's astral universe. The unquestioning acceptance of Petit-Âne's decision is similar to the way the pilot listens to, accepts and witnesses the Little Prince's death. These links point to a reading of Kozlov's tale in which Petit-Âne's death can be read as symbolising his spiritual rebirth (Derrien, 6–7). The links to *The Little Prince* are underlined in the blurb on the back cover: '*Tout le monde n'a pas la chance d'être le Petit Prince … Heureusement Petit Ours est là qui sait, lui, quell pays notre petit âne rêve d'atteindre …*' [Not everybody is lucky enough to be the Little Prince. Happily, Ourson is there and he knows which country our Petit-Âne dreams of reaching] suggesting that this is the reading author, illustrator, and publisher intend. Whatever the intention, the manifest story confronts readers with a suicidal figure who, like Ungerer's blue cloud, clearly represents a child.

There is a long tradition of using animals and toys as substitute child figures in children's literature because of the connections and affinities between them (see Kuznets 1994; Blount 1975). Anthropomorphising toys and animals (or, as in *Petit-Âne*, a combination of the two) provides a degree of disguise and distance which can be useful when dealing with sensitive or disturbing topics. In this case, it could be that the disguise is at least as much for the adult, for whom the idea of child suicide is devastating and unspeakable, as for potential child readers. Under normal circumstances (as opposed to conflict and natural disasters), children have little experience of death and find the concept strange – sometimes even amusing (see Goodall, 2000). Like sex, this area outside experience is something that interests them, and children's play often includes episodes of 'being dead', whether this is through being 'shot', or playing at being a ghost or acting out a story in which a character dies. Acting out violent impulses on toys is not uncommon either, though it is not always palatable to adults. The first page of Maurice Sendak's *Where the Wild Things Are* includes an image of Max's teddy, noose around his neck, hanging from a line, presumably one of the actions that causes Max's mother to send him to his room.

If a sibling, friend or classmate dies, children may seek to understand what this means and explore their feelings about it through fantasy and play. *Petit-Âne* can be understood as a narrative that enacts this curiosity about death as well as one that is concerned with suicide.[5] Although the donkey is certainly hanged at the end of the story, the final image shows him suspended from his middle, not by his neck as the preceding picture suggests he will be, and his death is presented as neither traumatic nor dramatic. This lack of tragedy may associate the events with the world of child's play, reflecting the reassuring things adults often say to children when someone has died (they are out of pain, they have gone to heaven or a similarly happy place, they are not really gone because they live on in our memories); however, it was precisely the beauty and serenity of the final images that appalled French critics. For them, Petit-Âne's smiling face on the last page of the book constitutes an invitation to young readers to imitate him. This ignores both children's understanding of the differences between fiction, play and reality, and the needs of those who, for whatever reason, have suicidal thoughts or know someone who has killed her/himself and are unable to articulate or understand their feelings, questions, and reactions.

For some readers, *Petit-Âne* offers a point of identification and way of relieving emotions. The potentially beneficial nature of juvenile novels which acknowledge dark and destructive feelings is discussed in detail in the next part of this chapter; before moving away from picturebooks, however, three more examples deserve attention. The first is a Dutch picturebook (references here are to the French translation) that explores the experiences and behaviour of the kind of child who might well develop suicidal thoughts. *Jules* (1996), by Gregie de Maeyer with illustrations by Koen Vanmechelen, features a character who is crudely made in the shape of a little boy from blocks of wood. He is tormented by his peers (who we never see) because of his appearance, beginning with his red hair.

To stop their teasing, he first cuts off his hair, then his big ears. Although he can no longer hear his abusers, he can still see them, so he takes out his eyes and so it goes on until nothing remains of him but a head without eyes, ears or tongue. Up to this point, nothing he does to himself eases his feelings of anger and self-loathing, and each time he attacks himself he looks more strange, provoking new bouts of bullying. Jules cuts, burns, and violently mutilates himself to the point where he has virtually ceased to exist. He even places his legs on the railway track so that a train detaches them. Suicide would seem to be the logical next step.

Jules does not kill himself, although his tormentors attack him and pull him to bits. The book's powerful representation of what it feels like to be bullied shifts to a more optimistic, more didactic, register with the arrival of a little girl, who finds what remains of Jules and begins to care for him. She puts his head in her doll's pram, strokes him, and draws a mouth on his blank face and inserts a pencil in it so that he can tell her his story. The last page sees him begin to write, but before he starts to explain how the others taunted him (' ... *un jour, on s'est moqué de moi'*), Jules announces that he likes his name, likes his red hair, his red cheeks, and all the things that previously had driven him to despair. This new self-acceptance and affirmation, a response to being shown – and recognising himself – as lovable, reassures readers that he will survive.

Not all children do survive, however, and the loss of a child is one reason why a parent may succumb to a period of depression. A rare picturebook that makes it possible for adults and children to share insights into what this is like is *Michael Rosen's Sad Book* (2004). Michael Rosen has been writing and performing for children in the United Kingdom for many years – long enough for some of his first readers to be parents themselves. He has a large following, and because he is also an active broadcaster, is in the public eye more than most writers for children. Rosen uses his own childhood and his observations of family life with his children as the basis for much of his material. When one of his sons, Eddie, who had appeared as a young child in Rosen's books but was by then a teenager, died without warning of meningitis, the loss was felt widely. Eventually, Michael Rosen talked about his experience in a radio broadcast for adults and, with long-time collaborator, illustrator Quentin Blake, created *Michael Rosen's Sad Book*. Both the broadcast and the picturebook can be seen as ways of dealing with grief; they also provide generous insights that may help readers understand their own, and others', emotions and reactions to bereavement.

The sombre front cover signals that this is not going to be one of Rosen's customarily zany and amusing books. It shows the usually exuberant Rosen as a grey figure walking under an enveloping grey cloud with Sid, a much-loved dog character from an early poem, also shown as grey. They are all contained within a frame, a controlling and distancing device that again is strikingly different from Rosen's usually explosive energy and Blake's response to it. Solemn grey endpapers continue the mood, but the first page shows the familiar, smiling face of Michael Rosen in the yellow and red palette Blake often uses when illustrating Rosen's work, although Blake manages to capture a haunted sense behind the smile. The text reads:

This is me being sad.
Maybe you think I'm being happy in this picture.
Really I'm being sad but pretending I'm being happy.
I'm doing that because I think people won't like me if I look sad.

Over the next thirty pages readers go through the various emotions Michael Rosen explains he has at different times in response to Eddie's death, and get to see how he behaves in different situations. Simple sentences and descriptions reveal how at times the feeling of sadness is over-whelming and that this can make him behave in ways that are difficult for those around him (including the cat!). At points it seems that putting his feelings on the page is making it possible to manage them and remember more of the happy times: towards the end of the book, brightly coloured vignettes of Eddie in the school play, and the two of them playing football on the sofa lead to associations with other good memories and happy moments. But this honest book does not suggest that the act of writing has been an instant cure. The final image is of a haggard, grey, Michael Rosen writing by candlelight at his desk in front of a framed picture (Figure 5.2). Since the immediately preceding images have been of birthdays, it seems likely that this shows what would have been Eddie's birthday, and his father is feeling the loss as much as ever. It is a powerful image, and not an opti-mistic note on which to end, though by this point the reader understands that the sadness is not a permanent condition but swirls round to catch him to different degrees at different times powerfully.

The insights Rosen and Blake offer in the *Sad Book* are clear enough to be understood by even very young readers – especially because the pictures

Figure 5.2   Final image from *Michael Rosen's Sad Book* by Michael Rosen, illustrated by Quentin Blake

show the moods so well. For children who are dealing with the sadness of an adult it offers insights into why the grown-ups behave as they do and how hard it is to overcome feelings of desolation and despair. Readers of whatever age who have suffered from depression themselves will recognise its symptoms and the strategies Rosen uses to manage it – not least telling others about what he is feeling and admitting his fear of alienating people if he cannot manage his emotions.

All of the picturebooks previously discussed in this section have featured child characters or figures who represent them, and with the possible exception of *Petit-Âne*, each has ended on an optimistic note. Perhaps because its central character is an adult, and because Rosen is trying to explain the long-term effects of bereavement to the children to whom he performs and who ask him questions about the death of his son, *Michael Rosen's Sad Book* does not provide a happy or consolatory ending. By contrast, a child's depression is handled in an equally powerful way by Australian author-illustrator Shaun Tan in *The Red Tree* (2001), but it does hold out the promise that things will get better.

The Red Tree is a visually stunning book. Large, complex, and eloquent images represent the feelings of fatigue, dislocation, inadequacy, inability to communicate, alienation, and purposelessness characteristic of depression. The first image, in place of a title page, shows a listless girl speaking through a megaphone, but all of the words are disintegrating and dribbling out of its bell as meaningless letters (you can see the image on the cover of this book). The following page shows a weathered grandfather clock in a field. The hours are represented by leaves; eleven of them are dark, though the twelfth is a brilliant red. The body of the clock seems to be an incomplete jigsaw puzzle, and through the holes it is clear that insects have infested the works. Time – the way we measure our lives – is broken and rotten.

The story proper begins with a picture of the same girl in her bedroom. She sits in bed, eyes downcast, blind raised only a crack. Apart from her red hair and a framed image of a red leaf on the wall, the image is effectively in monochrome, combining pink and grey tones in a subtle way to give the impression of sameness. Dark (dead?) leaves are falling onto the bed, floor, and surfaces. The text reads 'sometimes the day begins with nothing to look forward to' and is followed by images of the girl in a diving helmet trapped in a glass bottle (Figure 5.3), walking in a city like 'a deaf machine', marking off time on the back of a snail and other equally effective ways of representing the many bleak moods of depression. Yet the alert reader will soon spot that the little red leaf from the first page accompanies her somewhere in each of the surreal, confusing images. When she has struggled through the day – which has felt like an eternity – and returns to her room, she finds that the leaf has taken root in her floor, 'bright and vivid and quietly waiting'. The final page-turn shows the room filled with a beautiful red tree that is 'just as you imagined it would be'; the girl stands smiling beneath it.

Figure 5.3 'Nobody Understands' (detail) from Shaun Tan's *The Red Tree*

The minimal text works with the images to convey powerful feelings. Little is verbalised, but together the words and images convey a state of mind and, without a preachy or false sense of hope, reassurance that things change and in time will get better. The tiny leaf works in an unsentimental way to symbolise hope, survival, creativity, and the ability to nurture the resources necessary to make change possible. *The Red Tree* is a sophisticated response to depression that uses the picturebook as an art form to great effect. Much of its strength comes from the counterpoint between the eloquent, detailed, and complex visual images and the economical use of text; young adult fiction, on the other hand, relies on words – often presented as part of a 'talking cure' – to explore feelings of despair and self-loathing.

The tracks of my tears: self-harm in adolescent fiction

> ... he sees: a girl kneeling on the wet ground, head bowed over a task. The task is drawing a thin, shiny object (a pin? a needle?) across the inside of her left wrist. The track of the pin is marked by a line of small, bright blobs of blood, strung together like a bead bracelet. There are two or three of these bracelets running parallel across her wrist. The girl ... observes the red bracelets without emotion, and then she moves the pin, pushing it harder, jabbing it into a blood spot, pulling at the flesh, lifting it, making this one wound wider and deeper. The jabs are fierce, but she appears quite calm, maybe even she smiles, as though there is relief in this blood-letting.
>
> (Nicky Singer, *Doll*, 2002: 107)

Although some very young children may succumb to depression and feelings of terrible sadness, most do not, and very few resort to behaviours that put their health and even their lives in danger. Strong feelings of frustration, anger, unhappiness, and isolation are much more common in adolescence, and with age comes the power to take out these strong emotions on the self. Currently about 24,000 teenagers are admitted to hospitals in the United Kingdom each year after deliberately harming themselves (www.selfharmuk.org/facts).[6]

As was shown in *Jules*, self-harming takes a variety of forms, from suicide/para-suicide through overdosing, cutting, burning, hair-pulling, eating disorders, head-banging, biting, skin-scratching, and generally injuring the body in ways that may be both permanent and fatal. The behaviour is not new; what has changed are the numbers of reported incidents (the majority are believed to be unreported, so the potential number of young people participating in this behaviour is likely to be much larger than verified evidence suggests) and the length of time most young people engage in self-harming. In 2004, Childline, the UK telephone service aimed at supporting children and young people, reported a 65% increase in calls about self-harming; a

2003 poll in Ireland showed that 55% of young people know someone who has either committed or attempted suicide, and statistics show that in Britain, at least one in seventeen eleven to fifteen-year-olds is self-harming (Brennock, 2003: 1; www.selfharmuk.org/facts).

The profile of those who are self-harming has also changed. A 2006 study of *Adolescent Angst* by the Priory Group in the United Kingdom reports that,

> Adolescents who self-harmed were rare 30 years ago; then they tended to be extreme learning disabled or psychiatric patients who were very distorted in their senses. Today, adolescents across all regions and classes self-harm, although the practice is more marked among girls. (15)

This changed behaviour is being reflected in juvenile fiction, which may play a role in countering the trend by helping readers to understand what motivates it and being and introducing them to strategies for managing their feelings and actions.

Current patterns of self-harming among the young

Information about changing patterns of self-harming among adolescents and young people is currently being collected by a variety of organisations; *Adolescent Angst* confirms earlier evidence, not least the likely connections between self-harming behaviour and the large – and increasing – numbers of young people suffering from mental disorders of various kinds and degrees. A survey conducted by the UK Office of National Statistics in 1999 reported that one in ten children and young people suffer from mental disorders affecting their levels of happiness and producing feelings of depression, anxiety, and sleep disturbance, all possible instigators for self-harming (Quilgars, 2002: 348).[7] Also noteworthy is the fact that a number of studies have found

> a significant relationship between mental health and bullying ... [with] high levels of anxiety ... associated with bullying. They also found low levels of anxiety, but high levels of depression, associated with bullying others. (356)

Since bullying can happen at any age, the importance of picturebooks such as *Jules* for helping all those (both victims and bullies) caught in cycles of bullying to acknowledge and think about the consequences of their actions, should not be underestimated. At the time of writing, bullying has reached extreme levels in Britain, ranging from physical attacks through verbal abuse and psychological torments such as 'happy slapping', in which, among other things, humiliating pictures of peers are circulated on mobile phones and the Internet.[8] Bullying has specifically been blamed for several widely reported suicides by young people.[9] With this in mind, it is worth noting that while over the past decade an increasing number of British children's and YA books have addressed the dynamics of bullying, recently the number and range of such books have risen significantly. Their effect is to adjust the image of childhood associated with children's literature; at the same time, their intention (it is too early to judge their effect) is to change behaviour.

Quick to cut: narratives of despair

Suicide, the most extreme form of self-harm, is thankfully relatively rare;[10] it is also the form of self-harm that is least frequently written about for young people. Most books focus instead on wounds inflicted on the self that may be used not to end, but to prolong life. Foremost among these self-protective kinds of self-injuries is cutting. While there has been a rise in the frequency of self-harming, it is important to point out that teachers, who increasingly have to deal with the repercussions of self-harming episodes including the impact on other students, report that the increase consists almost entirely of 'episodic' incidents (meaning that they take place over a limited period of time in the young person's life rather than over a number of years).[11] These episodes are less ritualised and less bound up with the individual's identity than patterns of self-harming found in earlier generations.

Traditionally, self-harming behaviour has tended to be long-term, secretive and often compulsive. In the past, often only an individual and perhaps her (it usually is a 'her' since self-harming is considerably more common in girls than in boys) doctor would know the full extent of the self-harming behaviour. Today, however, it appears to be the case that many of the young people who self-harm do so for quite short periods of time, and they often find ways not to conceal but to confess to their concerns about their behaviour. Again, this suggests that the narrative of self-harming is moving in new directions – at least for some. Older patterns of self-harming have not gone away, of course, but new self-harming behaviours are now both more widespread and more widely reported.

The evidence suggests that a culture is developing in which self-harming is increasingly regarded as a way of dealing with anxiety and unhappiness in the young (*Adolescent Angst*: 15). Information volunteered by teachers gives some insight into the increased incidence of self-harming among pupils. The following comment from a British teacher who responded to an on-line questionnaire I circulated to others researching self-harming sums up the situation reported by many:

> Self-harming is becoming a real issue in schools today. I work in an independent boarding school and ... we have a number of boys and girls currently self-harming with a variety of possible motivations or causes. For some it is a genuine cry for help or their way of taking control of their

own lives, a way of coping. Unfortunately for others it is for attention or just copying others or even mimicking TV dramas such as Hollyoaks. (received 30 June 2003)

The sense that some of the behaviour is imitating plot-lines from popular narratives such as television soaps rather than a response to real stress is not uncommon, though in the United Kingdom, guidelines issued by the National Institute for Clinical Excellence (NICE: 2004) instruct hospitals not to judge individual cases but to treat all those who present themselves after self-harming 'with the same care, respect and privacy as any patient'.[12]

The problem is not unique to Britain. An Australian researcher responding to a questionnaire for a Nuffield-funded project on self-harming and schools volunteered the following information:

A school we consulted was having difficulty containing 'cutting out-breaks' and 'gloom clubs' among sub-populations of the school. These would tend to cluster around certain individuals, but would occasionally occur in non-related sectors within the school. (e-mail response received 24 June 2003)

The ubiquity of the behaviour is illustrated by Kate, a 22-year-old care assistant interviewed by *The Irish Times* as part of a 2003 survey of young people's behaviour and attitudes: 'We all did it [cutting]. ... There were just degrees of it. ... I just did it because everyone else did' (22 September 2003). Kate may make it seem casual and unimportant, but whether short or long-term, experimental or obsessive, such behaviour is damaging and worrying. While attitudes to self-harming may be changing among the young, making such behaviour more familiar, less stigmatised, and even regarded as 'nor-mal', it is nonetheless both painful and often permanently disfiguring to greater and lesser degrees. Usually, cutting or burning oneself would be both frightening and abhorrent, so the fact that more and more young people are deliberately breaking through the skin to reach flesh, blood, and in extreme cases even the bone below *to make them feel better* suggests bouts of high-level anxiety with which they feel unable to cope (see *Adolescent Angst*).

Cutting particularly is reported as bringing relief; it releases high levels of endorphins producing a 'high' that counteracts the depression often associ-ated with cutting, it makes the cutter feel detached from and able to purge her body, and provides a sense of control. In *A Bright Red Scream*, a study of women who self-harm, Marilee Strong explains:

As the first-person stories and narratives of the cutters make clear, they hurt themselves not really to inflict pain but, astonishingly enough, to relieve themselves of pain – to soothe themselves and purge their inner demons through a kind of ritual mortification of the flesh.

Rather than a suicidal gesture, cutting is a symbol of the fight to stay alive. (1998: xviii)

Three reasons are generally cited for why people self-harm; each seems to give an insight into the pressures of growing up in contemporary Western societies and evidence of the need to rethink the relationship between the ideal and the reality of Western childhoods. There are those who use cutting to relieve tension or to change an unpleasant emotional state; for this group, physical pain temporarily relieves emotional pain. For others, self-harming is used to give a sense of control over a situation they cannot manage, including bullying. Anorexia is generally regarded as the most controlling form of self-harm; it is also more likely to end in death than any other form of self-harm or psychiatric disorder (Mantel: 15).[13] The third category consists of those who use it to validate suffering – often because they have been violated in one way or another (such as through bullying or sexual abuse) but do not have any visible marks from the incidents. Self-harming allows them to create a physical manifestation of inner pain (Freeman, 2003: 10–11).

The relationship between inner states and the appearance of the body can give acts such as cutting an aesthetic dimension. At one end of this spectrum there are professional performance artists who use self-mutilation, bloodletting, and even forms of hanging (for instance, from hooks through the skin) simultaneously to entertain and to make statements about contemporary society (*ArtShock*, 2006). Such artists identify their bodies as human canvases, and this way of thinking can be applied to some self-harmers. The music industry includes figures such as the late Ritchie Edwards of Manic Street Preachers who deliberately display the damage they have done to themselves, and many testimonies from cutters acknowledge that they find the visual dimension of the act compelling and pleasing. In some cultures scarification symbolises a rite of passage; the lack of such formal ways of signalling changed status may attract some young people to a practice that will leave a permanent record of something they have done. Related to this is the fact that adolescence is a time when decisions about the future begin to be made, bringing with them an awareness of how little power, control, and even economic value most individuals have in a post-industrial society. When examinations and institutions begin to close doors on possibilities in what sometimes seem arbitrary ways, the attractions of demonstrating control over something – the body, pain, appetites – can be great. At some level, self-harming can be seen as dramatising the way some individuals feel compelled to shape themselves to fit their futures – like Cinderella's sisters, who slice off their heels and toes in an effort to force their feet into the glass slipper.

Although more girls than boys get caught up in self-harming behaviours, it is important not to ignore the fact that increasing numbers of males are now cutting and experimenting with other forms of self-harm. Writing about Susanna Kaysen's *Girl, Interrupted* (1994), Elizabeth Marshall argues that it reveals a deep-rooted association between female adolescence and susceptibility to mental illness. Kaysen's is a fictionalised account of her experience of being peremptorily placed in a psychiatric institution as an eighteen-year-old girl in 1968. Far from being disorganised and suffering from low self-esteem, the Kaysen character is rebelling against a variety of institutions (including family and school) and discourses that attempt to discipline girls' bodies (Marshall, 2006: 125). She is classified as promiscuous (and so sick), lacking structure (and so sick), and unmotivated at school (and so sick).

Girl, Interrupted is about events that took place in the 1960s, but it and the film starring and co-produced by Winona Ryder that came out in 1999 have both been popular with contemporary audiences of girls and young women. Much has changed in the more than thirty years since the events Kaysen describes, and though no one would argue that equality between the sexes has been achieved, the relative positions of adolescent boys and girls have changed significantly – and not to the advantage of boys. For that reason it is disappointing to see Marshall conclude that

> The bodily readings [evidenced by girls with arms bandaged because they had been cutting themselves] of Kaysen's text suggest that girls continue to ingest a cultural pedagogy that teaches girls to turn anger inward rather than outward, that instructs them to view self-destruction as the only viable option for resistance. It may mean that self-inflicted harm might be a cultural rite through which young women act out and resist the girlhood pedagogies that frame their passage from girlhood to womanhood. (128)

In the current climate, it seems important not to ignore the increasing numbers of boys who are dissatisfied with the way they look, uncertain about their futures, and unable to assume that traditional patterns of male hegemony will secure them desirable places in culture. With this in mind it is good to see that a number of books about boys who are overweight have recently appeared, suggesting that this is an area of anxiety. Among these are Catherine Forde's *Fat Boy Swim* (2003); June Colbert's *The King of Large* (2004), and Kevin Brooks's extremely powerful and interestingly written *Kissing the Rain* (2004). The books deal with young male obesity in different ways, not always insisting on the need to change the body: *King of Large*, for instance, features a boy who learns to create a fashionable identity rather than tone up and slim down. Moo Nelson in *Kissing the Rain* has two obese parents and no obvious way or motivation to change; he hates his body but food is his comfort. Louis Sachar's popular *Holes* (1998) has at its centre a male makeover story that compares very closely to the traditional female version as its protagonist changes from an overweight, unfit, and unlucky boy to a well-built hero.

Such books are a minority, however; by and large, we have become accustomed to seeing narratives that feature characters who turn on themselves through the eyes, experiences, and accounts of girls. It is undoubtedly the case that most adolescent fictions that feature self-harming are centred on female subjects; as in the case of bullying, over recent years, the numbers of YA novels dealing with cutting and related subjects/behaviours including anorexia, bulimia, and elective mutism have increased steadily. The central question about this new sub-genre concerns the role it plays in young people's understanding of and attitude towards self-harming. Do these books have a therapeutic function? Do they provide helpful insights? Could they be helping to normalise such behaviour and so contributing to its increased frequency? Are they participating in the creation of an aesthetic of self-harming?

Fiction, physiology, and the tendency to self-harm

These questions are predicated on the assumption that fiction, through its capacity to provoke empathetic identification and provide vicarious experiences, affects readers. At one level, however, the body insists on telling its own story, a story that neuroscientists are beginning to parse with increasing precision. In *Why Are They So Weird?* (2003), Barbara Staunch provides an account of what goes on in teenagers' brains. She reports that long-term studies in which teenagers voluntarily have their brains scanned on a regular basis show that the mood swings and what are often regarded as forms of aberrant behaviour associated with adolescence in the Western world (staying up all night, sleeping all day, bad time and task management, mood swings) coincide with and seem to be the product of significant changes in the brain. In layman's terms, this involves:

A surge of grey matter aptly called 'exuberance'. This overload of capacity and possibility is why teenagers can read a Russian novel a day, hack into military software, steal a car or want to save the world. It also causes a heightening of experience and emotion for which they are not fully equipped – like a roller-coaster setting off before every nut and bolt is in place. (Greenlaw, 2003: 13)

In addition to the physiological changes taking place in the brain, there are chemical explanations for many manifestations of behaviour associated with adolescence; for instance, 'A lag in their melatonin cycle prompts them to go to bed at two and sleep until 12. High dopamine levels make them crave sensation and risk' (13).

Information about adolescent physiology may provide insights into the adolescent psyche, but unless such physical and chemical changes are being affected by environmental and social changes (for instance, in diet, exercise, medications, allergies, and prolonged exposure to various aspects of information technology), it only implies a susceptibility at this stage to risky and exaggerated behaviour, not an explanation for why such behaviour is currently increasing or how to address it. Some psychiatrists take the line that teenagers are particularly prone to self-harming because their 'huge psychological task is to come to terms with their new body, so if things start to go wrong, it is taken out on their body' (Paul Gilligan, Irish Society for the Prevention of Cruelty to Children, in Sheehy Skeffington, 2003: 13). But again, it has ever been thus, so why the change now? In the absence of more obviously effective ways of addressing the problem, it seems important to look at the role of narrative – at the stories young people imbibe and generate – to see how far and in what ways self-harming behaviour is being explored in fiction for young people.

Fictionalising self-harming behaviour

Cutting is the behaviour that has been most thoroughly explored in recent adolescent fiction. This may reflect the fact that cutting is also one of the most frequent forms of self-harming, but it could also be that both the act and the state of mind/body it is associated with (distancing and cleansing) appeal to writers more than, say, head banging or burning. Patricia McCormick's *Cut* (2000), in common with all the adolescent novels discussed here, belongs to the mimetic tradition of writing about trauma in that it works from the assumption that the self-harming child can (though not without difficulty) identify and reprocess the event(s) that has caused the behaviour and in the process, change her feelings and behaviour (Knoepflmacher: 176).

Cut tells the story of Callie, who has recently both become a frequent cutter and stopped speaking (another form of self-harm). It is set in the institution where she has been sent for treatment, and significantly, given that she is not speaking, the narrative is her first-person, present-tense (though it includes flashbacks) account of her experiences there. While she is refusing to speak to those around her, she is talking to the reader.

The opening lines make it clear that she is refusing to participate in the treatment, which will involve her speaking to the therapist:

> You say it's up to me to do the talking. You lean forward, place a box of tissues in front of me, and your black leather chair groans like a living thing. Like the cow it used to be before somebody killed it and turned it into a chair in a shrink's office in a loony bin.
>
> Your stockinged legs make a shushing sound as you cross them. 'Can you remember how it started?' you say.
>
> I remember exactly. (7)

Usage here creates distance not only between Callie and the analyst, but also between Callie and the place – she regards herself as outside it though she is in fact confined within it. Because she doesn't recognise herself as part of the institution, Callie will not participate in its routines and requirements. The successive use of 'you' in this passage transmits to the reader Callie's feelings of rage at the analyst and her demands, which, in the course of the text subside as Callie begins to engage with the analytical process and to start to want to get well. Initially, however, though she 'remembers exactly' when she started cutting, she tells the analyst nothing. Although the analyst is left in the dark, the reader is given a detailed flashback of the afternoon when Callie took an EXACTO knife ('sleek, like a fountain pen, with a thin triangular blade at the tip' (p. 9)) and slid it across the palm of her hand.

> A tingle arced across my scalp [she has cut the palm of her hand]. The floor tipped up at me and my body spiralled away. Then I was on the ceiling looking down, waiting to see what would happen next. What happened was that a perfect, straight line of blood bloomed from under the edge of the blade. The line grew into a long, fat bubble, a lush crimson bubble that got bigger and bigger. I watched from above, waiting to see how big it would get before it burst. When it did, I felt awesome. Satisfied, finally. Then exhausted. (9)

The feeling of detaching or splitting out from the body described by Callie accurately echoes the description of many of the cutters in memoirs such as Caroline Kettlewell's *Skin Game* (1999) and those interviewed for studies including *A Bright Red Scream* (1998) and *Who's Hurting Who?* (1998). Importantly, while the initial description – and, indeed, all other accounts of the cutting itself – presents it as 'satisfying' and even aesthetically pleasing, this is a narrative that constructs cutting as an illness, and shows Callie not only wanting to get better, but also succeeding in getting better.

It transpires that Callie has blamed herself for an episode when her little brother nearly died; during her time in the institution, she allows herself to recognise that, in fact, her parents were at fault. Once this is understood, she no longer has the need to cut. The cause and effect as described may seem simplistic, but many autobiographical accounts of those who have or do self-harm point to similar moments when the feeling that this is what they must do first crystallises. Fiction makes it possible to highlight incidents and draw connections between them and subsequent feelings and behaviour more rapidly than is usually the case in real life and so to provide readers with insights and ways of thinking about what might cause someone to begin self-harming.

When trying to understand the relationship between not speaking and physically harming the self, it is useful to consider Serge Leclaire's theory of the internal *infans*. Maurice Blanchot summarises it well:

> … one lives and speaks by killing the *infans* in oneself (in others also): but what is the infans? Obviously, that in us which has not yet begun to

speak; but more importantly, the marvellous (terrifying) child which we have been in the dreams and desires of those who were present at our birth (parents, society in general). (in Kidd, 128)

Our articulate, functioning, self-accepting personae are laid over the pre-verbal *infans*, and our confidence to do this comes from the sense that who we are to some degree matches the childhood ideal that shaped the hopes and aspirations for us. When there is a crisis between the ideal self and the perceived self, the elements that hold us together – language and the body – often seem to represent everything that is wrong and so become the focus of aggression and control.

Callie's situation is much simpler than that of many long-term cutters whose crisis makes them feel unclean (sometimes in response to identifiable events such as sexual abuse or rape), and so cut as a way of getting rid of the perceived 'dirt' inside out. Because hers is presented as a relatively straightforward problem with a clear cause and effect, Callie's situation may be closer to that of the current generation of young people who are self-harming than would be someone who has experienced long-term abuse or other situations beyond their control. Although at first she rejects help, *Cut* shows Callie to be one of the new kinds of episodic and treatable self-harmers.

Nicky Singer's *Doll* (2002) offers its readers a more complicated back-story to the protagonist's impulses to harm herself. It gradually becomes clear that its central character, Tilly, belongs to a dysfunctional family that goes back for at least two generations. Her mother is an alcoholic, and her live-in grandmother has created a myth of perfection around her late husband, who eventually turns out to have been unfaithful and probably also had a drink problem.

The book begins with Tilly's account of the death of her mother, whose body she has discovered. Slowly it becomes clear that her mother has not died, but cut her wrists while drunk. This is not the first time she has tried to kill herself, but this time Tilly fantasises that she has succeeded. Anger at her mother and guilt for wishing her dead combine to make Tilly turn on herself during what appears to be a period of mild psychosis, when she believes that a doll she has created from her mother's clothes is the source of a voice that urges her first to risk death on a railway bridge and then to cut herself in imitation of her mother. This is the image in the epigraph to this section – the girl jabbing her wrist with a pin.

Again, the description of the cutting, with its sense of detachment and lack of pain, mirrors regular cutters' descriptions of how they feel when they cut, while the splitting of the self into other selves (Gerda, the doll, and an alter-ego, Tilly-Make-Believe) is also typical. Her mother's behaviour leads both to divorce and to Tilly's being bullied at school, which contributes to her mixed feelings of anger, self-disgust, betrayal, anxiety, and unworthiness. Already exhibiting anorexic behaviour, she now begins to behave in erratic ways, and as the cutting incident shows, is on the verge of becoming a serious risk to herself.

But like *Cut*, *Doll* declines to leave its character strapped to a seesaw of despair and self-harming. What changes things for Tilly is her first – and unexpected – romance. When someone else is attracted to her and encourages her to talk through what has been happening in her life, Tilly rapidly recovers. She begins to understand the family narrative more clearly and with a greater sense of perspective, seeing her own behaviour in the light of family history. Where previously she constructed herself as the victim of someone else's story, she now feels empowered to become the author of her own text and give herself a happy ending.

Although the happy ending may seem too easy, *Doll* perceptively depicts cycles of self-harming, the role of unexpressed emotions across generations, the overload of emotions built up over a period of time, the need to externalise inner pain and the added pressures brought about with the entry into adolescence. Despite acknowledging the complexity of many self-harmers' situations, it encourages readers to think about how such situations can be changed. In this, *Doll*, like *Cut*, conforms to an emerging pattern of YA books about self-harm, suggesting that when controversial subject matter is contained in books for younger readers, causing them to challenge ideas of suitability, the response is to default to a traditionally optimistic ending. Equally possible, however, is that the writers recognise that young self-harmers need not be condemned to lives of secrecy and self-loathing and are genuinely optimistic that many of the young people who are currently in distress will work through their problems and learn to accept themselves and be accepted by others.

One writer who knows that 'happily ever after' will not happen for many of the young people with whom she works and about whom she writes is E.R. Frank, an American clinical social worker as well as a children's author. Her novel, *Life is Funny* (2000), includes several incidents of self-harming, among them anorexia, cutting, and substance abuse. Unlike the other books discussed, it shows both boys and girls as self-harmers. *America is Me* (2002) is unusual in having a male central character. Both of Frank's books reflect the growing tendency for boys to be dissatisfied with themselves and the way they are perceived in society, presumably a response to changing social patterns in which male hegemony is no longer a given.

America is the young male protagonist of the novel (his name comes from his mixed race origins that make him a kind of melting pot). In many ways his situation at the start of the book is very close to that of Callie's in *Cut*. He too is in an institution where, he says, 'You have to watch what you say ... because everything you say means something and somebody's always telling you what you mean' (1). Like Callie, America decides not to co-operate with his analyst and to 'stay real quiet' (1). Also, like Callie, he gradually and painfully both makes a relationship with Dr. B and begins to reveal his life's story.

America's history does not emerge in order, and often incidents first seem to be unconnected, but gradually a story is pieced together in which the young, loving, bright child America who lives with an excellent foster mother is inexplicably returned to his mother (an addict and prostitute). He is unwillingly caught up in a brutalising life of crime and thuggery, and though he is eventually restored to his foster mother, she is then too old to look after him and America is in fact cared for by her half-brother, Browning. In many ways Browning looks after America well: he helps him with his reading, teaches him how to cook and clean and play baseball. But he also starts to abuse him sexually. Confusingly mixed messages about love and caring are offered to America; he hates what is happening, and one night sets fire to the house, killing Browning.

America blames himself for all the bad things that have happened to him, convincing himself that he is being punished because he is bad. Significantly for this discussion, once America has again been arrested and put into care, he fantasises that the files his therapist has been given contain the *story* of his life, a *story* in which he is the villain. The reader, of course, knows that he is the victim, and as the text goes on, it becomes obvious that this is a bright, capable, and loving boy, but one who has been much damaged. Additionally, because he *has* done things that are clearly wrong – among them stealing and causing the fire that kills Browning – *America is Me* is an ethically challenging novel at a number of levels. It also provides information about the state of mind young people like America are in: why, for instance, he sometimes splits out (or dissociates), which Dr. B explains to America – and through him the reader – like this:

> It's called dissociation. ... A lot of people do it when something's happening in the here and now that's upsetting to them. A lot of people find a way to go outside of themselves. They use their minds to take themselves away because it feels safer that way. (71)

Explanations like this help readers piece together the text, which is told through a patchwork of flashbacks, moments of dissociation, and third-person narration in the present tense. The reader assembles the story bit by bit as America allows himself to recall incidents from his past that he has repressed, until eventually his past and his present converge in a completed narrative. At this point America is effectively healed and is able to move out of the institution into a house with four other teenagers and a minder. He gets a girl friend, re-establishes his relationship with his foster mother, and ends the book with an image from his childhood of playing hide and seek and being found. America has found himself and stopped being invisible to the world that for a while let him get lost in its systems.

The emphasis in all of these texts is on talking – or more accurately, on telling stories – getting them out and joining up the bits so that they are seen in perspective and without the great holes in the psyche created by repression. The approach is classically Freudian, and the sense of hope and optimism that infuses the end of each is characteristic of children's literature, despite the difficult content employed. Are these weaknesses? My reading of all these texts is that though they deal with hopelessness and depression, they stand apart from the kind of literature of despair that characterises much of the most powerful contemporary adolescent fiction (see Reynolds, 2004). Although they focus on strategies for progress, perhaps implying too forcibly that there are always ways forward, they are also perceptive and credible. None of these books makes the world seem simpler or safer than it is, but through their insights into the motivations behind and behaviour of self-harmers, and their depiction of such behaviour as damaging and only temporarily effective, they convey the message that ultimately, self-harming itself is not a solution. At the same time, they help to dismantle the long-standing stigma associated with self-harming, thus encouraging those who self-harm – or who know people who hurt themselves – to talk about it and to seek help with both the causes and the behaviour.

Children's literature is one way through which children and young people receive stories about how the world works and ways of thinking about themselves and the things they do. Texts such as these can provide new narrative strands that for some will simply be interesting, but for others may offer alternative versions of the stories they are telling themselves about themselves. In this way, children's fiction may prove a valuable antidote to the current conditions that lead young people to harm themselves and so become a force for positive transformations in young people's lives.

6
Baby, You're the Best: Sex and Sexuality in Contemporary Juvenile Fiction

> Well, sex is great, isn't it? It's simultaneously filthy dirty and romantic, fun and deeply meaningful. It feels nice, tastes nice, looks both ugly and beautiful, it can be either obsessive or casual, can turn disgust into delight, it's absolutely hilarious and, of course, it's the source of the most meaningful relationships in our lives. When young people become sexual, we ought to throw them a big party, balloons, fireworks, everything. You've got sex – great! You're really going to enjoy this.
>
> (Melvin Burgess, 'Sympathy for the Devil')

Sandra Francy likes sex. In fact, she likes it better than anything else in her life just now. It makes her feel gorgeous and tingly and takes her mind off hassles at home and school. When boys snuffle in her ear she's like a bitch on heat, and that's just what she becomes in Melvin Burgess's comic allegory about adolescent sexuality, *Lady, My Life as a Bitch* (2001). As a dog, Sandra can do it wherever, whenever and however she likes – and that suits her just fine. Just as it did when she was a school girl, learning the ropes with her first boyfriend:

> I never minded sex on the floor. ... He used to bend and twist my legs all over the place. ... I remember lying there with my legs wide open and he was kneeling in between them, having a good look. Then he leaned forward and tickled me down there. ... and he was on me like a randy dog. (130–1)

Sandra Francy belongs to the new wave of sexually knowledgeable young people whose activities take up an increasing number of pages in the YA section of bookshops. With its light-hearted attitude to teenage sex and often raunchy language, *Lady, My Life as a Bitch* encapsulates the characteristics that make attitudes to and writing about sex, sexuality and relationships between the sexes, one of the most radically changed areas in contemporary children's literature. Burgess's book is a good example of how children's literature participates in shaping – it does not merely reflect – changing attitudes to young people in culture, and in the process generates and underpins new social dynamics and expectations around the young.

Children in postwar children's literature are essentially asexual, though they are vigorously gendered. Even in the late 1960s and early 1970s, the children's section of libraries contained little that was useful to sexually curious youngsters. However, the epoch of sexual liberation that occurred in the years after the contraceptive pill and before AIDs coincided with the rise of Young Adult fiction, and it was not long before pubescent and adolescent readers could find books about people of their own age, with feelings they recognised doing things with their bodies that they wanted to do – or indeed were succeeding in doing. Since that time, what was once one of the most vigorously patrolled boundaries separating fiction for adults from that for juveniles has been redrawn, although as many children's librarians will testify, the battle is not over. While groups of parents and educationists may continue to object to explicit sexual content in books written for the young, some writers and publishers have decided that it is has a legitimate place in juvenile fiction. It is now possible to find everything from the most chaste of kisses to explicitly described sex between adolescents in YA fiction, and a small number of picturebooks (notably Babette Cole's *Mummy Laid an Egg* (1995) and *Hair in Funny Places* (2001)) address children's curiosity about maturing bodies and what sex involves.

As well as acknowledging that the young are interested in sex, children's literature is participating in changes taking place in social attitudes to sexuality by moving beyond heteronormative stereotypes. As the final section of this chapter shows, writing for the young now includes a range of books that present characters who are exploring a variety of sexual orientations and partners.

An even greater shift has occurred in the attitudes that underpin many of these books; for most of the last century, efforts to protect and prolong childhood included attempting to shield the young from sexual knowledge and discouraging interest by associating sex with transgression and punishment. As Roberta Seelinger Trites points out in *Disturbing the Universe*, although teenage sexual activity has become a commonplace of YA fiction, until recently, the tendency has been to focus on the problems it can bring. For Trites this is central to the power/repression dynamic she sees as characteristic of YA fiction. She argues that by focusing on the possibly hurtful outcomes of sexual relationships – such things as regret, betrayal, pregnancy, disease, and restricted life choices – these books put forward the ideologically loaded message that in the young, 'sex is more to be feared than celebrated' (85). This is certainly not true of Sandra Francy, who revels in the fact that she gets to lose her virginity twice: once as a girl and once as a dog.

Trites's case that YA books attempt to curb youthful libidos is part of a larger argument about the way adult culture seeks to use this branch of children's literature to control adolescent power by simultaneously designating adolescent behaviour as deviant and redirecting its energies to approved ways of behaving. The premise is useful and her readings insightful, but in the six years since *Disturbing the Universe* appeared, the situation has changed. Moreover, reluctance to include sexual content in children's literature has always derived at least as much from adults' desire to keep the cultural space occupied by childhood registering as 'innocent' as from the instinct to curb youthful demonstrations of power (Rees: 173–84; Rose, 1984).[1] Because of her focus on the adult–adolescent power dynamic, Trites underplays other social factors at work in young people's sexual relationships in life and on the page. Foremost among these are poverty, class, education, biological sex, and sexual orientation – the same factors that affect life choices from cradle to grave. Although primarily read by educated, middle-class children, YA fiction's depiction of sexual desires, behaviours, and outcomes is more inclusive and less judgemental than *Disturbing the Universe* suggests.

Trites's chapter on 'Sex and Power in Adolescent Fiction' focuses primarily on books written in the 1970s and 1980s. While most of the books she discusses continue to be read, the context in which they now circulate has changed significantly, both inside and beyond the world of children's literature. As the section on British writer Melvin Burgess's *Doing It* later in this chapter shows, it seems likely that this change has largely come about as the next generation of writers – Trites's (and my) contemporaries – reacted to the patterns she identifies. Burgess, for instance, argues that he is not only addressing a long-overdue cultural need for books that show contemporary teenage life as it is, but is also bringing teenage books in line with other aspects of culture.

> If you are 15 or 16 and you want to read about people with sex lives, those people will have to be in their twenties or late teens at the earliest – no one writes for you. The whole entry into adult life is substantially unsupported by literature; which is so much bollox as far as I'm concerned. ... People recognise the realities of everyday life, are concerned but not scared by the fact that there are few secrets from children these days, and recognise [that]. ... in a world more embedded in fictions than ever, in the form not just of books but gaming, politics, film, TV, adverts, even education, kids are probably more able than their parents to appreciate the different ways stories are used. (Burgess, 2004: 293)

This is not to suggest that the underlying interest in young readers' well-being has disappeared; rather, that writers are taking into account the sources of information and influence available to young people in contemporary culture and trying to ensure that books specifically written for a youthful readership are credible and attractive items on the menu of sources of knowledge (not just facts but also such things as emotional insights and risk assessment skills) from which they choose.

Today, when even very young children may encounter (or using web cams, generate) pornography on the Internet or through DVDs, and teen magazines (often read by much younger children than their advertised audience) discuss virtually every kind of sexual behaviour and relationship, many adults believe that the best way to protect children from premature, unwanted, or risky sex is by providing accurate but not clinical information in forms and formats young people enjoy and trust. If they know how to read situations and signals, understand their feelings, and talk openly about how to prepare for sex, the hope is that fewer young people will find themselves coping with the negative consequences of sexual activity (see the discussion of *Pedro and Me* in Chapter 4). Research has shown that when it comes to learning about sex, reading is highly valued by young people. They like the fact that, unlike lessons in school or conversations with parents, they can choose when they want to engage with the facts and issues. They also like the privacy of reading and the ease with which books (as opposed to television or filmed material) can be consulted repeatedly to ensure that the content has been understood. Realistic fiction, which can chart a relationship over time and through stages such as wooing, sexual experimentation, and consequences, is particularly popular.[2]

Here we reach a paradox: since the 1990s there has undoubtedly been an increase in the amount and kinds of sex referred to in adolescent fiction; nevertheless, unless they have access to a copy of Judy Blume's 1975 classic *Forever*, young readers will struggle to learn from fiction written for them who does what to whom and how. As every previous generation has shown, in the absence of specifically targeted basic information, the young turn to less appropriate, often more explicit or salacious sources, however unreliable and despite the availability of officially disseminated literature. Even material that is aimed at adolescents and is deliberately informative and frank often fails to engage the young. In 'Sex and the Children's Book', Lissa Paul explains why this may be:

> Until recently there has been only one exception to the 'instruction and delight' rule of children's literature: books on sex education. Sex education is not about delight. Or toys. Only instruction – and the more clinical the better. (2005: 222)

Although there are increasing numbers of books that do now set out to entertain as well as instruct readers, even these rarely contain much in the way of detailed description of what sexual activity entails. Writing well about sex is extremely difficult, and outside the worlds of pornography, most writers for adults as much as for children ultimately opt to steer clear of detail; the restrictions associated with addressing a juvenile audience have resulted in some creative responses to the task in those who are willing to attempt it. The works I have chosen to discuss in this chapter, therefore, are concerned both with mapping changes in the sexual content and tenor of writing for the young and with identifying some aesthetically effective solutions to the problem of writing about sex.

Sex and the cerebral teenager: *Breaktime*

Probably the most intellectually and aesthetically interesting book about a teenager's first sexual experience is Aidan Chambers's *Breaktime*, which appeared six years before Jacqueline Rose was to argue that children's literature is stylistically conservative and has consistently rejected modernism. Although replete with sexual activity, far from offending critics and educationalists, *Breaktime* was applauded for its literary pedigree and stylistic panache. The National Association for the Teaching of English's *News* called it 'good intellectual fun' going on to note, 'The Joyce rhythms are strongest in the narrative, but all the great anti-naturalists are there somewhere: Sterne (a grey page), Beckett, Flann O'Brien, maybe even Dylan Thomas ...' (quoted on the back cover). The *School Librarian* similarly concentrated on its [meta]literary qualities:

> Like many other good novels, it is partly about writing and the nature of fiction, and that makes it first-class reading for everyone who has ever thought seriously about literature. Above all, it's very funny. (Quoted on the back cover.)

Neither mentions the fact that it is the first children's book to include a masturbation scene as well as a sexual encounter between two consenting but not romantically involved teenagers which contains no references to contraception, sexual health and responsibility, or love. Conceivably in the post-pill pre-AIDs 1970s, the stylistic challenges posed by Chambers were more novel than was the acknowledgement that teenagers are sexually active beings, but since the unwritten taboo against including explicit sexual content was to dominate juvenile fiction until the 1990s, this silence seems surprising.

Or does it? As the reviewers suggest, *Breaktime* is a very clever book, and its sexual acts are rendered on the page in stylistically challenging ways. When the narrating persona, Ditto, masturbates while looking at a picture of Helen, a former classmate with whom he later has his first sexual encounter, the reader has to deduce this from changes in the writing. For this scene, the prose takes the form of a stream of consciousness monologue that becomes less and less coherent as Ditto approaches and achieves climax.

> Her of course, the picture is of her ... those legs what legs what tits and a face to go with them a bit knowing though and maybe that's what held

me back though it doesn't now you brute but this letter now maybe all the time she was waiting was wanting was after it me me her after it was she me her me her legs breasts skin face legs o legs her her her there there there there there there. (20)

When Ditto and Helen have their sex-tryst, the events are described in three different ways simultaneously. Chambers achieves this by dividing his page into two columns. The one on the left consists of alternating lines of prose: the first is Ditto's narration of the events taking place, the second, set in italics, comprises his internal monologue as he struggles for control and then abandons himself to the sensations of his body once he enters and comes in Helen. The column on the right is an extract from the section on 'Patterns of Lovemaking' in Dr. Benjamin Spock's *A Young Person's Guide to Life and Love*, cunningly matched to Ditto's experiences so that, for instance, it explains how 'lips, tongue, hands may make loving contact with lips, tongue, breasts or genitals' (123) at the same time that Ditto and Helen are making precisely these kinds of contacts.

Although suffused with sexual desire and activity, *Breaktime* can hardly be described as a titillating novel. Its point is to stimulate the mind rather than the body, which presumably accounts for the critical response to the text: if readers are able to follow and enjoy what is going on, they are assumed to be sophisticated enough to deal with the content.

Despite its wit and humour, and the way it celebrates and acknowledges sex as part of young people's lives, the intellectual demands of Chambers's book have always prevented it from appealing to a mass readership. After nearly thirty years, it is also dated. But Burgess's charge overlooks Aidan Chambers's other books in the sequence in which *Breaktime* features, all of which deal openly and positively with teenage sexual relationships. Given that Chambers addresses the literary end of the YA audience, this is understandable. More surprising is Burgess's failure to acknowledge a landmark book which set out precisely to ease this transition in a very direct and accessible way.

Forever: fiction as teenage sex manual

In books penises are always described as hot and throbbing but Ralph felt like ordinary skin. Just his shape was different – that and the fact that he wasn't smooth, exactly – as if there was a lot going on under the skin.

(Judy Blume, *Forever*, 60)

Katherine, the protagonist of *Forever*, has clearly been reading books in which penises throb – and that is about as much as she knows about them. If she had read *Forever*, she would have known about such things as mutual masturbation, premature ejaculation, and that different sexual positions offer different kinds of sensations and satisfactions. She figures this out as she goes along, and for young readers, her open admission of ignorance ('Help me, Michael ... I feel so stupid' (59)) and the straightforward manner in which the couple set about exploring what gives each other pleasure is often revelatory and welcome.

Blume was the first children's writer to offer young readers a book about people their age having and, crucially, enjoying sex in a responsible and consequence-free way. The originality and power of *Forever* comes from its use of the novel form: factual material about sexual behaviour and health of the kind Lissa Paul has in mind has been widely available to the young for many decades, but until *Forever*, there had been nothing that followed a relationship in the way Blume decided to do. She also avoids clichés – there is not a single throbbing member – and includes plenty of unglamorous details ('I didn't mean to get you', says Michael, mopping semen off Katherine, 60).

Fiction offers a unique way to learn about and prepare for experiences to come, including sexual and romantic relationships. The combination of empathising with characters and following their actions over time encourages readers to think about how situations and relationships develop and the consequences of different kinds of actions and responses. They can work through a range of scenarios on the page, acquiring knowledge – not least about emotional and ethical issues – vicariously and without risk to themselves. It is important, then, that as well as books that extol the pleasures and pains of young love, young people have access to fictions that deal with the more everyday and prosaic problems and situations in which they are likely to find themselves, including how to put on a condom and how to work together to agree when both partners are ready and willing to start a sexual relationship. *Forever* does precisely this: Katherine and Michael plan and discuss everything: parts of the body (notably, only Michael's penis is given a name; he introduces it as 'Ralph'), what kind of contraception they will use, periods, other relationships, bellybuttons, and their future. Recent studies have shown that young people who talk through their relationships in this way are considerably more likely to practise safe sex and so avoid many of the problems associated with teenage sexual activity than those who don't; so despite critics' arguments that the book encourages promiscuity, Katherine and Michael have been providing good role models for more than two generations.[3]

Although Judy Blume seemed to be blazing a path for writing which provides information about what having sex involves and how to enjoy it without emotional or physical complications, the furore it provoked ensured that *Forever* had no imitators, despite the fact that it was a bestseller on both sides of the Atlantic for many years.[4] Indeed, indicative of the strength of anxiety about including detailed sexual content in writing for young people is the fact that Blume became one of the world's most banned authors, and in 1989, when US writers gathered to support Salman Rushdie against the fatwa that had been imposed upon him by reading aloud from his work, some also raised Blume's case and read excerpts from her novels (Oppenheimer, 1997: 44). Several of Blume's books fell foul of the Moral Majority and later the Religious Right in the United States for what was deemed their 'sexual content', whether this took the form of writing about menstruation and growing breasts, or masturbation, wet dreams, sexual intercourse, and birth control.

Tributes to the affection and gratitude which many of its original readers feel for *Forever* were offered in the media to mark the thirtieth anniversary of its publication, celebrated by the book's UK publishers with an anniversary edition.[5] Despite its many supporters, *Forever* is often criticised for lacking literary merit. Detractors deplore its banal and uncomplicated characters, its lack of moral ambiguity, and the way, they claim, it leaves nothing to the imagination. For some, its refusal to censure and punish teenagers who become sexually active and who do not even have the grace to stay together 'forever' is particularly problematic. Nicholas Tucker spoke for many adults when reviewing the first UK edition of the book (which appeared seven years after *Forever* was published in the United States) when he described it as being 'about two very dull young people, told in prose of the same soggy consistency as the used tissues that play such an important part in the couple's post-amatory techniques' (in Wilce: 2).[6] In fact, it is precisely the simplicity of the plot and the relationships that make the book so powerful for its young readers: *Forever* puts few stylistic distractions in their way and so allows them to read themselves into the text and experience vicariously its protagonists' ever-more satisfying sexual experiments.

Good adolescent role models such as Michael and Katherine are greatly needed. However, despite the fact that the majority of young people in Britain and the United States are sexually active by the time they are sixteen and that there is an urgent need to try to combat high levels of teenage pregnancy and sexually transmitted disease by every possible means,[7] there is still resistance in children's literature circles towards those who attempt to write openly and in a light-hearted and accepting way about the kind of things sexual activity may involve. When Melvin Burgess published *Doing It* in 2003 he was attacked by the then Children's Laureate, Anne Fine, for what she deemed the book's misogynistic, pornographic, and 'disgusting musings' (2003). Fine claimed the book demeaned both boys and girls, but though she quotes extensively from *Doing It*, it is not clear that she has actually read the book. Each of the characters becomes kinder, wiser, and more empathetic in the course of the book, and there is a clear association between growing up, embarking on relationships and ceasing to treat and talk about others as sex objects.

Burgess was undeterred by Fine's attack and since *Doing It* was published, he has regularly defended young people's right to read about the lifestyles they lead and the situations in which they find themselves. Significantly, while Judy Blume remained a lone voice, Melvin Burgess is rapidly being joined by others who are defying the accepted wisdom about children's literature. Where once 'doing it' in YA fiction meant boys and girls losing control and reaping the consequences – usually in the form of pregnancy – books for teenagers increasingly acknowledge that the sexual orientations of the young are just as varied and their desires at least as urgent as those of the adults around them. Perhaps more importantly, there has been a movement from guilt and unease to *jouissance* when writing about sex for this audience: the sexual experiences of young people in a growing number of novels are depicted as pleasurable and consequence-free. Fictional parents are also more inclined to accept and make provision for their children's sexual activities, a good example being Ron Koertge's *Where the Kissing Never Stops* (2005) in which Walker and his new girlfriend, Rachel, easily move from first kiss to a satisfying sexual relationship with his mother's approval.

Even when books show teen sex as natural, accepted, and enjoyable, most also continue to remind young people of the need to think carefully about and plan for sexual relationships. Liz Retting's *My Now or Never Diary by Kelly Ann* (2006) includes a typical scene in which the protagonist has to overcome embarrassment to get a prescription for the pill and a much longer scene where she embarrasses a young shop assistant while purchasing condoms. Significantly, however, such books now emphasise the need for sex to be safe rather than the need to avoid sex. Another notable change in recent fiction is that girls are no longer portrayed primarily as victims or reluctant participants, only giving in to pressure from their boyfriends.[8] Retting's Kelly Ann is caught in her boyfriend's kitchen in the suspenders and bra she has chosen to wear for what is to be the night she loses her virginity when his parents unexpectedly throw him a surprise party; Walker discovers that Rachel wants to have sex just as much and as often as he does. Neither are sexually active girls left to deal with the consequences – if there are any – on their own. As Michele Gill (2006) points out, a subgenre featuring teenage fathers has emerged in YA fiction in recent years, and books that show boys as more than uncontrolled and predatory bundles of hormones now make up a substantial portion of novels featuring sexual relationships.

The transition in YA books about teenage sex, from the careful didacticism of *Forever* and the cerebral safety of *Breaktime* to the current sub-Bridget Jones comedy of *My Now or Never Diary* and the in-your-face prose of *Doing It* or Julie Burchill's *Sugar Rush* (2004), came in stages. However, comparing books written at different times but which deal with similar kinds of sexual relationships suggests that the area of greatest change is not about how much sex is taking place but the importance attached to it and the strategies for writing about it. Perhaps unsurprisingly, as social attitudes to including sexual content in juvenile fiction have become less proscriptive in line with a generally more accepting attitude to sexual content in other areas of culture, writers have become less inventive. Books about affairs between teachers and pupils make up a small but useful case study through which this change can be mapped.

Teacher's pet

British writer Robert Westall was always prepared to push at the boundaries of what is regarded as suitable for children. *Falling into Glory* (1993) is built around an affair between seventeen-year-old rugby player and star pupil, Robert Atkinson, and his teacher, Emma Harris. This is no infatuation; once they become involved sexually, they meet often (though discretely), even spending whole days together, making love among the ruins of Hadrian's Wall and other antique sites they are studying. Although they have sex frequently and passionately and *Falling into Glory* conveys well the conflicting tensions arising from passion and the need for concealment, Westall never lapses into cliché or anatomical didacticism. Neither does he moralise or judge the relationship.

In many ways *Falling into Glory* is a rite of passage fantasy: she is experienced and Robbie a virgin, but he turns out to be as good in bed as he is on the rugby field. Ultimately, however, the age and professional distance between them begin to tell, and Robbie's prowess cannot disguise his emotional immaturity or her need for a more mature partner.

Although there is nothing in *Falling into Glory* to compare with the detailed lovemaking in *Forever*, it fully acknowledges teenagers as sexually powerful and competent beings and creates a highly erotic atmosphere. Robbie's physical response to his teacher's legs and smell as she drives him in her car (her skirt riding up, their shoulders touching) is much more sensuous than anything Katherine and Michael experience, and Westall finds many ways to convey the sensations of sexual intimacy without becoming graphic. Recalling the first time they made love Robbie tells the reader:

> I could tell you of the little things that surprised me; that a woman's skin is so much hotter than a man's, and so much smoother. I could tell you that the sounds a woman makes, her very breathing, is more like a symphony than anything else. ... Listen and you always know where you are with her. It tells you when you are winning, and when you are losing; like hunt the thimble, you are always getting warmer or colder. But those are just the details. (157)

Of course, the point is that there are no details – and precious little information. What masquerades as revelation and advice is in fact confined to allusion and metaphor. Robbie poses as the authority on what women's bodies are like, but can only compare sex to an abstract phenomenon (listening to a symphony) or a child's game (hunt the thimble). He goes on to try the landscape metaphor, a favourite throughout literary tradition, though in true Westall fashion it mutates into a military analogy:

> You creep on in fear and trembling, but there is no flare of sudden resistance, no sudden sniper's bullet of protest. ... Instead, a little arching of the back that leads you to the bra hook. ... And afterwards, a great peace ... (157)

Although *Falling into Glory* regularly reminds readers that such relationships between pupils and teachers are disapproved of, the narrative itself presents this one as an important and valuable experience for both Robbie and 'Miss' Harris. He helps her recover her sense of confidence and trust while she teaches him about relationships as well as sex. Under the guise of developing a cover story, Robbie starts dating a girl his own age and finds himself better able to enjoy their time together because of his relationship with his teacher:

> I suppose I was pretty pleased with myself, having two women on the go, when most of our lot hadn't even got round to kissing one yet. And it was nice to compare them. Joyce was all gentle and peaceful and legal. ... I wasn't minded to push Joyce along any faster. I supposed we might get there some day ... (219)

Adèle Geras's *The Tower Room* (1990), written close in time to *Falling into Glory*, offers a female perspective on a pupil–teacher relationship. The events take place at Egerton Hall, a boarding school based on Roedean, the well-known British girls' school where Geras herself was a pupil. It uses the story of 'Rapunzel' as an intertextual pre-text on which the narrative of the relationship between Megan, a pupil with remarkable hair who runs away from school with the handsome new teacher, Simon, is based. The pair set up house together in a small flat in London on his inadequate salary, and she quickly learns that love alone is not sufficient for happiness.

Like Westall, Geras creates a romantic, sexually charged atmosphere without mentioning so much as a breast. Although her roommates clamour to know what it was like to have sex, Megan simply tells them what they know already.

> 'Was it wonderful? Was it like Saint John of the Cross?' Bella wanted to know.
> 'Exactly!' I said. 'Like Saint John and Keats and everybody else.'
> 'And Buddy Holly?' Bella continued.
> 'Naturally. And Elvis, and Racine and Shakespeare, oh, everybody you can think of!' (134)

Where Robbie becomes dependent and demanding as his affair plays out, Megan discovers self-knowledge and strength through her relationship with

Simon. Eventually she leaves him to return to school and to have experiences more suited to her age. Although at one level she returns to a more childish condition, at another she has grown up and moved away from the fears and constraints of living with her domineering aunt (Megan is an orphan).

Both *Falling into Glory* and *The Tower Room* treat relationships between pupils and teachers as intense and meaningful but as ultimately doomed. Although Megan and Simon continue to love each other and work towards getting together in the future (when she is older and no longer his pupil), Geras, like Westall, shows that it is better not to leap over aspects of growing up, and that relationships demand levels of life experience most young people simply do not have. Despite the problematic nature of the relationships in these books, because they handle the sexual content 'sensitively' – meaning they avoid graphic descriptions, crude language, and sensational or voyeuristic episodes – neither Westall nor Geras found themselves in difficulties with critics or educationists over these love stories, and both books have regularly been reprinted since they first appeared. The teacher–pupil relationship in Melvin Burgess's *Doing It* (2004) was neither discretely described nor overlooked by adults.

Doing It follows the sexual exploits of three sixteen-year-old boys, one of whom, Ben, finds himself involved in what begins as the ultimate school-boy fantasy when his attractive young English teacher seduces him.

Miss Young – call me Miss – pulled him back on the cushions and kissed him even more deeply, making little moaning noises deep in her throat as though she was eating something surprisingly delicious. (27)

Miss Young turns out to be needy and sexually demanding. She initiates a variety of sexual activities, sometimes in school time, until Ben is both emotionally and physically exhausted. When he tries to leave her she cuts her wrists, and eventually he has to enlist her mother to help him disentangle himself from the relationship.

At its ethical and emotional levels, the way *Doing It* depicts sexual relationships between teachers and pupils is not unlike *Falling into Glory* and *The Tower Room*. Although at first Ben exults in his situation and sees it almost exclusively in terms of the sex, he learns to see Ali Harris as a fragile woman and tries to protect her. Like Westall and Geras, Burgess ends his novel with Ben's realising both that he wants to take things more slowly and work at a relationship with someone his own age and that females are more than sex-objects.

If I ever manage to get rid of her [Miss Harris] and go out with Marianne, I'll go ever so slowly. I wouldn't try to sleep with her on the first date. I'll try to kiss her and may try to slip my hands under her top, but if she didn't want it, that'd be OK. ... Some of my mates are really horrible, the way they go on about their girlfriends. ... I know what size and shape [Jackie's] tits are, I know what colour her nipples are. ... I know she hisses and whimpers when she comes. I even know that Dino can fit three fingers up her fanny but she doesn't like it much. (213)

The dynamics of Ben's relationship with Miss Harris and the way it is described indicate a very different understanding of young people's sexual attitudes and activity from Westall and Geras's books. Sex isn't limited to the exceptional student – all the young people in Burgess's book are shown to be sexually active and knowledgeable – and Ben's relationship with Miss Harris isn't a beautiful, meaningful and poignant interlude. He never deludes himself into thinking that he is in love with her, though she has made a good choice in Ben who is caring and discrete. For me there is also an important difference in the way Burgess addresses his readers. Westall lays down what is clearly meant to be mature advice about relationships and reiterates the popular wisdom that 'love hurts'; his is a one-way mode of address. Burgess, by contrast, deliberately avoids Westall's paternalistic stance and sets up a dialogue with his readers. He acknowledges that they bring their own experiences, needs, and assumptions to the text and trusts them to read intelligently and to separate fact from fiction.

Far from being 'filth any way you look at it' (Fine: 2003), Burgess believes that *Doing It*, like other equally contentious of his books including *Junk* (1996) and *Lady, My Life as a Bitch* (2001), accurately portrays young people's social and sexual behaviour and the way they (particularly boys) talk about sex. Partly in an attempt to redress the emphasis and validity given to female sexuality in response to feminist campaigns, *Doing It* focuses on a range of boy-behaviours and attitudes. It sets out to show that

young men aren't just blundering buffoons, teetering on the edge of sexual violence all the time, but sensitive as well as coarse, thoughtful as well as lustful, vulnerable as well as crude; and above all, irreverent and funny. (Burgess: 296)

Though it is sometimes hard to see characters in formation behind the endless references to tits and knobs, *Doing It* not only holds a mirror up to the young, but also offers adults and adolescents insights into each others' motivations and behaviours; it is extremely well observed and bold in its determination not to sanitise language or actions in the cause of preserving a misguided myth of innocence. This book plays its part in the ongoing shift towards greater openness about sexuality, and does so in ways designed to break down boundaries and bring generations closer together (though it does not encourage closer relationships of a sexual nature between young and old).

After all, as Burgess shows in the alternating narrative strands and through a range of vignettes, just about everybody is doing it in one way or another.[9]

Everybody's doing it: same-sex and transgender relationships

Although its repertoire of sexual pairings and fantasies is extensive, *Doing It* is exclusively concerned with heterosexual activities. Writers for the young have not been quick to take up the cause of sexual minorities, but the number of books about homosexual relationships is growing steadily and being augmented by works that explore a range of sexualities and behaviours. Most common are books about same-sex relationships between young men, including Aidan Chambers's fine novel, *Dance on my Grave* (1982), discussed in Chapter 4. Just as books about heterosexual relationships have now taken on board everything from first romantic love to energetic and lust-driven casual encounters, so the preoccupations in books about attraction between boys has ceased to be solely concerned with coming out and validating gay feelings.

Irish writer Tom Lennon's *When Love Comes to Town* (1993) was one of the first to provide a detailed and sympathetic portrait of the gay scene and to include a group of heterosexual characters who are relaxed and accepting of gay peers and siblings. Lennon's central character, Neil Byrne, is no limp-wristed, camp aesthete, either. As a rugby player and 'one of the lads', his sexuality is never questioned by his family or friends. When Neil finally tells his friend Becky that he's gay, she's not surprised and advises him to go to a gay bar in town and start living the life he wants to live. His sister and her boyfriend go with him to the bar, and together they are introduced to a circle of characters who are working hard at making relationships and being accepted.

It is not all easy for Neil. His parents and some of his friends reject him for a time, he is the victim of a homophobic mugging, one of his new friends dies from AIDs, and his first love eventually hurts and leaves him. But *When Love Comes to Town* places the events that happen to Neil after he comes out on the spectrum of the changes that accompany growing up and becoming sexually active. Homosexuality is neither sensationalised nor treated with kid gloves: it is presented as a way of being that, because it has been associated with a marginalised and oppressed group, has developed a lifestyle that can sometimes be both more outrageous and more secretive than most.

The drive to normalise same-sex behaviour is taken to extremes in David Levithan's fantasy, *Boy Meets Boy* (2003). Its central character, Paul, is gay but lives in a town where 'There isn't really a gay scene or a straight scene. ... They all got mixed up a while back ...' (9). This is not true of the surrounding area, where some of Paul's friends live, but there is never any trouble between gays, non-gays, or any sex or gender proclivity in Paul's town. Having set the scene, Levithan goes on to explore what falling in love would be like for gay couples in a world where sexual orientation is not an issue. Not surprisingly, it turns out to be just like falling in love for heterosexual couples in a world where that is regarded as the norm, as can be seen in the description of Paul and his boyfriend Noah's first kiss.

> I light the candles. The air smells like vanilla mist. Noah reaches over to touch my cheek. His thumb moves over my lips and down on the side of my neck. He leans me back against the wall and kisses me. I kiss him back hard. We breathe each other in. As the sound system tests itself out and orchids are floated atop the tables, we grasp at each other and explore each other and mark the time in movements and whispers. (216)

Perhaps to balance the conceit of a world in which sexuality is not an issue, Levithan resorts to stereotypical and hackneyed writing. Unfortunately, his characters are as devoid of style and interest as is the prose; nevertheless, *Boy Meets Boy* treats sex and sexuality lightly and offers a vision of an alternative world brought about not by new technologies or some form of Armageddon, but by adjusting the way we think.

Levithan works towards social transformation by encouraging his readers to think of all kinds of sex and gender behaviours as equally legitimate and important; Julie Burchill's *Sugar Rush* concentrates on making the case for lesbian sex, though despite having had lesbian lovers herself, Burchill's arguments lack both political and emotional force. Since this is one of a very small number of books that feature same-sex relationships between girls, *Sugar Rush* is a particularly wasted opportunity.

Where gay novels tend to have a reforming agenda, the relationship between Kim and Maria is characterised by all the worst aspects of juvenile infatuation. Once her protagonist, Kim, falls for her new best friend, Maria Sweet, she delights in the freedoms of lesbian love:

> ... this was PROPER sex, in a way that a boy and a girl our ages never could have had. It was sex without the rubbish, without the fear, without the you-made-your-bed-young-lady-and-now-you're-going-to-have-to-lie-in-it punchline; the pregnancy, abortion, disease, boy-boasting, bad rep, whatever. (113)

Maria is selfish, manipulative, and unfaithful, and eventually both girls are damaged by her behaviour. Where Lennon and Levithan present love between boys as romantic and fulfilling, Burchill goes for titillation. Maria and Kim 'fiddle' with each other in playgrounds, parks, and on the beach; they enjoy the sense of transgression and feel powerful in their otherness. Where the other same-sex books I have discussed work to promote understanding and change, *Sugar Rush* takes a less than analytical look at a single relationship as part of a particular moment in time. It captures the mood of youth culture at the start of the new millennium, but is more about charting the decadence of a culture on the wane than a vision of alternative ways of being. Julie Anne Peters's *Luna* (2004), by contrast, is committed to developing readers' understanding of sex and gender, encouraging them to move beyond the binaries of male/female, masculine/feminine into more nuanced ways of understanding sexual difference and orientations.

Luna is the chosen name for the female persona of Liam, a teenage transgender computer genius. Liam's sister Regan is his only confidante, and the story is focalised through her. She has watched Liam-by-day turn into Luna-by-night for years; the book begins at the period when Liam is no longer willing – or able – to suppress Luna. With Regan's help she is gradually allowed secretly to appear in the daytime, sometimes with frightening consequences. Eventually Liam decides to leave home, where his father cannot cope with the situation, and finance gender reassignment treatment using the money he has earned working for computer companies.

There is a highly unreal dimension to this book; Liam/Luna's talent, wealth, and beauty offer opportunities unavailable to most people, not least the ability to become independent and pay for sex-change surgery. To concentrate on these aspects of the novel is to undermine the work it does to give readers an insight into Liam/Luna's dilemma. Focalising it through Regan, who loves and admires both Liam and Luna and has seen the struggle between them, works well because it encourages readers first to care about Liam/Luna and then to accept that continuing to live out the masquerade is intolerable. And not just intolerable for Liam/Luna: Regan's life too has been consumed by the need for concealment and deception. 'Brother' and sister are both released from the stresses and restrictions of their lifetimes when Liam decides it is time to become Luna.

Although it attempts to provide insights into the experiences of those who do not fit comfortably into the 'normal' categories of male and female, *Luna* is more about the problems of living a transgender existence than an exegesis of current thinking about gender. For instance, Liam is always presented as a non-character; only Luna is allowed vibrancy and a sense of legitimacy. The possibility of accommodating the two selves or presenting a combined persona in circumstances where this would be acceptable is never put forward as desirable, although it is widely accepted in academic circles at least that gender is never a fixed, stable part of identity. Related to this is the fact that although Liam is conscious of performing his role as a boy and has to practise at behaving as a female, *Luna* is largely uninterested in how far identity is a social construct: Luna seems to come into the world fully formed and never to find herself torn between herself and Liam. This means that when Liam chooses to become Luna, the text suggests that the change will result in an unambiguously gendered 'correct' self; it ignores 'the neithers, the boths, the incoherencies' (Rabinowitz: 20) that queer theory has worked so hard to bring to our attention. Instead, it underlines the fact that in order to be what Judith Butler has termed 'culturally intelligible' (21) an individual must be recognisable as either male or female.

In one of the most telling moments of the book, Luna is turned away by the security guards as she attempts to board the airplane that is to take her off to her new life because her driver's license-ID is in Liam's name. She has to revert to Liam (in the ladies' room) before she can begin the process of metamorphosing into Luna. She is not allowed to be Luna *and* Liam. Most readers, however, will be aware that the lucrative computer skills that make the change possible – and possibly the ease with which Liam has found employment – are very much associated with the character's male identity and a set of skills associated with masculinity (and thus situated within traditional hegemonic power networks). Presumably these will continue to provide for Luna, suggesting some interestingly complementary mixtures of sex and gender elements.

Such subtleties invite readers to explore the limitations of thinking in terms of a single sexual identity. This is a compassionate book, but it would have been bolder if it had argued as much for new, less firmly delineated, ways of thinking about sex and gender as it does for the need to inhabit a body of the right sex. To do this it would have needed to be stylistically more complex, inviting different ways of reading and thinking, and to depart from the conventions of the rite of passage narrative.

Despite its limitations, the fact that *Luna* places a transgender character at the centre of a fiction for young adults is indicative of the changes that have taken place in the way sex, sexuality, and gender are represented in children's and youth literature since the postwar period. Far from the asexual, highly gendered, white, middle-class children and youths that dominated the children's publishing scene for most of the twentieth century, the last three decades have seen a steady pressure to be inclusive and, increasingly, to question the codes we use to think about childhood and adolescence in relation to sex and gender. As with the other chapters in this book, it is important to recognise that these changes are happening in dialogue with changes in culture, both responding to changes and helping to adjust the way readers think and behave. It is to be hoped that a generation that has grown up reading books that acknowledge and work at understanding a broad range of sexual relationships and gender orientations will be more flexible in the way it recognises and defines normal and legitimate behaviour.

7
Frightening Fiction: The Transformative Power of Fear

Chapter 4 raises questions about the way some popular forms of adolescent fiction encourage complacency and quiescence in readers. Reflecting attitudes associated with contemporary neoconservative politics, this kind of writing rejects many of the liberal ideas that were shaping children's and youth literature in the 1960s; its radicalism is anti-progressive in its assumption that mass political engagement is undesirable, and that the needs of the economy supersede those of democracy and the social and educational infrastructure that sustains it. At its best, fiction that deliberately promotes feelings of fear, unease, and disquiet in its readers has quite the opposite effect: it is 'visionary' and 'tests and shakes our complacency as individuals and as members of a larger culture' (Magistrale and Morrison in Stephens and McCallum, 2001: 174). Much contemporary frightening fiction, then, is characterised by an aesthetic of future-orientated transformation.

The history of frightening fiction encompasses a range of material, not all of it intended to test and shake complacency in the way Magistrale and Morrison suggest. As I will discuss later in this chapter, the early history of frightening fiction largely consists of stories designed to scare children into good behaviour, while some mass-market books that masquerade as frightening fiction are just as strongly implicated in the drive to produce 'useful idiots' as the hedonistic adolescent novels discussed in Chapter 4. Stories that use fear to promote change usually take the form of genres such as horror, thrillers, and mysteries: narratives that make the certain uncertain and in the process point to emotional and social cracks and fissures just below the surface of everyday reality, both individual and collective. Fictions of this sort generally achieve their effects by striving to expose the everyday as false and inadequate; often this means calling into question the intentions of those in authority. In the case of children's literature, this usually involves disturbing the adult-child power dynamic, the stability of which Jacqueline Rose claims is a central tenet of children's literature. With this in mind, it is perhaps surprising that frightening fiction is one of the largest and most diverse areas of writing for children.

Coercion and conformity: the early history
of frightening fiction

Fear can be produced in readers in a number of ways, to different degrees and effects, and for a number of purposes. Many of the oldest and most enduring kinds of narratives produced for children – such things as rhymes, games, folk and fairy tales, and even lullabies – contain violent incidents, frightening situations, and a variety of threats directed at children. The threats may take the form of injury, abduction, punishment or death. Babies fall from tree tops, children fall down hills, are beaten and sent to bed, or abandoned in the wood.

Such tales are staple nursery fare, even when they do not at first sight appear to feature children. Look, for instance, at the nursery rhyme (n.d.) about the 'man of double deed' who 'Sowed his garden full of seed' (Opie: 286). As one consequence follows another, the teller of the tale suddenly switches from third to first-person narration, in the process introducing a gothic feel, quite different from the matter-of-fact events reported in nursery rhymes such as 'Jack and Jill':

> When the door began to crack,
> 'Twas like a stick across my back;
> When my back began to smart,
> 'Twas like a penknife in my heart;
> When my heart began to bleed,
> 'Twas death and death and death indeed.

While the voice here is not specifically that of a child, the verse has entered into childhood lore as a ball-bouncing song, which means that the 'I' who suffers becomes the chanting child.[1]

Many well-known folk and fairy tales also recount more and less traumatic events experienced by infants and young children. Marina Warner's *No Go the Bogey Man: Scaring, Lulling and Making Mock* (1998) provides details of an array of frightening figures and characters associated with childhood from many parts of the world. Among the most common and potentially frightening stories are those in which parents destroy their own children: Cronus deliberately eats each of his children to stop one of them from usurping his place; the ogre in *Hop o' my Thumb* slits the throats of all seven of his daughters by mistake, and in *The Juniper Tree*, the father tucks into the curiously tasty stew made from his son's flesh.

The frightening element in most of these stories arises more from what they imply about the threat to children from parents, adults, and official institutions than from any elaborate bogeymen and monsters, prefiguring a theme that infuses the most popular form of contemporary frightening fiction, horror. As Freud pointed out in his essay on 'The Uncanny',

> ... the real horrors and monsters do not lie in some dimension behind or beyond the everyday, but inhere within 'homeliness'. The façade of the family home may conceal worse things than vampires, ghosts, or the living dead. (in Stephens and McCallum: 170)

Threats to children from those who should be caring for them permeate children's literature – from oral tales through nineteenth-century fantasies and contemporary urban thrillers – and underpin most juvenile examples of frightening fiction. When such stories are placed side by side, it is hard to escape the thought that, at least in the past (stories in which children are harmed or killed declined sharply during the first half of the last century), child readers might well have received the impression that most adults and even the Almighty wished them dead.

The most important text in which young readers of the past regularly encountered tales featuring threats to children was the Bible. Both in its entirety and in special editions for children, the Bible contains many examples of individual and mass murders of children by the adults responsible for them. These range from Herod's and Pharaoh's slaughter of boy babies, to the gory tale of Elisha, whose curse on a group of taunting boys results in forty-two of them being torn to pieces by a pair of she-bears. There are also parental sacrifices such as that nearly carried out by Abraham on his only son Isaac, and Jephthah's actual sacrifice of his daughter.[2] It would have been hard for child readers, for whom the Bible was a familiar and approved text, to ignore the incidence of child death at the hands of adults – not forgetting those who sicken and die because, as in the case of David and Bathsheba, God is punishing their parents!

Other approved reading of the past which today would be thought likely to frighten or disturb children includes tales of martyrs suffering gruesome tortures, which children were often given in the form of lavishly illustrated editions with the recommendation that they annotate their favourite bits. Few of the most famous martyrs were children, but martyrdom was an option open to children as well as adults, and the idea of inspired and meaningful suffering was often before them, not least in the widely read work we know as *Foxe's Book of Martyrs (Actes and Monuments of these latter perilous times touching matters of the Church*, 1554, trans into English in 1563).[3] Charles Lamb, born in 1775, provides an insight into how some child readers of earlier generations found pleasure and a stimulus to creativity in such books. He recalls loving 'a great *Book of Martyrs*' about 'good men who chose to be burnt alive' and where a child could play at putting his 'hands upon the flames which were pictured in the pretty pictures which the book had, and feel them' (in Tucker, 1976: 116). By contrast, a century later, E. Nesbit (born 1858) describes a book that sounds very like *Foxe's Book of Martyrs* – mentioning specifically illustrations of the kind that so pleased Charles Lamb – as

A horrible book – the thick tissue paper sticking to the prints like bandages to a wound. It was a book that made you afraid to go to bed, but it was a book you could not help reading. ('The Aunt and Amabel', 1912)

Its page-turning qualities made Percy Muir, in his influential history of children's literature, describe *Foxe's Book of Martyrs* as typifying the 'ghastly compilations ... [which] were intended as light literature to bring joy to the hearts of their young readers' and 'spare simple minds from the damnable influence of popular ballads and more pleasing narratives' (1985: 33).

Although it had popular appeal, Foxe's work was indisputably an approved text. The hugely popular and widely discredited tales, ballads, and literature that child readers of the past might encounter from a variety of unofficial sources including orally and in chapbooks and other cheaply printed materials, also contain myriad examples of terrible things done to children, almost always by the adults who were supposed to care for them. In the ballad *The Cruel Mother*, for instance, the mother in question rids herself of her unwanted babies by taking 'her penknife out of her pocket' and 'pierc[ing] those pretty babes to the heart'; in *Mary Hamilton*, another unwanted baby is tied in its mother's apron and thrown into the sea and she tells it, 'Sink ye, swim ye, bonny wee babe!/You'll neer get mair o'me'. Probably the most famous example told specifically for children, and found in chapbooks, ballads, and picture books, is *The Babes in the Wood*, in which a wicked uncle hires a pair of murderers to despatch his orphaned niece and nephew so that he can steal their fortune. The children are abandoned in the wood where, after fruitless wanderings, 'They sobbed and they sighed and they sat there and cried,/Those two little babies they lay down and died'.[4]

As these examples show, adults' murderous urges towards children are well documented in fiction, though this fact is often overlooked, repressed or denied. In her study of fantasy and children's fear of infanticide (1978), psychoanalyst Dorothy Bloch points out that Freud's version of the Oedipus story crucially ignores the fact that Oedipus's parents conspired to kill him at birth – and believed they had done so – focusing instead on children's fantasies of removing parental rivals. Bloch concludes that 'children are universally predisposed to the fear of infanticide' (3); this being so, it could be argued that the frequency with which the texts classified as 'children's literature' include images of dead and dying children act simultaneously as expressions of repressed adult desires and practical warnings to children.

Jacqueline Rose, also drawing on psychoanalytic theories, casts a slightly different light on this phenomenon. She maintains that the adults who write, publish, purchase, and introduce books to children are concerned not with eliminating real children, but with fashioning an image of childhood that is capable of holding off the threat of what adults – *not* children – fear most. According to Rose, the central fear in children's literature arises from adults' anxiety about the possibility that the maturity which has been negotiated with such difficulty through the unstable medium of language (language acquisition and management are closely associated with children's literature), could disintegrate if the adult were to be seduced by delights and behaviours associated with the preverbal, infantile stage. At an unrecognised level this may indeed account for the rigour with which writing for children has traditionally been expected to uphold the primacy of such less delightful attributes and activities as obedience, cleanliness, and the need for education.

Following Rose's line of thought, a great deal of children's literature can be understood as serving adults' needs by holding before them images of children – both child characters in the texts and those implied as readers of them – in the process of embarking on and valuing the progress to maturity and ultimately adulthood. The image of the child as reader, so integral to children's literature, represents the mastery of language, which equally signals the mastery of self as a subject in language. In Rose's account, however, this image of childhood is always phantasmagorical: it has no foundation and serves merely to hold off 'panic about the world and its unknowable, divisive and overwhelming nature' (10).

Rose points to both the ability of texts for children to awaken adult fears of self-destruction through regression, and the refusal of critics of children's literature to address the problematic nature of language. While this situation is changing, it is true that in studies of children's literature, the central existential fear that the self can as easily be unmade as called into being by language is rarely expressed. Instead, in children's literature and its criticism, the manifest expression of fear has focused on physical threats to the young. Significantly, in juvenile fiction before the mid-twentieth century, unless they are the acts of scoundrels like the wicked uncle in *The Babes in the Wood*, such threats, whether in the form of officially sanctioned punishments or more covert psychological tactics, are normally presented as beneficial to children. They are part of regimes designed to save young souls and teach them about the acceptable range of behaviours in the circles in which they moved, what was expected of them, and what the consequences of disobedience would be on this earth and in the hereafter.

Although many such texts include scenes that seem to be there for the purpose of frightening children, the kind of transformation they have in mind is quite different from that Magistrale and Morrison associate with modern forms of frightening fiction. Early children's fiction is about transforming the child by turning it away from sin and towards Christ, in the process creating what Foucault referred to as 'docile bodies': subjects who submit to and internalise the belief and value systems of their societies in ways that maximise their usefulness (*Discipline and Punish*, 1977). Since many of the popular tales which we now classify as children's literature were not originally intended to be exclusively for children, their messages about rewards and punishments were absorbed widely.

The difference between today's best examples of fear-inducing fiction and early children's literature can be seen clearly in the different stylistic devices employed. Most of the early tales in which children die or are seriously injured are treated as lessons rather than as works designed to provoke the thrill of fear and powerful sense of engagement that characterises the kinds of stories regarded as typical of frightening fiction today. This is achieved by, for instance, using a factual if sometimes sentimental tone in contrast to the heightened mode of horror, mystery or thriller writing, in which events and conversations are loaded with unspecified meaning. Early writers invariably choose third-person narrators while more contemporary forms of frightening fiction often make use of the first person or focalise events through the protagonist to achieve a similar effect of immediacy.

Despite their narrative restraint, frightening stories, poems, and ballads could have profound effects on young audiences. In *The Oxford Book of Nursery Rhymes* (1951; 1997, verse 293), Iona and Peter Opie include detailed notes to the verse titled 'Lady', which bear out this point. The verse is about a lady 'all skin and bone' who goes to church to pray one day, only to be met with a sermon 'gainst pride and sin' and the body of a dead man on the ground:

> And from his nose unto his chin,
> The worms crawled out, the worms crawled in.
> Then she unto the parson said,
> Shall I be so when I am dead?
> O yes! O yes, the parson said,
> You will be so when you are dead.

The accompanying notes quote the editor of *Gammer Gurton's Garland* (1810), who claims that the story 'has been bringing terror to listeners in the nursery' since it was first told. They include a recollection of the poet Southey of how he used to cry and 'beg his family not to proceed' when any member embarked on the tale, and an account provided by one of the Opies's correspondents who, in 1947, reported that this was one in a collection of verses that 'scared us so much as children, we fastened the leaves together'.[5]

Children's literature itself also provides fictional accounts of the effects such stories could have on young minds. In *Francis Fearful* (1775), for instance, the eponymous Francis, a clever boy whose parents have not paid sufficient attention to his upbringing, is terrified by all manner of things and because of this becomes a laughing stock when he goes to school. The reason for his timorous behaviour is that his nurse has filled his head with stories such as 'Valentine and Orson, the Seven Champions, the old woman of Ratcliff-highway, the tales of the fairies ... and ... stories about Witches and Ghosts, Hobgoblins, and the shrieking woman ...' (Anon: 57).

The fact that most of the earliest frightening tales that have survived in print make little use of the conventions now regularly employed to provoke fear on the page does not mean that such strategies were unknown. In fact, they were very familiar in oral forms including sermons, but tended to be excluded in literary works until the emergence of gothic tales, sensation fiction, ghost stories, and eventually horror fiction.[6] It is worth noting that each of these genres began in writing for adults, but with the exception of the short-lived sensation novel, quickly gravitated to the nursery, not least through popular periodical publications such as 'penny dreadfuls', 'bloods', and dime novels. Even more conservative and restrained examples belong to the domain of frightening fiction, since they were generally told with the intention of scaring children into behaving well by showing them the consequences of bad behaviour.

These cautionary tales may have been designed for readers' good – to help them avoid making similar mistakes – but this means that as well as the risks posed by malign adults and a vengeful God, children were given dire warnings about how they could harm themselves through faults such as greed, disobedience, envy, deceit, thoughtlessness, sloth, and carelessness. Probably even more disturbing was the fact that this kind of behaviour, they were assured, would lead not only to death, but also to damnation – which at various periods was the most frightening idea of all; especially since it was often linked to the idea that naughty children are no longer loved by their parents.

Although damnation is not the central idea of Lucy Lane Clifford's 'The New Mother' (1882), its account of the withdrawal of the loving mother in the face of repeatedly bad behaviour by two of her children who are under the influence of a seductively corrupting figure, and the arrival of the monstrous new mother, with her glass eye and wooden tail, has frightened generations of children. Clifford was writing on the cusp of modernism, with its questioning of religious orthodoxy, and her tale has only obliquely religious overtones; the non-conformist tinker turned preacher, John Bunyan, puts the same message rather more starkly in 'Upon the Disobedient Child' from his *A Book for Boys and Girls; or, Country Rhymes for Children* (1686):

> Children become, while little, our delights,
> When they grow bigger, they begin to fright's
> Their sinful Nature prompts them to rebel,
> And to delight in Paths that lead to Hell. ...
> Thus they who at the first were Parents Joy,
> Turn that to Bitterness, themselves destroy.

While Clifford's later, psychologically complex and compelling tale offers a metaphoric warning about what happens to parent–child relationships when children behave badly, Bunyan's poem specifically tells young readers that the longer they live, the more likely they are to disappoint their parents and go to perdition. To modern eyes, one of the most disturbing elements of this kind of frightening fiction from the past is the way it creates a lexis and model of death as desirable – something to be sought – and life as problematic and damaging. This idea became so commonplace that in some contexts it was eventually stripped of much of its fear and became capable of a more light-hearted treatment. Take, for example, 'The Mansion of Bliss', a game published in 1810 by the firm of William Darton, which involves players in a race to see who can get through life most quickly and virtuously, making as few errors as possible on the way (for purity take an extra turn and collect a counter from each player; for swearing lose three turns). The winner is the first to arrive at the 'Mansion of Bliss' for, the instructions tell players,

> Who enters the mansion of bliss,
> Will have cause to rejoice at his claim;
> So well has he travell'd thro' life,
> He has happily ended the game.

Heinrich Hoffman's long-lived and influential *Struwwelpeter* (1845; English translation, 1848) also contains blackly comic tales of child death, including 'The Dreadful Story of Pauline [or Harriet, depending on the edition] and the Matches' in which Pauline/Harriet, when left alone one day, does what she has been told not to do. Ignoring the warnings of her cats, she plays with matches,

> So she was burnt with all her clothes,
> And arms and hands, and eyes and nose;
> Till she had nothing more to lose
> Except her little scarlet shoes;
> And nothing else but these was found
> Among her ashes on the ground.

Stories featuring the death or threatened death of children do not have the monopoly on what is considered frightening fiction, however. For many children, more frightening and memorable than the stories from *Struwwelpeter* that end in death are the ones that feature grotesque ways of dealing with mundane behaviour such as thumb-sucking (the great, long, red-legged scissorman cuts off thumb-suckers' thumbs 'and then/You know they never grow again'), refusing food, or playing in the rain ('Flying Robert' is carried away by his umbrella and never returns). Over the years it has become apparent that precisely what frightens children in the books and other forms in which they encounter narrative is unpredictable. While some find Hoffman's tales terrifying, others enjoy their dark humour.[7] What is clear is that early children's fiction tended to use fear to promote social conformity. As the texts discussed in the following sections will show, populist forms of frightening fiction for the young carry on this tradition, but there are many more innovative and more thoroughly frightening contemporary texts in a variety of genres, formats, and media that evoke fear as a way of exploring a range of topical issues with a view to challenging the status quo and working for social change. Such works are transformative in the way Magistrale and Morrison suggest: they unsettle and reposition readers so that they are less inclined to accept the world around them at face value.

Fear, fiction, and the adolescent

As readers of early children's literature demonstrate, many people remember vividly the stories and games from their early years that frightened them significantly. Adults responding to questions about frightening children's books on an Internet discussion list were often able to recall vividly the circumstances of encounters with texts that frightened them, whether this was private reading at bedtime or a shared reading.[8] They also provided accounts of themselves/their partners/their children having been so scared by particular books or films in childhood that, like the Opies' correspondent who stitched the pages of the book containing 'Lady' together, these books had to be physically disarmed by being wrapped up, hidden from sight, and sometimes removed or destroyed.

Such extreme reactions were inevitably the product of being unprepared for the way a story unfolds. In *Tales of Innocence and Experience*, the writer Eva Figes recounts precisely such an incident which took place when she began reading *The Juniper Tree*, a fairy tale she did not know, to her granddaughter. Both were unprepared for the stepmother's violent beheading of her husband's son, the horrible stew, and the pile of bones that were all that remained of him. Figes describes their reaction:

> I am appalled by the words coming out of my mouth. Now I know why this story was never read to me as a child.
> I think this is rather horrid. What about a different story?
> Speechless, knees tight together, she nods. I fetch a jolly picture book and she sits quietly enough whilst I turn the pages, too quietly.
> I shut the book with a cheerful, reassuring smile. ...
> Can they put the boy's head back on again?
> Do you want me to find out? (72)

Both grandmother and child feel the story is out of their control because they cannot anticipate what is coming. It does not hold to the patterns familiar in the other tales they have shared, where the wolf's belly is slit open and the grandmother and Little Red Riding Hood escape, or Hansel and Gretel save themselves from the witch's oven and return home in triumph. Because they cannot predict what will happen, they succumb to the fearful elements in the narrative and eventually have to flee from it. But this too is unsafe – unfinished, the story lives on in their minds and emotions, so it must be confronted again. This time, however, the grandmother is prepared, and rightly or wrongly, she edits the remainder of the story, giving it familiar twists and turns to arrive at 'They all lived happily ever after.' 'Where does it say that?' the child demands (73), a story the wiser after this unexpected foray into the narrative outback.

Fear arising from a narrative that unexpectedly slips behind a reader's defences is quite different from the experience of consciously choosing a book that advertises itself as frightening – and anticipating the pleasures that can arise from being frightened under the right circumstances. This kind of pleasure is about control – choosing what, when, and where to experience frightening fictions – so it is not surprising that the period of adolescence, a time notoriously about learning to manage the self in a society that often seems overwhelming, is particularly associated with an appetite for this kind of narrative. At least since the 1950s and the vogue for American horror comics, many young people of both sexes have actively sought narratives in the form of books, comics, radio and television programmes, films, and now computer games that include and may even primarily be about incidents which combine horror, violence, and the supernatural, all staple elements of contemporary frightening fiction.

A number of theorists have attempted to explain this predilection. From the moment deliberately ghoulish stories first found their way into print, commentators were pointing to the adolescent propensity to read them, and worrying about their possible effects. In the Victorian era, British publishers who distributed 'penny dreadfuls' were characterised as vampires, polluting the minds of the young and 'smoothing the way that leads to all destruction' (in Barker and Petley: 155). These hugely popular examples of frightening fiction came to be associated in the public mind with the social discontents associated with the approach of modernity and the accompanying perceived rise in anti-social behaviour, thereby adding another meaning to the idea of 'frightening fiction'. This tendency to implicate by association mass-market forms of frightening fiction in a wide range of illegal, immoral, and dangerous behaviours continues to this day. The press in particular is quick to condemn them as addictive and perverting – a kind of literary contagion – blaming them for everything from young people's rejection of high-quality writing to acts of extreme violence (see Murdock in Barker and Petley).

While educationalists and journalists have tended to vilify high-profile examples of frightening fiction, calling them 'vile and truly pernicious' (McCarron, 1994: 28), others have been more interested in understanding their appeal and possible effects. For instance, in his exploration of how readers are created, J.A. Appleyard suggests that the popularity of such narratives with adolescents stems from the fact that:

> Teenage readers have discovered that the conventions of juvenile litera-
> ture do not match the complexity of their new experience. And as a result
> they demand that stories not just embody their wishes and fantasies, but
> also reflect realistically the darker parts of life and the newfound limits on
> their idealism. (1994: 97)

Specifically, Appleyard is alert to the way that the element of fear in these texts frequently functions as a metaphor for the experience of change and separation characteristic of adolescence and the growing sense of 'a split between the "me nobody knows" and a changing personality' (97). Such an analysis focuses on the difference between the experience of fear in real life and attempts to create sensations of fear on the page. The first is a biological response stemming from the fact that organisms are programmed to assess situations in very basic ways: our bodies look for signals that tell us whether something offers an opportunity (to eat, to mate) or a threat (to be eaten, to be denied the opportunity to reproduce). Threats produce a feeling of fear, often accompanied by aggression. Primitive reactions such as these are inad-equate in a complex world, however, and familiarity with many experiences, whether derived from life or forms of narrative, can aid in predicting the most advantageous way to behave.

Adolescence is widely recognised as a time of confusion, not least, as Appleyard points out, about the extent to which the self feels threatened by physical and emotional changes and constrained by outside forces. This is why Rosemary Jackson sees fantasies which present the self as divided between the benign familiar and a hostile/aggressive other as manifestations of adolescent alienation, developed during a period when the libidinal drive is high but society tends to limit or even prohibit its expression. Fictions dealing in images of divided or doubled selves frequently act as wishfulfilment fantasies that allow vicarious fulfilment (1995: 70–86).

Both Jackson and Appleyard offer well-rehearsed psychoanalytic explanations for adolescents' attraction to narratives that deal in frightening images and events. Such texts, the argument runs, mirror maturing children's recognition that the world is not always as pleasant a place as they may previously have been led to believe, and this feeling is corroborated by the fact that they themselves have feelings and drives that sometimes seem strange, overwhelming, and threatening. As has long been recognised, the image of monsters, aliens, or other kinds of supernaturally powerful beings who take over the body of an ordinary person (a frequent motif in conventional horror and one which is used regularly in contemporary forms of frightening fiction) provides the perfect metaphor for this stage in a young person's development.

Through it, 'the beast' many teenagers suspect they harbour within themselves can be externalised, encountered, and finally overcome. A sensitively evoked version of this experience is found in the Japanese picturebook, *Sleepless* (1996), written and illustrated by Shuhei Hasegawa (translation provided by Akiko Yamazaki).

Sleepless tells the story of teenage boy, Kentaro, who can't sleep because he is obsessed with thoughts of growing up, getting old, and dying. Although he feels isolated and emotionally outside the mainstream of society, Kentaro recognises a sense of power in himself; the illustrations suggest that he is apprehensive about whether this is the exciting and legitimate new-found power of adulthood, or something more malign. In one image he is shown exhaling a mighty breath across the sleeping town; its force strips leaves from the trees, makes a dog's fur stand on end, and pushes against a middle-aged man, striding along with his briefcase. It seems as if he could blow them all away, and yet nothing has changed when morning comes. His sleepless vigil generates disturbing thoughts and images of death and destruction; one night he imagines his friend Kagami coming towards him, and in his vision she is on fire. He opens his mouth and swallows her.

Hasegawa's illustrations convey a variety of complex and conflicting emotions: desire, destruction, repression, and perhaps guilt. Kentaro is shown as divided between the self his friends see and the self he experiences alone at night. *Sleepless* clearly presents an image of adolescence that conforms to the interpretations offered by Appleyard and Jackson; however, if such explanations are evoked too readily when examining the frightening fiction to which adolescents tend to be attracted, it is likely that they will all be understood as providing the same, ultimately cathartic experience – a reading experience that would seem to work against change. Moreover, focusing on the emergence and demands of sexual drives in adolescents ignores other possible ways in which such narratives tap into and shape young people's views of the world.

A critic who takes a different though also largely psychoanalytic approach to analysing the appeal of the kind of frightening fiction classified as 'horror' is Julia Kristeva. In *The Powers of Horror: An Essay on Abjection* she explores why readers of any age seek out the feelings of disgust or loathing typically encountered in texts which employ the modes of horror. According to Kristeva, this urge stems from the need to reinforce the transition from what she terms the maternal semiotic realm to the paternal symbolic realm, begun through processes such as weaning, toilet training, and the entry into language. While the mother/infant relationship of the semiotic phase is a symbiotic one, outside the demands of civilised society and characterised by connection based in shared bodily rhythms and sensations, the symbolic belongs to the civilised social world and the autonomous individual. As Rose also reminds us through her focus on adults' fears about the instability of language, entering the symbolic is achieved at a cost – separation from the blissful condition of unity with the mother – and maintained with difficulty. This means that anything which threatens to undermine the self-identity achieved by the transition to the symbolic is construed as fearful; as a way of defending the new state, images associated with the domain of the semiotic come to be regarded as loathsome and repugnant. Following Kristeva's logic, it is not surprising that many of the images employed in frightening fiction are connected with the semiotic. Think, for instance, how many monsters are inarticulate, infantile in their constant demands, which can never be met, and leak bodily fluids like an untrained infant.

Kristeva's explanation is helpful for understanding the images, lexis, and functions of frightening fiction: 'anything that threatens to send the subject back into the semiotic is accompanied by sensations of dread' and provokes the urge to re-enact and so reconfirm the transition to the symbolic (in Vice, 1997: 163). The images that frighten us are perverted and disguised images of what we long for; perhaps especially during the turbulent years of adolescence, when the process of separation begun in infancy tends to be reactivated, creating a desire to return to the sense of complete and satisfying connection of infancy. Since this state can only be achieved through regression and ultimately the destruction of the self, it must be vigorously rejected and its appeal denied by those who have barricaded themselves inside the stockade of maturity.

As the historical overview with which this chapter begins shows, damage or destruction of the self or the beloved, whether corporeal or psychic, affecting child or adult, seems always to be immanent in frightening fiction. While Julia Kristeva explains the feeling of loathing stimulated by horror as a response produced by the need to reject the seductive and ultimately destructive appeal of the semiotic, feminist critic Helen Cixous understands fascination with the bizarre and uncanny, equally common in narratives concerned with generating fear, rather differently. It is, she says, 'not merely ... displaced sexual anxiety, but ... a rehearsal for an encounter with death' (in Jackson, 1981: 68).

It is often observed that adolescents frequently believe (or act as if they believe) that they are immortal. Texts which provide vicarious encounters with ghosts, the undead, and others who exist outside the conventional definitions of life may be read as confirming this belief: seeing a ghost is frightening, but it can also be taken as evidence that death is not the end of the self, and even that interaction with the known world remains possible after death. J.K. Rowling follows precisely this logic in the Harry Potter series. Ghosts and similar manifestations – for instance, the interacting characters in portraits – talk, move, and observe events. They may be dead, but they have not ceased to exist.

If ghosts in Rowling's series are benign, her treatment of the undead is a different matter. The range and variety of such creatures has increased with each book in the series: from the dementors who reflect the many people of all ages who struggle to fight off depression or who have been damaged by abuse and torture, to the hooded wizards who launch a brief but recognisable terrorist attack during the Quidditch World Cup. Their significance goes beyond symbolising some of the anxieties and tensions Harry feels as he enters adolescence. In fact, from its light-hearted beginnings the series has become an important barometer of public response to post-9/11 circumstances.

It has been revealing to observe the changes in the amount and kind of frightening material Rowling has included in successive books now that unexpected, violent deaths no longer seem as remote as they did to most people in the West over the previous fifty years. Particularly powerful is the climate of uncertainty and paranoia which pervades *Harry Potter and the Half-Blood Prince* (2005) as the extent of Voldemort's network of the undead and potential martyrs becomes clear. Rowling has significantly adjusted the series's representation of the kinds of actions and events that are frightening and in doing so has increased the books' capacity to stimulate debate, function metaphorically, and offer social comment.

While Voldemort himself increasingly resembles a Bin Laden figure, evading capture, controlling events from constantly shifting vantage points, and by some accounts even capable of returning from the grave (whether in the form of Bin Laden's audio and video tapes or through Voldemort's magical/supernatural means), Rowling thus far has refused the ultimate fear: the descent into meaninglessness. As the series moves towards its conclusion, the childish utopia of Hogwarts has largely been dismantled, but the narrative has replaced simple forms of gratification with the deeper sense of purpose that comes from striving to uphold the tenets of humanism. Harry and his companions believe that there is value and meaning in what they do, win or lose, and readers are required to accept this view if the books are to engage them. Significantly, however, they know they cannot restore the old world; their job is to help create a new world order, the nature of which has yet to become apparent.

Rowling's series is taking on more and more attributes of frightening fiction, not least in its inclusion of evil children, which disturbs the myth of childhood as a time of innocence, inexperience, and vulnerability. The Harry Potter books are also notable for having been translated into a variety of new media and formats. In the case of Rowling's series, the transition into film and PC games – the two most radical transformations of the books – has tended to dilute the element of critique, usually by making Harry less complex and more heroic.[9] This inevitably makes the new narratives less frightening since heroic Harry is always cast as the victor, and most viewer–players already know the outcome of the stories before they begin watching or playing. This diminution of fear is neither a necessary or usual outcome of changing the mode by which a story is delivered, however. As the following examples will show, fear is often used to sell fictions to children and young adults, while blurring the boundaries between media is central to much contemporary narrative innovation.

Fear on screen

There was an unprecedented vogue for frightening fiction for and about young people in the run up to the new millennium, not all of it in the form of books. There were films such as *The Blair Witch Project* (1999), *The Sixth Sense* (1999), and *The Others* (2001), while the genre of computer games known as survival-horror games proliferated during this period and now has both a huge following and many successful products. Survival-horror games have names that, through references to darkness, evil, hauntings, and vulnerability, clearly evoke some of the most enduring genres that make up frightening fiction. Popular games include *Nocturne, Alone in the Dark, Thief – the Dark Project, System Shock, Resident Evil, Veil of Darkness, Doom,* and *Realms of Haunting* (many of these are parts of series with sequels appearing on a regular basis); reviewers' plot summaries and analyses of 'fear factors' show how closely related to gothic and horror fiction they are.

While those who do not play computer games may think of them as primarily a visual medium, the most successful employ professional writers as well as directors and actors, and strong story lines are central to the games' appeal and playability. Some, like the early cult game *Myst* (not in the horror mode), overtly merge the worlds of book and game; in *Myst*, the player learns by reading the accompanying manual that s/he (identified as 'you' – there is no invented protagonist) has discovered and read a book titled *Myst*. At the moment of closure, the book disappears to be replaced by the world of the book, an island, from which the reader must escape.

Frightening PC games are particularly dependent on strong plots. Angelina Sandoval's overview of one season's crop of games includes a description of *Clock Tower 3* for readers, starting with an overview of the plot (referred to by developers as 'the script'). From its origins in the school story (the central character, Alyssa Hamilton, is at boarding school), it mutates to the familiar frightening fiction setting of an empty house with a secret passage which seems to be implicated in the disappearance of Alyssa's mother. Add a nightmare chase scene and a science fiction twist through the introduction of a time portal, and you have the story line of *Clock Tower 3*. Despite piling cliché on cliché, the game is deemed to have the necessary 'fright factor' that Sandoval is seeking for her reader-players:

> *FRIGHT FACTOR:* Have you ever had a nightmare where something was chasing you and you had no idea what it was but it wasn't a good thing? Clock Tower 3 is like that and many of the things that chase the main character aren't chasing her down to get her phone number. No these things are spirits of murders long gone but still homicidal. Chilling? Oh, yeah.

As the plot summary shows, PC games such as *Clock Tower 3* are not the non-linear puzzles novices and non-players often imagine them to be, but developmental narratives with beginnings, middles, and ends, though they do include complicated digressions that add multilinear dimensions to the narratives. This is not surprising since games have their origins in the highly popular gamebook typified by the Fighting Fantasy series by Steve Jackson and Ian Livingstone in the 1980s and 1990s (see Chapter 8).

The plots and narrative devices employed in survival-horror games may be familiar, but that doesn't stop them from drawing players into scenarios, though just as experienced readers/viewers tend to find mass-market horror books and films either boringly predictable or comic (see Cullingford, 1998 and Barker and Petley, 2001), so regular players and players who also explore other media widely seem to be less susceptible to the 'fright factor'. The fact that the games periodically require players to withdraw from the action to acquire additional information or perform analytical tasks also disrupts the long-term power of the narrative. Finally, the fact that if they are to complete games, players need to return to or restart them repeatedly (in many ways analogous to rereading or watching a film for the umpteenth time) means that for most, the fear that comes from being taken unawares rapidly dissipates; games quickly cease to be frightening fictions and become exercises in gaming skill and problem-solving exercises. Like Eva Figes and her granddaughter, however, unprepared players can find themselves genuinely disturbed by PC games. One player described for readers of the site *PC Game* his reactions to playing the game *Scary*:

> I have never been more horrified by a game in my life. I only got maybe a half hour into the game, at that point I had enough, and decided to uninstall. What made me uninstall you ask? I'll tell you. These zombies with these worms coming out of their chest [*sic*] and entering their head were chasing me. I couldn't kill them, there were too many. I had to run. They kept screaming ... and. ... chased me right down this elevator. This elevator was going down the side of a great pit, in the center of the pit at the top was a little metal bridge going from one side to the other. As I was huddled ... at the bottom of the pit, the zombies preceded [sic] to walk 'drag, clank; drag, clank' across the bridge saying 'I can smell you', 'kill me', and other assorted things. I couldn't take it. I flat couldn't handle that game. I uninstalled and never looked back. (http://pc.ign.com/mail/2003–11–03.htm, accessed 22/07/05)

To many readers, the *Scary* scenario will seem highly derivative; however, the player's account of it is reminiscent of someone describing a nightmare; especially in his (?) strong identification ('I') with the character in the game, showing clearly that some players are drawn into the game through the same processes of interpellation and identification associated with popular fictional genres. A game's ability to scare players is very much a product of its fictional components, thus locating such games firmly in the domain of 'frightening fiction' (Mummer: 24–25); more significantly, the fusion of established conventions and new technologies they have fostered has the capacity to reinvigorate and redirect contemporary forms of frightening fiction as well as to enable games to capture players.

The need for such fusions – strong on traditional narrative conventions yet reinflected by awareness of the modes of new media/IT – becomes apparent when looking at the 1990s craze for children's and adolescent horror fiction. This arose early in the development of PC games, but in the midst of the 'video nasty' vogue (Rose, 2005: 11). With hindsight, it is clear that series such as Point Horror and Goosebumps failed to capitalise on either the literary legacy of frightening fiction or the possibilities for narrative experimentation provided by new media/IT. For instance, the books tended to avoid strong empathetic characterisation, despite the fact that the most enduring examples of frightening fiction, whatever the medium, implicate the self in whatever awful events unfold, whether this takes the form of a Mr. Hyde alter-ego or the taint in the blood caused by the vampire's bite.

Series horror almost invariably shows evil as something from outside, and thus Other/not me, weakening the books' ability to provide metaphors for the hidden, multiple, and sometimes transgressive selves that lurk within us all and which are so powerfully evoked in classic horror fiction. Neither do they play with or challenge ideas about the book as a form, beyond a jocular level of parody. As a consequence, despite their phenomenal sales during the 1990s, Point Horror and its imitators have largely become passé. Moreover, although there was considerable anxiety that such books were corrupting child readers and turning them against established ways of behaving, textual analysis reveals juvenile horror series to be deeply conformist. Like earlier children's fiction, they use fear to show the consequences of failing to conform (McCarron, 2001).

By contrast, those texts that successfully mingle techniques and ideas derived from new media and developing areas of information technology with long-established narrative conventions and deeply embedded sources of fear are capable of making lasting contributions to both children's literature and culture. The hybrid nature of many of these texts may explain why they often attract adaptors, resulting in multiple versions of narratives (book, film, comic, game, graphic novel, and Internet fan-site), more than one of which will be known to most 'readers'. The complex intratextual dynamic that results can in itself be transformative. A good example of this is the film adaptation of Catherine Storr's *Marianne Dreams* (1958), a powerful children's fantasy about two ill children whose time is divided between their sickrooms and a fantasy world where they meet, which subtly makes use of many of Freud's insights into the nature of the uncanny.

In Storr's novel, the two children, ten-year-olds Marianne and Mark, are trapped in a house where they are subject to hostile surveillance and unexplained interference on the radio. The sense of menace owes much to the Cold War period in which Storr was writing, with its fear of spies, and anxiety about threats to individuality from monolithic and unaccountable regimes. Thirty years later, Bernard Rose's 1988 film version, *Paper House*, turned Storr's children's book into a horror movie by evoking the late-twentieth century's fearful fascination with child abuse and violent murders. The film's central female character, Anna, is on the cusp of adolescence and full of anger against her father, who is always away. In her delirious dreams she encounters a fantasy father who wants to attack her, perhaps because she is sharing a house with another male. This change, as well as the deliberate use of cinematic devices derived from horror films, translates a children's 'modern classic' aimed at readers of ten and up into a certificate 15 film (USA, PG-13): a rare example of an adaptation raising the audience barrier.

Adaptations are just one way in which cross-media fertilisation can result in highly original forms of frightening fiction. Writer Neil Gaiman has produced several innovative works that challenge assumptions about what is suitable and appealing for juvenile audiences. Gaiman's *Coraline* (2002) and *The Wolves in the Walls* (2003) have created anxiety in some adults because of their atmosphere of uncanny menace. In *The Wolves in the Walls*, the feeling of unease owes as much to illustrator Dave McKean's images, which insert real objects introduced digitally into pictures created through a combination of drawing and collage, as to Gaiman's text. Both *Coraline* and *The Wolves in the Walls* create worlds which blur the boundaries between reality and fantasy, placing Gaiman's books for children firmly in the realm of the uncanny, which is always frightening.

Before the publication of *Coraline*, Gaiman was best known as the writer of the influential Sandman series of graphic novels. Just as works in that series frequently draw on myths, legends, and canonical texts such as the plays of Shakespeare, so *Coraline* references several landmark children's texts and especially Lewis Carroll's *Alice in Wonderland*. It also alludes to the grimmest fairy tales and some classic horror films, contributing to a melange of classic storytelling and new forms.

Like Alice, at the start of her adventure, Coraline is bored; she is also angry at her parents. Like many characters in juvenile fantasy fiction, she and her parents have recently moved to a huge old house (though as a late twentieth-century family, they only occupy a converted flat). Although her parents both work at home, they are always too busy to play with Coraline and make no concessions for her tastes and interests:

'Why don't you play with me?' she asked [her father]. 'Busy' he said. 'Working', he added. He still hadn't turned around to look at her. (24)

As she explores the house and grounds, Coraline encounters a host of stock scary elements: in addition to the creepy old house and a dangerous well, there are two witch-like old women who read tea-leaves, a bizarre man upstairs who trains mice for his mouse circus, a talking cat, the ghosts of previously kidnapped children, and a locked door in the sitting room, where Coraline is not allowed to play. Things start to get genuinely frightening when Coraline's parents disappear after she's been cross with them and wished them gone. In their absence, Coraline goes into the forbidden front room and explores the mysteriously sealed door behind which, in another gesture to Carroll, she discovers a flat that is exactly like her own but in reverse. The uncanny is at work, transforming the familiar into the unfamiliar and animating the inanimate. In the flat are her parent-doppelgangers – her 'other parents' – calling to mind Freud's observation that as children mature, they often turn against their parents and fantasise about replacing them (or that they are not their real parents) with superior parent-figures who nevertheless resemble their own in some fundamental ways (1985: 40).

The other parents do everything that Coraline's real parents do not – they play with her, cook her favourite meals, and in their world, the toys are alive and so more fun to play with. However, it soon becomes apparent that the new parents are not quite what they seem. Coraline discovers that if she wants to stay with her other parents, they, like the Sandman from E.T.A. Hoffman's short story of that name, which Freud writes about at length in 'The Uncanny', must remove her eyes, which will be replaced with shiny black buttons like their own.

Not surprisingly, Coraline is alarmed at this suggestion and begins to long for her real parents. Her other mother puts into words what Coraline has been thinking about her parents: 'If they have left you Coraline it must be because they became bored with you, or tired. Now, I will never become bored with you, and I will never abandon you' (69). When she hears her thoughts from the mouth of the other mother, Coraline recognises that they are not true. By this point the text has become extremely disquieting; like Alice, Coraline seems to have no control over events, and the other parents' behaviour is increasingly sinister. But she determines to be brave and to find and restore her real parents, and when she eventually succeeds, she discovers that the fantasy or adventure has given her the ability to see with new eyes, and to appreciate what she has previously taken for granted: 'The sky had never seemed so *sky*; the world had never seemed so *world*. Nothing, she thought, had ever been so interesting' (146).

The book doesn't end here, however. As well as enabling her to realise that she loves and is loved by her parents, Coraline's journey into the frightening realm of the other parents has put to rest another anxiety that she had been refusing to acknowledge – starting at her new school: 'Normally on the night before the first day of term, Coraline was apprehensive and nervous. But, she realised, there was nothing left about school that could scare her any more' (170–1).

While the use Gaiman makes of his frightening fantasy is ultimately in line with the ethos of traditional children's fantasy fiction – Coraline uses her time out from real life to deal with the problems and anxieties of her real world which she finds exaggerated and disguised in the reverse world of her other parents – the modes he employs often challenge in precisely the ways that Rose claims adults do not want children's literature to do. For instance, adult–child relationships are certainly called into question, and the book's celebration of the bizarre and macabre challenges notions of childhood as a time of innocent pleasures. Perhaps most importantly, meanings in the book are unclear: Coraline may rescue her parents, but she does not represent 'a pure point of origin in relation to language' (Rose: 8), neither is she 'rendered innocent of all the contradictions which flow from our interactions with the world' (8–9). In many ways, *Coraline* is precisely about such contradictions and the initiation of both the child in the book and child readers into the knowledge that the world is 'unknowable, uncontrollable, divisive and overwhelming' (10).

This defiant rejection of long-standing models of childhood in children's literature is the central force behind Gaiman's radical contribution to children's literature. I regard *Coraline* as one of the innovative texts discussed in the course of this book that have opened the door for writers and illustrators to re-present childhood in children's literature, just as *Alice in Wonderland* broke from an earlier set of constraints. How many makers of children's books will step through the door remains to be seen, however. Arguably, the label 'children's literature' has come to stand for a certain kind of experience; particularly for younger children, it is important to think very carefully before taking away this security. Often key to how young readers deal with frightening material is how closely it mirrors real-life. The final section of this chapter deals with books for a variety of ages in which the fictional worlds where frightening things occur are analogues for the real world children inhabit.

The shock of the real

The recent rise in fictions dealing in fear can be linked to the zeitgeist associated with the approach and arrival of the new millennium. In *Hystories* (1997), feminist literary critic and historian of medicine and psychoanalysis, Elaine Showalter, argues that Western civilisations at this time became increasingly prone to epidemics of hysterical disorders typified by Gulf War and Chronic Fatigue (ME) syndromes; accounts of alien abductions; anxiety about unidentified viruses, fluoridation of water; chemical warfare; anorexic and bulimic behaviour; tales of satanic ritual abuse; recovered memories of childhood sexual abuse; Multiple Personality Disorder, and the widespread conviction that hugely powerful governmental, economic, and medical cartels deliberately withhold and manipulate information vital to the well-being and health of the population. Since the end of the twentieth century, children's literature has reflected many of the themes and areas of anxiety identified by Showalter. Significantly, however, their *modus operandi* can be beneficial. In ways similar to the fairy tales discussed by Bruno Bettelheim in *The Uses of Enchantment* (1976), popular adolescent horror stories such as the books that make up 'The Saga of Darren Shan' (1999–2005) externalise and symbolically enact topical anxieties, turning them into coherent stories, each with its own closure. Although they show the world as dangerous, and people and places as unstable and unreliable since they constantly mutate, conspire, and betray, the important thing is that in the majority of these books, ultimately all enemies can be identified and overcome.

The need for books that both acknowledge and help to manage topical fears has increased in the new millennium following major international terrorist attacks; there are currently very clear channels and focuses for fear, which are gradually being reflected in writing for children of all ages. While many writers find it most appropriate to write about horrifying events in cathartic and reassuring ways, some require readers to grapple with the social and political complexities which have given rise to them and the consequences of failing to address such problems.

As is true of many children's books that push back the boundaries of what is acceptable at the level of content, there is nothing ground-breaking about the form or style of Gudrun Pausewang's *Fall-Out* (UK edition translated by Patricia Crampton, 1994; originally published in German 1987), but in its detailed depiction of the events surrounding a fictional accident at a nuclear power plant in wealthy and well-informed Germany, it breaks many of the boundaries associated with children's literature. It deliberately sets out to frighten and disturb readers as a way of causing them to engage with the issues it raises. It also challenges adult and institutional authority by questioning the decision-making of most of the adults with whom Jana, the central character, comes into contact.

The opening sequence of events is frightening by any standard. Fourteen-year-old Jana is at school when an emergency siren goes off signalling that there has been an accident at the nearby nuclear power station. She and her little brother, Uli, flee on their bicycles, pursued by a radioactive cloud and obstructed by convoys of cars full of panicking people. Fights break out, shots are fired, pets are executed, and eventually the children are forced to head across a field and onto a track, where Uli is shockingly run over. When Jana reaches him she sees, '… Uli's head, half shrouded by the cap, … strangely flattened, in a pool of blood which was visibly widening' (36).

This series of events takes only the first thirty-five pages of the novel – a beginning that deliberately takes readers unaware and so recreates at some level what it would be like if such a disaster should happen in reality. *Fall-Out* follows Jana through radiation sickness and her decision to join the 'Hibakushi' (the name used for survivors of Hiroshima), a group of politically committed victims of the accident. While the rest of the country tries to ignore their fears of what the Hibakushi represent, this band makes it their business to remind them of the hundreds and thousands who died and who will die because of the accident, bad management, and poor policies.

Gudrun Pausewang is a political activist who uses her books to disseminate information and to shock people out of the complacency that results in the kind of scenarios described so vividly in *Fall-Out*. While many children's writers create novels that deal with important topical issues, from global warming through conflicts in the Middle East and the plight of refugees, few are prepared to frighten young readers into engagement in the way Gudrun Pausewang does. Pausewang's is not a lone voice, however. Outside Britain and America, a number of writers and illustrators have tackled the problem of how to handle the many horrific events taking place in the world.

'Pef's' picturebook *Une si Jolie Poupee* (2001), for instance, tracks the experiences of a doll, created by scientists on a computer to be the most beautiful and appealing doll ever made. Based on a news story, and written in the hope that it will 'provoquer une prise de conscience chez adultes qui ont le pouvoir de sauver des enfants' [*be a wake-up call to those adults who are in the position to save children*] (text from author's notes; my translation), *Une si Jolie Poupee* is focalised through one of the dolls. She tells us that they have been designed to come apart to reveal a secret hiding place. Pictures show the dolls being mass produced and loaded onto lorries for distribution. At this point adult readers may begin to feel less concerned about the cynical manipulation of childish markets than about the purposes for which the dolls will be used, since the vehicles into which they are loaded are recognisably military. The following images confirm that all is not what it should be when a man in goggles and gauntlets is shown hiding something which is clearly not sweets, a toy or some other pleasant secret (what the doll has imagined children will place in her) in her special compartment.

Carefully packed in a wooden case, the doll, still imagining being cuddled in the loving arms of little children, is transported with her many 'sisters' by helicopter to a country ravaged by war, where men in balaclavas hide them among the rubble. The narrating doll is discovered by a little girl who hugs the 'si jolie poupee' to her, causing, the anti-personnel mine inside to explode. Limbs fly from doll and child; the final image shows the doll's head with the words, 'Maintenant il ne reste de moi que ma téte et ma téte a honte, tellement honte' [*Now there remains only my head, and my head is ashamed, so very ashamed*].

The French have been among the most willing to push back the boundaries of children's literature at all levels, but elsewhere too the kinds of frightening incidents real children live through every day are being incorporated in books for children. Roberto Innocenti and Christopher Gallaz's picturebook

Rose Blanche (1985), for instance, ends with the death of a child who has discovered and tried to help prisoners in an East German concentration camp towards the end of the Second World War. Another picturebook, *My Dog* (2001), by Australian John Heffernan, illustrated by Andrew Mclean, is set in war-torn Yugoslavia, and shows ordinary families turned into refugees, and the implied rape of the mother of the boy who tells the story. Both of these books deal with real events in the known world and attempt to defuse frightening incidents and ideas by encouraging children to talk about them. Whatever the content of the texts, then, the underlying message is optimistic: all hold up the possibility for healing and change. My final example, set in the not too distant future, is more ambivalent.

Fear of the future

Meg Rosoff's *How I Live Now* (2004) is narrated by Daisy, an anorexic fifteen-year-old from Manhattan. She does not get on with her father, who has recently remarried and whose new wife is expecting a baby, so Daisy is sent to stay with cousins in England. Shortly after Daisy arrives, her aunt travels to a peace rally in Oslo, and immediately terrorists attack England, which has so many troops in other countries 'keeping the peace' that there are not enough at home to defend the country. For a while the children live quite happily in the country, looking after themselves, during which time Daisy starts a passionate affair with her thirteen-year-old cousin, Edmund. War breaks out, the children survive, and eventually Daisy returns to her father, no longer anorexic; however, Daisy's return to her father is forced and unwelcome. She has to wait until she is 21 and England has started accepting visitors again before she can be reunited with Edmund, whose mind has been seriously affected by his experiences in the war and particularly by what he thinks is her betrayal of him.

How I Live Now breaks many long-established rules of children's literature. It contains graphic violent incidents, indicts modern parent–child relationships, and presents as pleasurable and positive under-age sex between close cousins. Rossoff's text confronts many areas of anxiety about the world we live in, including fears of war, terrorism, and invasion; the inability to be self-sufficient in cultures based on supermarkets and service industries, and young people's sense that their parents care more about their work and the world outside the family than for the family itself. At its heart is the sense that at all levels in Western society families – once the bastion of children's security – are failing to work, and that this is both a symptom and part of the cause of national and international cultural failures. The book's response is not a return to basics and a call for conventional families to be reasserted and strengthened (this is what Daisy's father does when he carries her off to his home with its mother, father, and sibling set-up). Instead, it suggests that strength will come from groups bound together by mutual empathy, identification, interests, and accumulated experience: in other words, self-selected.

Very few children's books since the 1980s have offered anything other than dystopian visions of the future. *How I Live Now* regards the world as we know it as a dystopia in waiting, and suggests that the only way it can be avoided is through entirely new ways of thinking about how societies work. It remains to be seen whether Rossoff's readers will take up the challenge and avoid the frightening future she sees in prospect if they do not. If they are to do so, however, they need more than texts that warn them of the risks, problems, and assorted environmental and political time bombs that have been set by previous generations. They need new kinds of texts and new approaches to problem solving; they need playfully experimental narratives that not only make gestures towards but creatively embrace new media and technologies. While books such as the picturebooks from France discussed in Chapter 3 are engaging with a range of ideas about form and narrative, other aspects of cultural change are largely resisted in books for children. One area where creative experiments might be expected is in books that respond to new media, thematically, stylistically or in terms of format. As the following chapter shows, however, one of contemporary British society's greatest fears circulates around the domains of technology and cyberspace and their impact on culture. It may not be until the current generation of young people, who have grown up as readers, viewers, and players of fiction, take to the keyboards that these new forms and formats will come to fruition. Meanwhile, frightening fiction is likely to include a high proportion of texts that regard this very fusion as the most frightening fiction of all.

8
Back to the Future? New Forms and Formats in Juvenile Fiction

Computers are ubiquitous in the lives of young people in the West, and their influence is beginning to impact on what is written for the young, the forms in which they encounter text, and how they read. In some ways the effects are similar to the influence of radio, film, and television on writing for previous generations, when ways of constructing and interpreting narratives in the new medium altered how writers and illustrators of printed texts worked. The proliferation of media – and particularly those associated with computers and cyberspace – is giving rise to eclectic textual forms such as email, blogs, and hypertext that mix codes and modes resulting in 'transtexts' or writing that combines elements from fixed print and different media.

Decoding transtexts requires more than conventional literacy skills and often involves new ways of approaching text – for instance, deciding whether or not to activate hypertext links and in what order they should be read. While the young increasingly provide evidence of their 'transliteracy'[1] – literacy that crosses between media (Thomas: 26) – writers and publishers have yet to engage fully with the requirements and opportunities represented by transtexts and transliterate ways of reading. Neither are they preparing for the fact that soon it will no longer be necessary to sit in front of a computer to access electronic texts: people will be reading from 'digital paper and a variety of mobile media in buildings, vehicles, and supermarket aisles' (26). This lack of professional engagement in the future of narrative means that there is currently a gap between technological innovation, how users are generating and responding to text online, and developments in narrative fiction.

This final chapter looks at the extent to which children's literature is participating in the challenge to find aesthetically satisfying new narrative forms capable of capturing the globalised, high-speed, communication-saturated experience of growing up in the twenty-first century. Like the French picturebooks discussed in Chapter 3, such narrative platforms are central to stimulating new ways of thinking suited to the contemporary world, where writing increasingly needs to operate within or in response to digital contexts.

Tradition and transformation

There is every reason to look for examples of fictional transtexts in the domain of children's literature. From the earliest days of commercial publishing, printers, and publishers who produce work for children have sought to find ways to make their books and related items attractive to the young by introducing novelties such as pictures, colour, new kinds of bindings, and toys. The relationship between children's fiction, computer games, Internet chat rooms, fan sites and blogs, and developments in Virtual Reality (VR) is also well established, not least because writing for children began experimenting with the narrative possibilities now associated with computer games and VR long before they took shape and started to be mass produced in the form of arcade, video, and Internet-based computer games.

Arguably, the earliest experiments with breaking the boundaries of the printed page and exploring the possibilities of interactivity and remediation occurred in the formative years of commercial publishing for children. The vogue for harlequinades, movable books, and toy theatres (traditionally regarded as part of the children's publishing industry) began in the eighteenth century, when publishers started to experiment with ways of creating the illusions of movement and/or transformation in books. This was usually done by inviting readers to lift a flap, pull a tab, or rotate a volvelle. By the early twentieth century, the interactive potential of movable books made of paper had been thoroughly explored, notably in the very complicated and entertaining works designed by Lothar Meggendorfer (1847–1925). Even in the age of digital media, pop-up, movable, and other novelty books continue to be popular; the American artist Robert Sabuda's elaborate, surprising, and entertaining creations including *The Wonderful Wizard of Oz* (2000), *Alice in Wonderland* (2003), and *Encyclopedia Prehistorica: Dinosaurs* (2005) in particular have revived interest in the form. For the most part, however, such books tend to be celebrated for their creative exploitation of the sculptural potential of paper engineering or as a nostalgic category of publishing rather than as an anticipation of the interactivity and hypermediacy associated with electronic/digital narratives.[2]

More recent examples of textual prefiguring of electronic narratives are the adventure gamebooks that became a publishing craze among young readers – particularly boys – in the 1980s. These precursors of the computer game offered readers opportunities to interact with texts by combining the roles of player and reader: having assumed a persona, the player/reader was required to make decisions at various points which moved them on to different sections of the book. Sometimes this involved choosing which plot line to follow, sometimes rolling a die or using a similarly arbitrary device to decide what happened next. As in most computer games, the persona had special attributes and gained and lost power points through battles and by solving problems or collecting weapons and similar items. The popularity of gamebooks such as the Fighting Fantasy, Lone Wolf and Choose-Your-Own-Adventure series coincided with the rise of role-playing games led by Dungeons and Dragons.

While role-playing games continue to have keen supporters and can be played in online versions, printed gamebooks are essentially obsolete, having been superseded by computer games, whose appeal is that they give the illusion of breaking through the screen and allowing their users to get inside the world of the game: 'The active involvement and sense of control over the images offered a degree of identification that was much higher than in watching movies or videos' (Berghaus: 246).[3]

Gamebooks are a good example of the way printed texts have traditionally anticipated narrative developments that are fully realised in other media. For instance, nineteenth-century novels often made use of techniques now associated with film – such things as close-ups, dissolves and cutting between scenes – before cameras capable of taking 'moving pictures' had been developed (Murray: 28). Now technology develops so rapidly that the situation is largely reversed. Professional writers have yet fully to explore the possibilities for narrative offered by new media (the lively and often innovative contributions of amateurs are discussed in the Conclusion), and IT specialists involved in creating game-fictions have tended to concentrate more on individual aspects of technology – particularly the extent to which it can make virtual experiences seem real – than on developing a symbiotic relationship between texts and technology. (The emphasis on technological rather than narrative innovation is not surprising since most of the most advanced computer work is financed by governments for military applications. The high costs associated with cutting edge research and development with computers suggest it will always be the case that innovation is driven by needs other than creative.)

Transtexts will only become 'transliterature' when a balance is struck between the aesthetic and technological opportunities provided by new media. Achieving this balance requires exploration of narrative possibilities at all levels and in every medium. Where once this was the prerogative of professionals, a great deal of textual experimentation is now being conducted in cyberspace, often by enthusiastic nonprofessionals including the young, who are among the most active users of computers and the Internet. One way they do this is through participation in MUDs (Multi-User Domains), where people meet in characters of their choosing and collaboratively create stories.

In her study of the future of narrative in cyberspace, Janet Murray suggests that MUDs are the crucibles in which narrative forms are being combined to create new kinds of textualities. Both the nature and the pleasures afforded by the resulting narrative forms are new, she suggests; moreover, since the roles of author and reader are merged, the creative act is collective rather than individual, and the resulting fictions have no reader or audience but only participants (1997: 47).

Murray sees the pleasures arising from these emerging narrative forms as an intensification of the immersive satisfactions of realist fictions. Her ambition for narrative is to reach a point where readers will be able to participate in and shape the narratives they read; for instance, in such a version of *Little Women*, it would be possible for a Jo March character to decide to marry a digital Laurie and so completely change Alcott's original novel and the subsequent series. In such a case not only is each reading individual, but also no two texts will be identical.

For Murray, this way of customising fiction is the ultimate goal of narrative in cyberspace; she predicts such texts will 'have a transformative power that exceeds both narrated and conventionally dramatized events because we assimilate them as personal experiences' (170). It seems more likely that her vision of the future of narrative would result in texts that are essentially wishfulfilment fantasies of the kind familiar from dreams and daydreams. As Freud points out in 'Creative Writers and Daydreaming' (1907), most people struggle to make such material interesting to others. Nevertheless, Murray's analysis of the dynamics of MUD-generated fiction provides a useful starting point for thinking about directions in which electronic media seem to be taking narrative and how children's literature is responding to them. There will eventually be ways of combining the strengths of new media and existing narratives that draw on more than the immersive opportunities available in cyberspace.

Participation and experimentation: electronic texts and narrative evolution

The narrative innovation associated with MUDs and other electronic fictions tends to be of two kinds.[4] The first is the level of participation they offer through opportunities for interactivity, 'interactivity' on-line referring to how far texts, including game-fictions, allow reader–players to affect fictional environments and narrative development as they move around the text's terrain and make choices about what they will do and what will happen. Interactivity is the means by which reader–players participate in the creative act (Ascott in Berghaus: 239). Great claims are made for the interactive potential of electronic fictions; however, except in the case of MUDs and multiplayer games which attain a critical mass of players and variables that mean choice is truly inexhaustible, the extent to which players can affect what happens is ultimately limited by a game's program.

The second area of narrative innovation in electronic texts arises from opportunities for digression, extension, and embellishment via hypertext links – what Dresang calls 'connectivity' (1999: 13) – that direct players to different episodes and encounters which build up information. In keeping with the principles of remediation explained below, these currently tend to be delivered in the form of fragments of texts that evoke traditional – often classic or antique – books. For instance, in Romain Victor-Pujebet's CD-ROM version of *Robinson Crusoe*, reader–players are presented with a digital copy of Defoe's novel in the opening sequence which includes text, illustrations, and a map. Successfully negotiating Victor-Pujebet's game-fiction requires that the text be consulted periodically in ways that set the scene, offer instructions, and provide clues (for a full discussion of this CD-ROM, see Sainsbury, 2006).

Intertextuality is a narrative device often associated with textual experimentation. Many electronic fictions are highly intertextual; in the case of game-narratives, pretexts tend to be drawn from the genres of high fantasy, sword and sorcery, myth and legend, vampire, and cyberpunk, and often take the form of generic intertextuality (see Stephens, 1992: 85); for instance, the inclusion of dwarves, elves, wizards and mythological weapons, the landscapes of antiquity, and familiarly stylised archaicisms in language.

Electronic narratives' frequent references to literary texts are characteristic of the phenomenon Jay David Bolter and Richard Grusin term 'remediation,' referring to the way one medium is represented within another (1999: 45). Remediation, they maintain, operates a double logic: on the one hand, there is a seemingly inexhaustible appetite for new media and innovation within media which they call 'hypermediacy'; on the other is a desire to 'erase all traces of mediation' (5) and give the illusion that the earliest forms of print-based and electronic media are still the most important and respected in culture (5). It is this aspect, which they term 'transparency' since it involves trying to make users oblivious to the effects of remediation, which characterises the textual level of most of the best-known electronic game-fictions. By contrast, their visual dimensions almost always make use of and celebrate the latest hypermedia design elements, illustrating perfectly the double logic of remediation. Overriding both characteristics of remediation in most successful games is the narrative; no matter how technologically advanced, games with inadequate storylines inevitably fail commercially.[5] To date, with very few exceptions, game-fiction narratives employ structures, voices, and strategies familiar from the classic realist novel; despite the opportunities to experiment with temporal and spatial elements made possible by the medium, game-fictions are deeply conservative narrative forms.

The child and the electronic book

If the narrative dimension of game-fictions depends on traditional modes of storytelling, can children's literature be expected to do otherwise? Eliza Dresang argues that in fact many contemporary children's writers and illustrators are being inspired by digital media to create radical texts for children. However, the majority of her examples involve visual texts and especially picturebooks: juvenile fiction lags behind and for the most part is more cautious about exploring the way narrative is changing as it responds to new media.

There are a number of possible reasons for this, beginning with long-held perceptions of the child reader which have largely been shaped by pedagogical and developmental concerns. These hold that there are limits to what children's literature can do stylistically because, as new readers, children have to learn to deal with textual conventions, irony, and similar devices, before they can interact playfully or inventively with texts. Following a similar line of thought, it is argued that because children are still developing cognitively and emotionally, they need texts that are reassuring and confidence building rather than potentially unsettling and destabilising. Indeed, until the last two decades of the twentieth century, most publishers, educationalists, and parents subscribed to the belief that because children's literature is bound up in language acquisition, its writers had to confine themselves to grammatically correct, well-expressed language, however inappropriate this might be for a character or situation. Writing at much the same time that Jacqueline Rose was putting forward her thesis that children's literature depends on a child that has access to 'pure' language, Margaret Higonnet summed up the situation thus:

> It would seem that, as a specialized children's literature developed in the modern West, it [children's literature] has been made to carry and inculcate our norms of literary unity and structure. Just as literature written for children reproduces social norms, it also crystallizes formal norms, innate only in appearance, which serve ideological purposes. (1987: 52)

In other words, there has been a reluctance to experiment with narrative form in writing aimed at the young because traditional form symbolises social coherence and is associated with continuity through the transmission of cultural values linked to 'correct' use of language and style.

Reluctance to engage with changes to narrative in response to developments in new media and information technologies is fed by other concerns too. One of these is an aesthetic of the book: readers, writers, illustrators, typographers, designers, collectors – all kinds of book enthusiasts – value the physical characteristics of the traditional printed book. The feel and smell of the paper, the drama of the page turn, the pleasure of a well-designed cover, the crispness of good quality printing – sometimes even the remembered taste of books sucked and chewed when young – are redolent to many. Book lovers also point to the practicality and durability of the technologies behind the printed book: books are portable, pages contain comfortable amounts of information, and the only 'software' needed to access their contents is literacy, which is presumed never to go out of date.

Added to these attributes are practical considerations; for instance, printing technology tends to be affordable (though costs vary considerably between mass-market popular fiction and academic or artists' books) and relatively long-lived, while electronic books regularly become defunct because the software used to produce them is constantly being upgraded. Currently the costs of innovation and the need to keep hardware up to date make texts purchased in the form of CD-ROMs relatively expensive. If texts are downloaded from the Internet, they may be affordable – or even free – but until the arrival of digital and electronic paper[6] and other technological developments that mean electronic texts can be viewed in supermarkets aisles and a host of other locations – they then either have to be read at a desk or require expensive portable equipment (for instance, a hand-held screen) if they are going to be read on the move. Readers generally object to scrolling through long passages of text on a screen, and while it is possible to print most kinds of electronic texts, doing so results in an inferior but probably no less costly (if the price of paper, ink, hardware, electricity, and time are factored in) final product than a traditionally published book.

For all of these reasons, the relationship between books, new media, and Information Technology tends to be ambivalent, not least at the level of plot, and to be governed by the double logic of remediation. For instance, to date electronic books have been so preoccupied with demonstrating that they are genuinely books – foregrounding remediation strategies of transparency – that they generally fail to embrace the possibilities offered by new media.[7] They display transparency by, for instance, being designed to resemble the pages of a book, and providing electronic 'page turns' at regular intervals. This mimicking of the way books work belies the underlying structures and organisation of many kinds of electronic books – the source of their potential to provide new narrative possibilities. The most important of these for fictional purposes is the hypertext link, which enables readers to access a range of information, often through pictures, film, animation, or sound as well as print and the main graphic level of the texts.

Hypertext is also capable of forging connections between texts, media, and users far beyond what can be offered even in books that aggressively push at the boundaries of what print can do, such as the picturebooks described in Chapter 3. Some of the puzzles that have intrigued writers from the earliest days of the novel – such things as how to escape the linearity of text, disrupt chronology, and create a textual equivalent of the multiple thoughts, sensations, and actions every individual experiences simultaneously at any given moment – have been, if not obviated, at least transfigured by hypertext. Yet, to date, few writers have publicly engaged in exploring the intellectual and artistic potential of electronic fiction. In the sphere of juvenile fiction, those who have, have tended to do so as part of an experiment in marketing; for instance, linking popular television programmes, magazines, and Internet fan sites, or, as in the case of Philip Pullman's US publisher, Knopf, publishing individual chapters on the Internet as a way of creating a market for

The Golden Compass (Dresang, 42), rather than with a view to exploring the potential of the medium as an art form.

The perceived need to make the new medium resemble the old – and vice-versa, since printed books also make use of characteristics of new media such as e-mail and text messages – is currently so dominant in children's literature, both on page and screen, that it is important to look more closely at the forces that shape the relationship between children's books and new technologies. Particularly revealing is the way IT and cyberspace are represented in fiction for younger readers.

Textual technophobia

Bolter and Grusin's 'double logic' is symptomatic of a deeply rooted ambivalence towards new technologies in many aspects of Western culture. With children in mind, there is specific concern associated with the amount of time young people spend interacting with devices such as PCs, mobile telephones, and gaming products. Jacques Ellul traces the roots of this ambivalence to the shift from magical/spiritual societies to those governed by technology.

> When science and technology replaced magic, what was removed was that physical-mechanical part of the magical system that simply could not compete with a new world based on scientific method and technological efficiency. That part of magic that functioned for its adherents in the spiritual realm was never replaced. Machines cannot do the work of gods. Machines cannot calm fears, or provide answers to our deepest questions. All the technology in the world cannot repair the human spirit, or locate the soul. (in O'Har, 2000: 863)

If, as Rose maintains, childhood functions as a cultural signifier of an imagined, idealised pure point of origin which the adult is perpetually seeking to regain (1984: 19), it follows that it is also allied to pre-technological epochs, primitive/supernatural/spiritual thinking, and the sense of integration that Ellul identifies as being overlaid in culture by the advent of technology and scientific rationalism.

The child–machine, magic–technology, pastoral–mechanical dichotomies are problematic at a variety of levels, and arguably underpin some of the most popular works of late-twentieth and early twenty-first-century children's literature (see Harris, 2005; Oakes, 2003; Sconce, 2000; Stivers, 1999). For instance, it is conceivable that one of the attractions of the Harry Potter books is the way they replace the Muggle world of televisions, computers/IT, and modern transport with ancient spells based on natural ingredients, handwritten communications, libraries and steam engines, flying broomsticks, and floo powder (Chevalier, 2005: 408; O'Har, 862): 'What matters is that things work in the wizarding world without magic ...' (Chevalier, 408). Similarly, the Artemis Fowl books of Eoin Colfer display a fascination with technology, but it is repeatedly shown to be unsafe in the hands of humans, and even those who belong to the fairy world are prepared to abuse it (see, for instance, *Artemis Fowl: The Arctic Incident*, 2002). In Irish writer Conor Kostick's *Epic* (2004), the virtues of gaming technology – in this case evidenced in its capacity to let people work out their problems and conduct their battles virtually while living peacefully together – are soon perverted so that the population is in thrall to the game and its mysterious masters.

Alec Broers used his five Reith lectures (an annual series of lectures on a topic of public interest on BBC Radio 4) to warn against the technophobia he believes is endemic in British society. According to Broers, technology shapes our lives; its influence is paramount and inexorably increasing. While many emerging countries such as India and China appreciate and engage with the intellectual challenges posed by technology in all its forms, others are failing to do so precisely because of the kind of ambivalence that rejects or seeks to contain rather than celebrates new media and new applications of existing media: the mindset that values – even requires – transparency over hypermediacy, sometimes to the point of constituting a new Luddism. This kind of rejection of technology, he prophesies, will lead to technophobic countries falling behind in intellectual, social, and material development. Moreover, since technology alone will be able to address many of the key problems facing the world, among them global warming, viral epidemics, and food shortages (some of which themselves are products of technology), those countries that fail to provide the necessary conditions in which technological innovation thrives, will be at a distinct disadvantage.

Implicit in Broers's lectures are the questions, 'How have we come to hold technology (which includes all the applied sciences, from engineering to the Information Technologies) in such low regard, and why are so many of us frightened of it?' There are certainly many factors at work in society to explain the current situation, but for the purposes of this chapter I am interested in the interactions between children's literature and technology as it is manifested in new media and Information Technology.

Out with IT!

The majority of those books for children that deal with computers, the Internet, and other forms of IT/electronic communication actively perpetuate the kind of negative stereotype of technology Alec Broers warns against, so any discussion of children's literature's response to technological innovation needs to consider both what lies behind this hostility and what its implications might be.[8] This attitude to things scientific and technological is not unique to children's literature; indeed, it can be understood as a vestigial cultural reflection of the positions adopted by first Matthew Arnold and

T.H. Huxley (classical versus scientific education) and then, in what is often referred to as the 'two cultures' debate, by F.R. Leavis and C.P. Snow (English versus Science). However, if a more constructive relationship between the ways of knowing and thinking offered by traditional texts and new media is to be forged, this deep-rooted suspicion of science and technology needs to be challenged in the books and stories given to children. In the same way, fiction for a generation that is already predisposed to depend on and inter-act with new technologies needs to acknowledge that how the young under-stand narrative is changing and to see this as a creative opportunity rather than a threat.

Rodney Philbrick's *The Last Book in the Universe* (2000) typifies the hostility many children's books display towards new technologies in its depiction of a future generation that spends its time immersed in fantasies in cyberspace and grows intolerant of books and writers. So much so, indeed, that the last writer of traditional books is horribly hanged resulting in a text that presents books as the last bastion of civilisation against a relentless tide of electronic media. While it is important to value and perhaps even to protect the book as attractive new alternatives become available, we must also accept that young readers today acquire media literacies alongside conventional literacy, meaning that they come to texts of all kinds as transliterate readers. It is pos-sible that those who seek to defend printed texts by denigrating new media may in fact be putting the book in danger: if it becomes an ossified form, how well is it likely to appeal to a transliterate generation?

The response to technology in children's literature currently falls broadly into three groups. The most pervasive of these are 'Prometheus stories' in which humankind's thirst for knowledge is shown to have transgressed what 'ought' to be known. The result is Armageddon of one form or another; for instance, nuclear catastrophe, famine, or the earth's having turned into a wasteland of various kinds (too wet, too dry, made toxic by chemical/nuclear waste, or otherwise unsustainable). Some scenarios show populations ravaged by uncontrollable, often human-made diseases, others what happens when the products of vivisection or cloning run amok.

A related motif that owes much to the scenarios of cyberpunk, features robots or other mechanical devices that have been developed too far in the sense that, like Victor Frankenstein, their creators have played God and attempted to give life to mechanical inventions but have either neglected or failed to make them compassionate. These ambiguously situated creations – highly intelligent, capable of independent ratiocination and certain kinds of emotions – are almost inevitably shown attempting first to liberate themselves from human control and then to achieve domination over their creators.

Narratives that take the form of 'technological dystopias' are preoccupied with the extent to which humans increasingly depend on technology. Reliance on technology means that day by day and generation by generation knowledge and skills acquired by our ancestors are being forgotten because we no longer use them. Arithmetic, for instance, has largely been rendered redundant by calculators and computers, which also check spelling and provide templates for the organisation of charts and data. Many aspects of navigation, architecture, engineering, graphic design, pharmacology, stage lighting, research – even domestic laundry skills – are now regularly managed by computers, which means that fewer individuals are now capable of passing on first-hand knowledge. Technological dystopias take this tendency to a catastrophic conclusion by presenting visions of the world in which the master/slave relationship between humans and machines has become a threat to human creativity and existence, sometimes culminating in one of the apocalyptic scenarios characteristic of the Prometheus plot line.

The antidote to such dystopias is invariably a pastoral world that has not been contaminated by technology, where food is grown and gathered by hand, and contact with the natural world restores agency and morality. Young people reading these books are offered a choice between 'good' nature and 'bad' technology, though in fact the problems were created by human abuse of technology rather than the technology itself (for a detailed discussion of this polarised view of nature and technology, see Applebaum, forthcoming 2008). An exception to this pattern is provided in Peter Dickinson's early and extremely thoughtful *The Changes* trilogy (1968–1970) in which the population of Britain is infected with machine-hatred and rapidly degenerates to a medieval way of life. This is no pastoral retreat but a return to the dark ages with feudal barons, fear of witchcraft and primitive lifestyles and outlooks. The vindication of technology provided by *The Changes* is highly unusual.

The villain in juvenile 'IT pandemic fiction' is Information Technology, often in the form of cyberspace, though in earlier versions, computers generally, as well as robots and cyborgs, tended to pose the threat. The specific anxiety in books about malign IT or evil lurking in cyberspace largely stems from the fear of what is not understood and so is constructed as threatening to a human-centred view of how the cosmos should operate. For most people IT – and especially cyberspace – is like magic. It is unfathomable and operates invisibly, which means that at some level we distrust it in the same way that previous generations suspected other devices whose workings are not visible to the eye such as electricity, the telegraph, the camera and the telephone (Sconce, 2000). Even the book was once a new medium and reading, for the illiterate, regarded as a kind of magic (hence the associations between grammar and gramarye);[9] as this chapter has already shown, the tension in the relationship between the book and new and emerging technologies has never been dispelled.

The mistrust of technology, then, is ancient, wide-ranging, and serial in the sense that as each new innovation is introduced its predecessors take on a patina of age and respectability (the underlying rationale of remediation). Nevertheless, in Britain and many parts of the West, new media and technologies continue to be seen as threatening, and some predict that this threat is reaching crisis point. Sarah Kember points out in *Virtual Anxiety* that there are those who see the new Information Technology as signalling that we are entering the 'final phase of human history', a phase of chaos and run-away, self-organising technologies where 'rotted by digital contagions, modernity is falling to bits' (*Plant and Land* 1994, quoted in Kember, 1998: 1).

In many quarters of British society, IT, especially when in combination with cyberspace, is charged with ushering in a philistine age, resulting in people sitting in front of screens instead of reading books, going to museums and galleries, or exploring the landscape. There is an anti-IT discourse that implies it is eroding public virtue, and that what is termed 'technological progress' in the area of IT (smaller, faster, more life-like) is either nugatory or dangerous. As Kember points out, this danger is expressed through metaphors of the body (102–3): we talk in terms of viruses and contagion; we're nervous about sharing files because, just as a virus can be transmitted through the blood, so the fluidity of information as it pours through cyber-space makes it metaphorically like blood. Information is the bodily fluid of cyberspace, and the condom of the PC – the fire wall – has a high failure rate. The media resounds with stories about the risks posed to our bank accounts, our professions, and our very identities by IT.

Adults working in the social spheres inhabited by children are inclined to be highly risk-averse; the fact that children's literature is almost invariably written, published, and purchased by adults for children undoubtedly con-tributes to the negative way IT tends to be represented in many books for the young. Those writers who think of IT as dangerous, dubious, or who hold it responsible for dumbing down culture damn it through the kind of story-lines outlined above. The efficacy of this strategy for engaging young readers is questionable.

It seems likely that the tendency to depict IT negatively in children's literature has its origins in a double-vision of self by writers: at one level, they project their own current (adult) sense of anxiety about using IT onto child readers, while at another, the implied reader they have in mind has more in common with the pre-IT children they themselves were than the post-IT children growing up today. I am not suggesting that all adults, or all children's writers, are technologically incompetent but that their relation-ship with new technologies tends to be less comfortable and intuitive than that of the young. This undoubtedly owes much to having lived through developments in technology which began with cumbersome and badly written manuals rather than the user-friendly devices now available.

There are other, more deliberate and valid reasons why children's writers may underscore the potential dangers of IT. Some, for example, have clearly defined agendas about the impact of IT on language, social divisions, com-munity, the environmental impact of technologised societies, or concerns about over-dependence on IT. Often, however, it seems authors worry that IT in its various manifestations will be harmful to young users imaginatively, morally, and even physically, particularly when it creates a space in which otherwise taboo or outlawed behaviour is permissible (Barry Atkins, 2003: 22; 141; 142). Whether environment, social, pedagogic, or creative, these areas of anxiety help to explain the widespread appropriation of tropes from gothic fiction by writers for children whose books feature IT – and especially the Internet (Crandall, 2004).

Nadia Crandall draws some illuminating parallels between nineteenth-century versions of gothic fiction and juvenile cyberfiction. Both are responses to times of rapid social change and scientific advancement, including changes in the way we think about the self. Gothic writers anticipated and then responded to ideas about the psyche given shape by Freud's theories of the conscious and unconscious. In the same way, Crandall suggests, cyberspace seems to embody the postmodern construction of the self as unfixed and multiple and to give expression to the ideas of scientists working on theories of time and the possibility of multiple worlds. In cyberspace it is already possible to inhabit multiple realities (1). A final point of comparison is that just as nineteenth-century gothic fiction addresses a pervading sense of aesthetic ennui and exhaustion, juvenile cyberfiction is in part a literary response to the equally fatiguing phenomenon of information overload and the disorientation that, according to Jean Baudrillard (1998), means it is no longer possible to distinguish between what is real and what is simulated.

Similarities in context are reflected in shared narrative strategies. According to Crandall, 'the metafictive conventions which permeate nineteenth-century gothic novels have been adapted for contemporary child readers by writers writing about the Internet (1). She identifies a 'transgressive chronotope' in both gothic fiction and children's cyberfiction, where characters act out – and often enjoy – forbidden behaviours including violent and aggressive actions (in juvenile fiction, the kinds of erotic transgression typical of gothic fiction are considerably more limited).

One way this behaviour is countenanced in both cyber and gothic narratives is through the use of ancient settings – central to many PC games and their online counterparts and equally familiar in much fiction featuring IT. For instance, twenty-first century children may take on the roles of Greek heroes or chivalric knights and act out beheadings, blindings, stabbings, and other kinds of actions that would be completely unacceptable in real life or for personae that inhabit virtual worlds closely modelled on contemporary reality (5).

One of a growing number of children's books which explore this kind of experience is Alan Gibbons's *Shadow of the Minotaur* (2000), in which Phoenix, the central character, is sucked into the world, based on Greek myths and legends, of a computer game his father has been developing. He finds himself becoming increasingly aggressive, a better and better fighter, and someone who, unlike his nerdy image in real life, *enjoys* battle, even when it involves killing.

Significantly, however, this behaviour is shown to be wrong – both gothic texts and cyberfiction counter the new with highly conservative moral viewpoints based on an allegiance to the past. In juvenile cyberfiction, the protagonist's cyber self must capitulate to the real self if disaster is to be avoided, and this often means steering clear of the agent of change – the computer – and spending time with friends out of doors or in the real world. In *Shadow of the Minotaur*, for instance, Phoenix destroys the VR suits used to play the game and goes to Greece. Although while there he discovers disturbing evidence that the game has not in fact been terminated, for the moment at least he is out of the house, out of the game, and enjoying experiences in real life.

Before arriving at this stage of recovery and resolution, Phoenix has been so immersed in the game that he loses track of time and is frequently unable even to distinguish between night and day, game and reality. This kind of disorientation is typical of another parallel between gothic and juvenile cyberfiction: the way each conjures up forces of darkness through associations with night-time, the dark and sleep deprivation, which leads characters to lose track of time and find it difficult to distinguish between fantasy and reality – or between Virtual Reality and real life (Crandall: 5).

A book that makes this blurring of the boundaries between gaming and being its narrative subject, is Lesley Howarth's complexly structured novel, *Ultraviolet* (2001). Because the central character, Violet, lives in one of the toxic wasteland worlds characteristic of Prometheus stories, where people must stay inside since the rays of the sun have become life-threatening, she and her peers play reality-based computer games constantly. As the plot develops, it becomes increasingly difficult for Violet to separate game, dream, and reality, and only the most alert reader is able to do so, even on successive readings. Effectively, Howarth creates a series of the kind of 'consensual hallucinations' invented by Gibson in *Neuromancer*, in which users agree to share experiences in a cyber world with others. In *Ultraviolet*, the hallucination is experienced equally and simultaneously by characters and readers. Realisation that this is what is going on is denied until the final pages of the novel, when, in a very effective twist, a fault in the new generation game Violet is playing causes it to degrade. A child visiting Violet's house complains to her father that Violet is monopolising the PC game and behaving strangely:

> 'I want to run *Cohorts* or *Ravendale*, but Violet won't take the headset off.'
>> Nick raises his eyebrows. 'Use the other one.'
>> 'She's got priority gameplay.'
>> 'Edition Eight has a guest-room, if she's Questing. Go in and
>> fight her for it.'
>> 'It's like she's fighting someone already.'

'Practicing self-defence?'
'With the headset on? You should see her.' Rawley's eyes widen.
'You should.' (193)

While this is happening outside the game, inside fragments of conversation and random objects, thoughts and memories from real life begin to permeate the game in ways it can't control so that Violet and the reader find it confusing and nonsensical in the same way that a compelling dream begins to disintegrate just before the sleeper awakes.

Violet knows that the game used objects from the 'feelie' tray she had prepared: this is an assemblage of props that players hold both to enhance tactile sensations and to give the game real world material to paste into its scenarios, though they are often disguised in the way material from our conscious worlds is re-presented in dreams and daydreams. However, when she and her father examine the tray after he has forcibly removed her headset and attempt to identify how the game built its virtual world and plot, she remains unable to separate game, dream (she has periodically fallen asleep while playing over a period of more than a day), and reality.

This kind of disorientation is a classic feature of gothic fiction and is clearly associated with fears of invasion, originally supernatural but now technological. While the affinities between gothic and juvenile cyberfiction are striking, gothic is not the only mode used by children's writers when writing about computers, games and cyberspace. Two early and particularly good examples of books about computer games that make no use of gothic motifs are Orson Scott Card's *Ender's Game* (1985; the companion volume, *Ender's Shadow* did not appear until 2000) and Terry Pratchett's *Only You Can Save Mankind* (1992). Like some gothic cyberfiction for the young, both raise interesting ethical questions about the fights and levels of violence in computer games by revealing that they are not simulations – these are real battles with real consequences, though the players are not told this.

Pratchett's hero, Johnny, an outstanding player of video games, is contacted by the aliens who are being killed by players using a new video game. Since the other players do not realise what is going on, Johnny finds himself trying to protect the alien fleet from other gamers. Written as the first Gulf War was drawing to a close, *Only You Can Save Mankind* reverses the scenarios and anxieties associated with gothic cyberfiction. The alien 'others' are not invaders and it is not set in the past; indeed, the casual, uninformed way in which they are killed parallels the much-vaunted use of highly accurate unmanned missiles in Gulf War I.

At first, *Ender's Game* seems to be a simple tale of humans versus invading aliens. After a near invasion by aliens, adults prepare for the future by selecting and training the next generation of military leaders. Children specially selected for their intellectual and physical prowess and an innate ability to be effective fighters are sent to a military academy in space where the hope for the future, six-year-old Ender Wiggin, is rapidly promoted. The book culminates in the children, led by Ender, practising to fight the 'buggers' by playing games on very detailed simulators. As the games get harder, Ender loses increasing numbers of fighters, and in his last game, has to sacrifice the majority of his fleet to blow up the enemy's home world. At this point the adults tell the children that they have in fact been engaged in real battles; they have not only massacred the 'buggers', but have sent human fleets to their deaths. The questions this raises about adult–child relationships and the responsible exercise of power are profound and made more so when Ender discovers a 'bugger' cocoon full of eggs and recordings that reveal that they were a peaceful race that had no intention of invading earth.

Whether gothic in mode, futuristic in setting, or featuring characters familiar from contemporary everyday reality, juvenile cyberfiction tends to reflect anxieties about interactions between children and new technologies. These are the concerns that lead to attempts to erect safeguards such as imposing (or trying to) limits on the amount of time that children spend using computers, creating legislation and agencies designed to prevent paedophiles from lurking in cyberspace, and guidelines about communication masts that may pose health risks. While it is important to be alert to potential problems caused by new technologies, we need also to be aware that we are creating a new generation of cautionary tales for young readers about the dangers caused to individuals and the world by invisible presences that may be seeping into our minds and bodies through such things as the computers and mobile phones that we have installed in our homes and carry in our handbags and pockets. I have yet to find a children's book that unreservedly celebrates such things as the way cyberspace makes it possible to transcend the self and operate outside the economic and practical restrictions of reality.

In a discussion of Stuart Clark's *Thinking with Demons*, which looks at how those who in all other ways are accepted as sane and normal can believe in devils, Marina Warner develops Clark's identification of the way language authorises beliefs; the way we represent the world in language controls how we think (2005: 41). If we demonise technology through language – and especially through the stories we use to make sense of the world for young people – we are not only in danger of impeding narrative development, but also of stifling speculation and the urge to explore the imaginative possibilities technology itself may offer. Children's literature has been good at sounding a warning note about the misuse of and overdependence on technology, but that should not mean rejecting new thinking or new technology and offering almost exclusively dismal and frightening fictional visions of a technologised future. As Warner points out, 'Children's literature ... writes the future, and this has given it its deep affinity with fantasy, fairy tale, romance, and other wishing, emancipatory modes which can branch in imaginative and surprising ways' (27).

For much of the late-nineteenth and early twentieth centuries, technology and science were equated with progress and exciting possibilities. Even in the post-war, post-atomic period, when they featured in children's literature (which happened more frequently in books and comics produced in America than in British children's fiction), science and technology were seen as stepping stones to the future. Children's books with a scientific/technological dimension tended to focus on heroic challenges (as in Madeline L'Engle's Time Trilogy 1962–1978) and life-improving or labour-saving aspects of technology (e.g. William Pène Du Bois's *The Twenty-One Balloons* (1947) or Jay Williams's Danny Dunn series (1956–1977)). Such books celebrated technology and science and anticipated inventions now in regular use. In this way they encouraged young readers to anticipate the future and the possibilities it offers and to recognise that these often have their roots in technology.

Once the fall out from nuclear fission and the ethical problems it poses began to be fully understood and experienced, the negative consequences of unfettered scientific experimentation increasingly came to dominate children's books featuring technology and science. The publication of Rachel Carson's *The Silent Spring* (1962) ushered in a new strand of environmental awareness that has had an enduring and profound impact on future-orientated publishing for children. Important as such counterbalances to the dominance of science and technology in modern life are, it is important to be sure that children's literature does not automatically reject IT and other technologies, or cease to offer optimistic visions of future worlds. To do so would be to limit the capacity of children's literature to be emancipatory, imaginative, and surprising, qualities future thinkers will need to shape a world better than the one they have inherited. For that reason, I have chosen to end this chapter by discussing a number of texts that offer less dismal views of technological futures and point towards innovative fusions between the narrative techniques of traditional and electronic texts. These are the books that envisage new models of society or point the way forward from transwriting to transliterature.

Skip forward: emancipatory modes of electronic fiction?

Alexandre Jardin's *Cybermaman* (1997) offers an interesting image of human–PC interaction that culminates in a healing vision of IT.[10] When Lucie Plume, much-loved mother of three, dies, her family is doubly bereaved when they discover that all the images, letters, and other keepsakes of her that have been digitally stored in the family computer have been erased during an electrical storm. The original materials have been destroyed by the children's father, who has come to believe that while physical objects will deteriorate, digital images of them will be preserved exactly as they were when his wife died. Digitally she will have a kind of immortality.[11]

This idea has come from conversations with his neighbour, Zeig, a scientist and inventor who is passionate about computing technology. Zeig has invented a machine that the children use to transport themselves virtually into the hard drive of the family computer (in this case virtual reality means that their bodies remain in this world, but only as empty shells as in all other respects the children have disappeared into the computer's memory). Their aim is to recover the lost files that contain all the memorabilia relating to their mother. After crossing landscapes composed of images and text from their online encyclopaedia and other material stored in the computer, and overcoming various threats and obstacles, they finally succeed in finding the lost images. Having reconnected with their mother virtually, they return to the real world comforted and with the conviction that though they no longer have a mother in real life, they do at least have a cybermaman.

Alexandre Jardin's text acknowledges both the limitations and the possibilities of technology. *Cybermaman* at one level is a cautionary tale, warning against the seductive power of IT: the Plume family learn that the screen and the technology behind it cannot substitute for reality, and used incorrectly, they can create devastating problems. At the same time, this large and lavish book shows readers that technology can also provide unique solutions to problems – especially when the attributes of humans and machines are mingled. In this way *Cybermaman* offers a more radical vision of new technologies than most children's books in which IT features.

The idea of combining the strengths of human and machine is not in itself new: Donna Haraway's ground-breaking 'A Manifesto for Cyborgs: Science, Technology and Feminism in the 1980s' argues that as they function in fiction, cyborgs – hybrids combining machines and organisms – decouple biology and social organisation, allowing us to rethink the way we behave and how society is structured. In a cybernetic future, she suggests, reproduction would no longer be a biological process. This would mean that women's bodies could be released from the chains of associations, expectations, and controls arising from their roles as wives and mothers – especially as these have been given shape in patriarchal cultures leading to changes in their positions in society. Equally profound, the essay proposed, would be the impact on the psyche, which would be freed from the dictatorial outcomes of the Oedipal drama; in Haraway's vision, cyborg existence offers a post-Oedipal, post-gender, post-human world, untroubled by sexuality.

'Untroubled' is the state Haraway associates with a cybernetic future: the anomalies and transgressive behaviours that are currently classified as disturbing will disappear, she maintains, when the line between animal and machine has been crossed more completely than it has to date (though even in the 1980s the boundary was already elastic and since then successive developments in genetic modification techniques are constantly stretching it to new limits):

> ... a cyborg world might be about lived social and bodily realities in which people are not afraid of their joint kinship with animals and

machines, not afraid of permanently partial identities and contradictory standpoints. (468)

A recent children's novel that begins to explore some of the potential for social transformation that Haraway identified more than two decades ago and in so doing rings the changes on the Prometheus storyline by mooting the possibility that advances in robotics/technology do not have to result in catastrophic scenarios is Helen Fox's *Eager* (2003). *Eager* pits an unscrupulous corporation against a morally and ethically righteous individual to make the point, generally underplayed in children's cyberfiction, that technology-based problems and disasters are rarely the fault of the technology itself but of what humans do with it.

Although it takes a broadly optimistic view of technology, there are many inconsistencies in the book's basic scenario, which depicts a world divided into have alls (the technocrats) and those whose lives are severely constrained by limited resources and restrictive legislation. While the lack of resources is a direct result of the unchecked use of technology by earlier generations, the problems are mediated to some extent by technological developments, and most people live comfortably in what by contemporary standards are very high-tech environments. Smart houses and domestic robots undertake most mundane tasks, while education, advice, and simulated experiences such as underwater exploration and visits to other countries and epochs are facilitated by the 'gobetween', Fox's vision for the Internet, which includes a highly developed, fully interactive virtual reality component.

While there are places where children gather for sporting and educational purposes, and other designated buildings for work and recreation, in many ways the world Fox creates conforms to Haraway's prediction of how a society in which humans and technologies continue to move closer together (a post-human world) will function. Different environments interface polymorphously, and they need to since restrictions on movement caused by limited amounts of fuel make many kinds of actual experiences impossible for most.

This is not a technological dystopia; nevertheless, it is clear that many basic skills are no longer practised and are consequently in danger of atrophying. More importantly, *Eager* includes moments when humans interact with machines or cyber–personae exchange information. In this book, such interactions are offered as part of a future vision and often take place in Virtual Reality (the gobetween generates exceptionally successful VR simulations); however, such exchanges between artificial and human intelligences are already beginning to occur in real life. For instance, in an article extolling the use of simulated computer games as models for 'situated learning' (learning that takes place in virtual environments rather than abstractly from models of one kind or another), the American educationalist David William

Shaffer and his colleagues offer several examples of what they regard as effective learning through VR and other kinds of simulations including Full Spectrum Warrior:

> ... the knowledge that is distributed between the virtual soldiers and real-world player is not a set of inert facts; what is [sic] distributed are the values, skills, practices, and (yes) facts that constitute authentic military professional practice. This simulation of the social context of knowing allows players to act as if in concert with (artificially intelligent) others ... (2005: 107)

The authors go on to explain that such games 'are already being used by corporations, the government, the military and even by political groups to express ideas and teach facts, principles and world views' (110). Although Shaffer's team praise the way simulations make learning meaningful, others sound a cautionary note. Psychologist Dave Grossman's study of military training methods used in the United States since the First World War looks specifically at the way video games have been used to desensitise troops and increase both their willingness to fire on the enemy and the frequency with which they do so. He concludes,

> If we had the clear-cut objective of raising a generation of assassins and killers who are unrestrained by either authority or the nature of the victims, it is difficult to imagine how we could do a better job [than encourage them to play video games involving shooting']. (in Berghaus, 247)

While, as Grossman shows, there are reasons to suspect the uses to which some agencies may be putting computer games that use simulations, in *Eager*, simulations not only compensate for actual experiences that have been lost, but are also used benignly in the formation of the robot's character (significantly, Eager's subjective sense of self is acquired through interactions with humans). The eponymous EGR3 is a new generation robot that has been designed to acquire knowledge through experience – most of it through VR simulations of many real-life situations and environments – in the same way that humans do, in the expectation that this will make it not just rational and capable of independent thought, but moral as well. Significantly, Eager, as he becomes known, contains no human parts; the fusion of human and machine comes through modelling the robot's development on the human entry into the world, though at an accelerated rate. Eager is effectively a blank slate when he is created, but as he builds up layers of experience, he begins to speculate on their meaning and relationships. In other words, he becomes reflective and develops a nascent sense of subjectivity.

Although Eager is a prototype for a new generation of robots, living in close proximity has already begun to cause confusion in both humans and machines, calling into question what it is to be human. The Bell family, where Eager is sent to test how he functions in the real world, are constantly debating how to behave with the robots and the house (the house wakes them up, tells each member of the family what is happening in different rooms, reports to the robots and other equipment what the family needs and so on). Although Mr. Bell insists that they are only machines, the children and their mother find it hard not to read emotions and personalities off them; particularly their out-of-date butler, Grumps. When Grumps serves tomato soup for breakfast, Mrs. Bell can't bring herself to point out the mistake and makes sure he has left the room before allowing the family to voice their complaints.

> 'He doesn't have any feelings, Chloe', Mr. Bell said to his wife. 'He's a machine.'
> 'You know what I think', she retorted. 'Grumps cares for us just like one of the family.'
> 'He's programmed to care for us. The fridge cares for us too by looking after our food, but we don't get sentimental about it.' (11)

The machines too, seem to find the boundary between themselves and the humans they serve more blurred than it used to be. The house insists that it is not a machine (8), and it is clear that Grumps is worried about what will happen to him now that his timer has broken and he can no longer tell what time of day it is, resulting in assorted domestic problems including soup for breakfast. When Eager arrives, the problem becomes acute. The text reaches its crisis when Eager sacrifices himself to save the Bells and, indeed, the world, from a degenerate line of copycat robots created by a profiteering corporation.

By the end of the book, Eager, who has been reassembled, is recognised as a sentient being capable of having and eliciting emotions. Indeed, in conversation with a philosopher whom he visits on the gobetween in the final scene, Eager voices the thought that in fact the new generation of robots he represents are charged with the task of restoring people's humanity:

> 'Human beings are funny', he mused. 'Sometimes they get so caught up in their emotions ... that they can't think properly. ... And other times they try to behave like machines as if they had no feelings. That's when they really start to hurt each other. ... Professor Ogden hopes the next generation of robots will help them to remember what it means to be human.' (298)

Eager ends with a cybernetic epiphany, when Eager realises that just like humans, he is fully subjective and announces to the philosopher, 'I am' (298).

Another example of writing that broadly welcomes closer interactions between humans and IT is the Golem series by Elvire, Lorris, and Marie-Aude Murail launched in the United Kingdom in 2005 after a successful debut in France. Whereas many of the writers who develop plots around IT do so in order ultimately to reject it, these French siblings are more willing to see its attractions and particularly to explore the range of relationships and roles open to those who regularly communicate with others via the Internet. For instance, while in the five Golem books IT is certainly problematic in that it is being used by a multinational corporation to infect young people with mind-controlling messages, it is also through IT that the company is defeated. Characters in a mutant computer game step out of the PC to help players identify what the company is doing and together, using a combination of human and character skills, and ways of problem solving learned through gaming, they sabotage the B Corporation's plans for world domination.

As well as showing how IT skills can be harnessed to good social ends, the Golem series also shows communities of IT users and players of different ages, backgrounds and abilities working together, underscoring the potential for inclusivity in Internet communication, and the ways in which even what seem to be time-wasting games can be creative. Although they raise some ethical questions about interactions between humans, computers, and IT, ultimately the Golem books celebrate their ability to bring people of different kinds, ages, and backgrounds together in ways that encourage them to recognise each other's abilities and personalities, freed from the automatic stereotypes that operate in everyday life.[12] Golem 1–5 also see cyberspace as one of the new horizons for adventure: the world entered through the Internet represents unexplored territory in much the same way that unchartered seas, desert islands, and outer space did for readers of previous generations.

Such examples are few and far between, however. More typical is M.T. Anderson's *Feed* (2002) – notable for, among other things, being one of the very few works in this subgenre to experiment with style and form, creating usages, metaphors, and syntax inspired by electronic communications.[13] In this sense *Feed* evokes or simulates characteristics associated with hypermedia, but its ultimate point of reference is the book; indeed, the power of the final line owes much to a deliberately created page turn (see below).

Feed is a cautionary tale – a Baudrillardian nightmare of sign-value spiralling out of control – and it is unusual in its exploration of what happens to the human body, intellect, and psyche when human and machine merge. Anderson's novel features the first generation of young people to have a chip inserted in their heads at birth. The chip hooks them up to the version of the Internet (called the Feed) that has evolved since it has been harnessed by multinational corporations to serve their own ends (they've also taken over schools, where young people study logos, brand names, and shopping while being served the latest fast food in the cafeterias).

While the rest of the world struggles to survive the effects of exploitation and pollution resulting from the need to service western consumers, the young people in Anderson's novel are barraged with advertisements and soap operas and a media flow that keeps them from ever sitting back and thinking about the world. The only purpose of the Feed is to get them to shop. Significantly, although these young people are all constantly in communication through the Feed, the world depicted is one in which privatised, atomised existence has been taken to an extreme. It is also a mode of existence in which change is so constant and rapid that there is no time to reflect on what they experience, and where feelings are swamped under a barrage of information. The sheer volume of information now available can make it difficult to know what we think, and to separate significant facts from media spin. This problem is magnified by many factors for the young people in *Feed*, so they give up trying to think for themselves entirely, and allow the Feed to turn all aspects of their lives into consumer opportunities. For instance, when their polluted environment causes lesions to form on their faces and their skin to rot away, the Feed constructs the new look as a fashion statement so those whose skin is less affected pay for surgical enhancement in the form of cosmetic lesions.

The book culminates in the death of the main character, Titus's, girl friend. Because her parents are academics and so both suspicious of and unable to afford to have her chip fitted when she was born (this is not a culture that values academia), Violet can't manage the connection and eventually dies. Standing by her bedside Titus, who through her has gained some insight into the global situation, has his emotions read by the feed which instantly sends him a personalised message:

Feeling blue? Then dress blue! It's the Blue-Jean
Warehouse's Final Sales Event! Stock is just flying off the shelves at prices so low you won't believe your feed!
    Everything must go!
        Everything must go.
Everything must go.
          Everything must go.
[Page turn]
        Everything must go.
[The numbered last page is blank.] (pp.235–7)

Feed is an innovative and radical book in many ways – and it is as hostile to new technologies as anything I have read. It plays through scenarios of hyperreality and simulation, both in the form of simulated experiences and an unrelenting demand simultaneously to consume and to measure others by their consumer choices. The final scene, then, can be read as an enactment of 'the end of transcendence', as Baudrillard termed the state when 'individuals can neither perceive their own true needs or another way of life' (in *The Consumer Society* cited in the entry on 'Jean Baudrillard' in the *Stanford Encyclopedia of Philosophy*, accessed online on 30/11/2005). If *Eager* ends with a cyborg epiphany, *Feed* closes with a moment of reification, as its central character is absorbed into the Feed and becomes inseparable from it.

Reboot: next generation player–reader–writers

Unsurprisingly, all of the texts discussed so far were written by adults for children. It seems likely that it will be the rising generation – who have simultaneously ingested narratives about IT and grown up interacting with computers/IT, fostering an intuitive understanding of electronic logic – that finds ways of realising the potential in electronic narratives to tell new stories in new ways. As yet, however, there is no landmark text, author or device that decisively points an aesthetic way forward.

As this chapter has shown, the books currently being written for children tend to be more concerned with calling attention to the potential ethical, philosophical, environmental, and social dangers of the brave new cybernetic world than with devising transfiguring narratives that make it possible to revision the future in the optimistic, energetic, and emancipated mode that has characterised the best writing for children in previous epochs.

Equally important is the fact that while historically children's publishers have been quick to seize on mechanical innovations that have offered new ways to captivate young readers, finding such developments both aesthetically and financially rewarding, to date, forays into electronic publishing have brought neither accolades nor commercial gain. The CD-ROM format was a spectacular commercial failure, and no publisher has yet found a way to combine on-line activities with serious children's publishing in a profitable way.

Eliza Dresang suggests that digital-age readers are remaking the texts they have by transferring reading skills from one form of literacy to another in what she refers to as a text's 'connectivity'. In other words, they are using their transliteracy to convert traditional texts into a proto-transliterature. Her specific claim is that those familiar with hypertext respond to cues in texts and so

> interact with these books by making decisions as they read; they may approach the text in various nonlinear or nonsequential ways that the author does not determine in advance. Readers not only interact with the visual format but may interact with the context by mentally exploring levels of meaning or plateaus of story. (12)

As this suggests, currently we have transliterate readers, but are still waiting for the first fully transliterary texts. Meanwhile, there is a frenzy of electronic narrative activity. At the time of writing, it is estimated that more than

300 million people around the world currently experience game-fictions regularly, whether on consoles, PCs or mobile telephones; the games industry was forecast to make $34 billion [US] in 2005 (Hamm: 86) and online social networking or 'Me Media' are stimulating millions of people to create mini life stories on personal websites. In the process, new ways of thinking about how to combine textual/hypertextual, visual, and digital characteristics of the medium are being discovered and narrative conventions are not only taking shape but being widely used. When the first genuinely transliterary texts appear, it seems that unlike innovative texts of the past, which had to wait for readers to understand what they were trying to do, large numbers of readers will be ready to appreciate and work with the forms of storytelling they employ.

Thus it seems that while ideologically children's literature may be struggling to construct new visions of how society could function, aesthetic transformations are in process. Chapter 3 looked at the exciting ways in which picturebooks are responding to new media; currently developments such as the use of electronic whiteboards in school are being observed by publishers with a view to adapting the technology for publishing purposes when they feel the right combinations of texts and technology start to come on stream from the rising generation of writers and illustrators. Meanwhile, narrative on the Internet grows apace; all those who are currently meeting in MUDs, creating autobiographical social networking sites, writing blogs, and serious fiction are helping to map the narrative terrain of cyberspace. As the Conclusion indicates, transliterary pioneers – many of them children and young people – are navigating the shifting boundaries of the book as a narrative art form in a digital age. As the next generation of writers emerges, children's literature will provide the same kind of creative spaces for playing with and introducing new ideas in [digital] fiction that have made it so culturally valuable over the centuries.

Conclusion: The Foundations of Future Fictions

Although print-based children's literature is only beginning to feel its way towards creating transliterary texts, a major transformation of children's literature itself is taking place in cyberspace. As critics in the field regularly observe, children's literature is the only body of writing to be defined by and named for its audience: children read children's literature, they do not produce it (see Rudd, 2004 for a discussion of children's relation to children's literature). The situation is changing, and a great deal of writing by children is finding audiences via the Internet. As this trend continues, the nomenclature of writing read by the young may be forced to adjust. 'Children's literature' may indeed come to refer to writing by the young for the young, meaning that the work produced by adults for children to read will have to be relabelled.[1]

The most dynamic arena in which young people are producing fictions – and so preparing to become the next generation of established writers – is fan fiction, or fiction written in response to narratives already in circulation, be these on the page or screen. Alison Evans's study of this emerging genre gives an indication of the scale of the activity: having tracked a single fan fiction site (www.fanfiction.net) she estimates fans are producing the equivalent of 8,200, 50,000-word novels annually. As Evans observes, if these books were finding their way into bookshops, this would be heralded as a publishing revolution (2006: 27).

Who are these new writers and what is their relationship to children's literature? Fan fiction is currently produced primarily by girls between 15 and 20 (17), and since by definition fan fiction is based on pre-existing narratives, they are responding to the fictions about which they are most passionate. Among the most active sites are fictions based on the Harry Potter books, generating between 130 and 200 postings a day (27). In this sense they can be seen to be intimately connected to the fictions of childhood. Although inspired by existing fictional works, fan fiction does not simply replicate their styles, conventions, and narrative voices in the manner, say, of writers who attempt to complete another author's unfinished novel or who produce prequels or sequels to famous novels. Instead, fan fiction shares many characteristics with children's literature in the way it brings together characters and settings from more than one work in the 'canon' (the body of original narratives on which they draw),[2] experiments with new points of view, and develops relationships between characters that may seem to run counter to the manifest storylines in the originals.

While such scenarios go a long way towards achieving through text (rather than VR) the kind of wishfulfilment fantasies Janet Murray predicts will comprise cyberfictions when technology makes it possible for them to be fully visualised and interactive (see Chapter 8), fan fiction is not as focused on personal satisfactions and motivations as is Murray's vision for the future of narrative. Fan fiction sites have some very clear rules, many of them derived from the practices of traditional book publishing. Before they will be posted, texts must be deemed by webmasters to be well written, well presented, and their content must be appropriate for the target audience – different sites have different intended readers and fictions are given audience ratings analogous to those used for films signalling, for instance, whether a story contains explicit sexual material.

The fundamental rule of fan fiction is that characters must behave and speak as they do in the original: they may make different decisions and change alliances, but they must not act Out Of Character (OCC). What is deemed to be 'in character' can seem outlandish to those who have not engaged with the originals to the same extent or from the same perspective as the writers so, for instance, one of the popular romantic relationships in Harry Potter fan fiction is known as DM/HG (Draco Malfoy and Hermione Granger) (30). Fan writers provide evidence, rationales, and motivations for new relationships, and this is one way in which they are able to be genuinely innovative. In keeping with the combination of genre incubation and innovation characteristic of children's literature, writers of fan fiction often make use of forms, characters, and devices from literary tradition – for instance, battles between good and evil or character types drawn from myths, legends, and sagas – to generate new kinds of stories. Henry Jenkins, whose *Textual Poachers: Television Fans and Participatory Cultures* (1992) initiated the academic study of fan fiction, suggests that this is a healthy response to a world in which major corporations have taken control of myths and other traditional folk materials: fans reclaim basic themes, plotlines, characters, and structures through their writing.

Genre innovation in fan fiction takes several forms including 'slash' stories – stories based on same-sex character pairings – the most famous being Kirk/Spock (the genre is named after the slash between the names) which envisage relationship scenarios between *Star Trek*'s Captain Kirk and Mr. Spock. Jenkins argues that such stories reconfigure romantic relationships as a way of compensating for the inadequacies of the media representations of female characters (his study was written before popular series featuring autonomous female characters such as *Buffy the Vampire Slayer*). According to Jenkins, 'slash explores the possibility of existing outside of these [sex and gender] categories, of combining elements of masculinity and femininity into a satisfactory whole' (in Evans: 22). Again, an affinity between fan fiction and children's literature becomes evident since such fictions are not only giving rise to a new genre, but also to a new vision for sex and power relationships in culture. Slash stories contest certain norms and pilot alternative ideas about how relationships could function just as some of the novels discussed in Chapter 6 are doing.

Sexual behaviour and relationships are central to another way in which fan fiction is pushing at the traditional boundaries associated with children's and youth literature. Although Chapter 6 points to ways in which attitudes to the inclusion of sexual content in writing for the young have become more open, even Melvin Burgess's *Doing It* falls well short of the sexual content of some fan fiction – despite the ratings. It is perhaps not surprising that a generation that has grown up with online pornography, web cams that allow them to send intimate pictures of themselves into cyberspace and many of whom send and receive sexually explicit text messages is producing writers who seem uninhibited about producing sexually graphic material and posting it (albeit anonymously) for the world to read. In her study of teenagers and fanfiction, Rebecca C. Moore observes:

> Sexual content [in fan fiction] ranges from innocent handholding to hardcore kink, and writing of both types often inhabits the same sites or even the same stories. Even the most 'kid-safe' archives ... contain R-rated stories. While fanfiction offers 'safe' ways to explore sexual issues, what sensitive readers find may shock and disturb them. Discovering how young adults slake their voracious hunger might equally shock and disturb adults. (in Evans: 24)

This clash between what actual children write and the idealised image of childhood that Jacqueline Rose places at the centre of children's literature gives an insight into the possible consequences of the shift from a literature for children to a literature by them. Though adults may find reading young people's sexual fantasies disturbing and distasteful (just as the young are horrified by imagining sex between their parents or other 'old people'), the phenomenon deserves closer scrutiny. On the one hand, it underlines the disjunction between the sexual context in which young people circulate and the prohibitions about sexual content in children's and YA fiction discussed in Chapter 6. On the other, the confrontation between the real child's voice/imagination and the fictional child associated with children's literature can be seen as challenging adult views in a way that throws them off course and requires them to be adjusted – precisely the creative function Lyotard associates with the 'monster-child'.

The inclusion of sexual fantasies, mixing characters and plotlines, adjusting perspectives, and otherwise playing with fictional forms are some of the ways in which the young writers of fan fiction are exploring fictional strategies and sometimes blazing new narrative pathways. Although they are working in a new medium, novelty on its own is not the primary motivation of most young fan fiction creators. Many aspire to becoming authors of books and see what they are doing as preparation for future careers as professional writers (Evans, Chapter 4). With this in mind, it is not surprising that fan sites reproduce the quality and regulatory activities associated with traditional forms of publishing. One way in which they are unlike most mainstream publishing activities, however, is that they tend to be directed to special interest groups. By sampling different fan sites it is possible to identify groups who share similar interests and who read in similar ways, making it likely that they will enjoy similar kinds of stories. Many young writers are encouraged to share what they have written precisely because they know their core group of readers to be sympathetic (40).

Another difference is that fan sites are about watching texts grow, and having the opportunity to feed back comments to the writers in the process. Although they exist in an age of instant communication, this aspect of their publication resembles earlier forms of serialised fiction, from nineteenth-century novels to comic strips and regular features in popular juvenile magazines. In the case of fan fiction, feedback to the writers is more direct and faster than was previously the case, and the writers expect to receive readers' comments. (Some well-known published writers such as Stephen King and Terry Pratchett participate in related fan activities through web sites, blogs, and serialised publication of work in ways that allow readers to comment and shape work as it evolves.)

Perhaps the greatest impact on the experience of narrative currently associated with fan fiction is on what Roland Barthes (1975) identifies as one of 'the pleasure[s] of the text'. For Barthes, when reading, pleasure is bound up with knowing from the first page that a book will end – it has a last page. Fan fiction denies this pleasure since it exists to extend indefinitely the textual experience, and it does so by imagining the 'real' lives of characters in a way that literary criticism has for long regarded as unsound. In place of the pleasure of the known conclusion are the temporary conclusions reached at the end of each published instalment and the very different satisfaction that comes from knowing fictions featuring favourite characters will be available indefinitely. In these ways fan fiction can be seen to be pointing in two directions simultaneously. Like remediation, it is excited by and uses new media, but it often does so in traditional ways.

Nevertheless, it is through the experiments of those who are serving their literary apprenticeships online that the next round of narrative innovation is likely to occur. These new apprentice writers are moving between narrative forms and media and are accustomed to encountering different versions of the same text in different formats: as they develop it will be they who see the potential for new kinds of stories delivered in new kinds of ways. In the process, they may change the meaning of children's literature for future generations, but like generations of writers before them, their understanding of narrative, culture, and self will continue to be indebted to the fictions they encountered in childhood.

Notes

1 Breaking Bounds: The Transformative Energy of Children's Literature

1. I do not recognise Karin Lesnik-Oberstein's insistence that the majority of academics who write about children's literature are primarily concerned with finding the right book for the right child (*Children's Literature: New Approaches*, 2004: 1–24).
2. Although publishing for children includes many innovative and important non-fictional works, my concern is specifically with narrative fictions for children.
3. See Rumer Godden's entertaining 'An Imaginary Correspondence' featuring invented letters between Mr V. Andal, an American publisher working for the De Base Publishing Company, and Beatrix Potter for an entertaining insight into this process. The piece appeared in *Horn Book Magazine* 38 (August 1963), 197–206.
4. Peter Hunt raises questions about the regard accorded to Hughes's writing for children suggesting that it derives more from the insecurity of children's literature critics than the quality of the work: 'It is almost as if, with no faith in their own judgements, such critics are glad to accept the acceptance of an accepted poet' (2001: 79–81).
5. See Reynolds and Tucker, 1998; Trites, 2000 and Lunden, 2004.
6. Although writing in advance of Higonnet, Rose would have been familiar with many of the examples on which *Pictures of Innocence* is based.
7. By the time she reaches her conclusion, Rose has modified her position to emphasise that 'children's literature is just one of the areas in which this fantasy is played out' (138), undermining her claims that the child-audience is key to the work of children's literature in culture.
8. A useful comparison of what Rose has in mind can be found in Stanley Fish's *Surprised by Sin* (1967). Fish suggests that Milton recreates the Fall in the reader, who as a post-lapsarian user of language, anticipates the events because Milton describes Eve in words such as 'wanton' that *now* have 'sinful' connotations which they could not have had before the Fall.
9. According to James Bartholomew, two of five robberies are committed by ten to sixteen-year olds during school hours as are a quarter of all burglaries and a third of all car thefts (see 'Academies of Crime' at www.Telegraph.co filed on 14 May 2006).
10. Pullman in fact quotes Singer ('events never grow stale') at the start of his speech.
11. Peter Hollindale discusses the differences and similarities of writing for adults and children and having pointed to particular requirements for writers addressing young audiences he concludes, 'Some of our greatest novelists work within the narrative constraints of children's literature [that is, they are alert to and work with the same issues and requirements that inform how successful children's writers work]; the difference is that they do not have to' (1997: 41).
12. It is important to keep in mind the fact that memory and influence are complex phenomena: memory is not always accurate and influence can operate at many levels. The importance attributed to certain texts by those who subsequently became writers may not have been recognised at the time of reading; nevertheless, it is interesting to observe how often writers credit childhood reading with shaping their own literary practice and how specific they are about individual books they regard as formative.

13. Carpenter identifies the source as *The Tale of Ginger and Pickles* in which the dog and cat shopkeepers are sorely tempted to eat their mouse-customers (272).

14. See Justyna Deszcz-Tryhubczak's 'A Writer on the Yellow Brick Road: Salman Rushdie's Ozian Inspirations' in Greenway (pp. 51–68).

15. The page numbers referring to Nelson's chapter were taken from an incomplete manuscript and will inevitably be different when the book is published. To indicate that they are provisional they have been set in bold. Many of the same anxieties are being expressed in relation to today's crossover books – again because it seems only to involve adults reading works written for children rather than children annexing works of adult fiction. Of course, when children read adult texts a whole new set of concerns based on the need to preserve childhood innocence comes into play.

16. Smiles specifically addresses young men, 'some perhaps still in their teens, most in their twenties' (Nelson, 179).

17. I conducted an informal survey through the pages of the Society of Authors' newsletter, the findings from which suggest that Victorian and Edwardian writers continue to influence the current generation of writers for children. The authors mentioned most frequently as influences on their own work were Charlotte Bronte, Charles Dickens, Kenneth Grahame, Charles Kingsley, C.S. Lewis and George MacDonald. Some volunteered specific titles: the Alice books, *The Lion, the Witch and the Wardrobe* and *Little Women*. Influential genres were myths, legends, hero stories and fantasy. Comics were mentioned as both a genre and a format by several respondents. The author and texts to be mentioned most frequently were C.S. Lewis's Narnia Chronicles; however, one respondent provided the following interesting information on the basis of research he did for a possible programme to celebrate the fiftieth anniversary of Anthony Buckeridge's first Jennings book:

> I conclude that a whole generation of comedy writers (aged between 40 and 60 – Alan Ayckbourn, Jonathan Coe, Robert Leeson, Susan Hill, Stephen Fry, Griff Rhys Jone, Victoria Wood) were influenced by the ... surreal humour of Linbury Court School and its pupils. (e-mail correspondence with Lee Pressman, 21 March 2005)

18. It strikes me as significant that the only equally focused response on this scale in children's literature has been to the possibility of a nuclear (or similar) holocaust. Currently, environmental threats and developments in robotics are stimulating a new generation of dystopian fiction.

19. This has been well documented in relation to Charles Dickens and Robert Louis Stevenson who regularly draw on the stylistic and narrative conventions of popular childhood narratives (from toy theatres to penny dreadfuls) but who have gained and sustained the respect of the cultural establishment.

20. Although technically Magic(al) Realism and Carpentier's 'Marvelous Real' are separate terms, the first referring primarily to the mode of narration and the second to its subject, this description of the marvellous captures the essence of the transformative power at the heart of Magic(al) Realism.

21. Similar and related terms ('*Magischer Realismus*' [Magical realism] and '*Neue Sachlichkeit*' [New Objectivity]) had been applied by art critics and historians since the 1920s.

22. In other ways, Bowers's reading of the relationship between children's literature and magic(al) realism is rather simplistic, not least her suggestion that 'we should question the extent to which readers of magical realism are simply reluctant to give up

their childhood approach to stories' (108–9). It should be noted that some scholars of children's literature are seeking to establish a specific vocabulary and tradition of this kind of writing as it developed in children's literature. Eva Kaum's unpublished MA dissertation, *For All of Us Can be Transformed: A Study of the Ordinary and the Extraordinary Worlds in David Almond's Teenage Novels* (Roehampton University, 2001), for instance, proposes the term 'fantastic realism' which she suggests stresses not just an interaction between a real-world setting and fantastic experiences but also the change which takes place in the characters as a result of their experiences.

2   Breaking the Frame: Picturebooks, Modernism, and New Media

1. The account is contained in a brief correspondence between Hildick and Leonard Woolf in January 1965; Hildick suggests publishing the story in picturebook form, possibly with illustrations by Brian Wildsmith. Woolf acted on the suggestion but had Duncan Grant provide the artwork. The result is a book that looks very much of a piece with the Bloomsbury-Charlesworth-Hogarth Press productions of the time, but which makes a less creative use of the picturebook format than perhaps an experienced picturebookmaker such as Wildsmith would have done. Julie Vivas's 1991 illustrations have proved more successful.
2. My attention was drawn to Stein's story by Roni Natov's discussion of it in *The Poetics of Childhood* (2003), pp. 103–10. Natov's interest is in the way the story explores gender, identity formation and socialisation, and the way even a child, once having taken on – or entered into – language, is compelled at some level to impose her identity on the pastoral world.
3. The site for 'Yesterday and Today: Children's Books of the Soviet Era', organised by the Rare Books and Special Collections Division of McGill University, notes that there was an overall increase in book production during this period and that 'Children's books naturally followed the mass trend and a first printing of 100,000 and up was common'. See http://digital.library.mcgill.ca/russian/intro.htm, accessed 20/02/2006.
4. Günter Berghaus makes the point that to be effective in their challenge to prevailing aesthetic, social, and political forces, avant-garde artists 'need to possess a reflective consciousness and be aware of the conceptual framework within which they are operating' (xxi). In other words, they must be fully versed in the rules before they can dismiss them or anticipate what will take their place.
5. Belsey discusses this in Chapter 8 of *Culture and the Real*.
6. Eugene Ostashevsky discusses the circumstances of the deaths of the members of OBERIU.
7. The books were created by Harlin Quist. Originally the stories stood as codas to sections of Ionesco's memoir.
8. This work has yet to be translated into English so I am relying on critical accounts of its contents. According to Debattista (2005), the collection is gaining in critical stature and attention making a translated version more likely.
9. Aidan Chambers was to pose precisely this conundrum at the end of *Breaktime* (1992), another example of a fully modernist (in some ways even postmodern) text for young readers.
10. Beckett (2002, 55–65) discusses this technique with reference to Lavater's *Le Petit Chaperon Rouge*.

3   And None of It Was Nonsense

1. Thanks to Dr Jill Barker, University of Luton, for this and several other examples of nonsense incorporated in plays of the 1500s.

2. There is no record of when this challenge ostensibly took place, and Carpenter and Prichard (1984) note that the piece is sometimes attributed to the eighteenth-century actor, James Quinn. It also exists in an Irish version, but the Irish writer, Maria Edgeworth, who includes it in *Harry and Lucy Concluded* (1825), credits it to Foote ('The Great Panjandrum' in Carpenter and Prichard).

3. This tendency was demonstrated by Stanley Fish in an impromptu experiment. On entering a classroom which had previously been occupied by a linguistics class and seeing a list of linguists' names on the board, Fish told his students of religious poetry that the list was in fact a poem that he wanted them to analyse. This they proceeded to do, producing a succession of plausible readings of the 'poem' (McHale, 7).

4. As Marcus suggests, this kind of behaviour was not unusual for Victorian men, and is often imaged in terms of a veil, dividing the public and private. Significantly, like an ambiguous figure, a veil is not rigid and excluding, firmly dividing what it conceals. Instead, a veil is yielding and suggestive – and almost always associated with women. In *Sexual Anarchy* (1992), Elaine Showalter discusses Victorian men's fascination with the veiled female form, suggesting that its attraction stemmed in the way it threatened to reveal the thing men feared most: the castration-desiring female body. It was in this sexual milieu that Dodgson/Carroll grew up and worked.

5. The Lewis Carroll Society issues compilations and reprints of many of the games and puzzles Carroll created for himself and his child friends.

6. Martin Gardner's *The Annotated Alice* (1960) discusses Carroll's parodies of Watts in detail.

7. For Donald Thomas (1996) this distinguishes Carroll from the paedophile, placing him instead in the category of the onomatomaniac: one who suffers from the compulsion 'to fill the mind with endless problems, puzzles and calculations, in order to crowd out unwholesome bedtime thoughts' (2).

8. See Showalter (1992: 147–8) on the way nineteenth-century men constructed women as fearful and castrating.

9. Thomas points out that the age of consent was not raised to 13 until 1875; campaigning journalist W.T. Stead managed to get it raised to 16 in 1885 and received a curt published response from Carroll in the process (259; 279).

10. Thomas provides details of several of these relationships (260–1). It is important to remember that this practice began earlier; for instance, following Rousseau, whom he met in Paris, Thomas Day (1748–1789), author of *Sandford and Merton* (1783–1789) attempted to find the ideal wife by raising two twelve-year-old orphans and educating them according to Rousseau's methods as set out in *Émile*. The experiment was not a success.

11. As Lecercle points out, the prefix 'non' is comparable to 'un': it indicates denial and so associates nonsense with the domain of the unconscious (2). However, while nonsense *may* conceal psychological revelations and invite psychoanalytic readings, it does not always do so. The tendency for critics to unveil hidden meanings was itself parodied by a critic in the *New Yorker* in a piece on the great American nonsense writer, Theodore Geisel, better known as Dr. Seuss. Geisel was given the task of writing a book using only the 225 words his editor had selected for their ability to teach phonics, and eventually came up with *The Cat in the*

Hat – a book undoubtedly in the nonsense tradition. The *New Yorker* article offered readers a tongue-in-cheek analysis of the text as a story about an 'alarmingly polymorphous cat' intruding on a scene of repression against the wishes of the household superego (the fish) to introduce two uptight little persons to their libidos – Thing One and Thing Two!

12. Daniel Heller-Roazen provides examples of and consequences for those (usually men) who have lost language and regressed to the noises associated with infant babble in *Echolalias: On the Forgetting of Language*, Cambridge, MA: Zone, 2005.

13. Shires (1988) develops this point in a powerfully argued essay, which can usefully be read alongside Karen Coats's (2004) discussion of new readers and nonsense (pp. 64–6).

14. Tigges suggests that by the nineteenth century, nonsense was often valued as a way back to childhood or as an escape from everyday reality (6). Robson (2001) suggests that some Victorian men desired to regress to a state of girlhood.

15. Sewell, by contrast, firmly separates dreams and nonsense. In *The Field of Nonsense* (1952) she observes that, 'Far from being ambiguous, shifting and dreamlike, [nonsense] is concrete, clear and wholly comprehensible ... Nonsense verse seems much nearer logic than dream' (in Malcolm, 110).

16. The translations are taken from Derrien (2004; 2005). My knowledge of Cox's work – and indeed what familiarity I have with French picturebooks – owes much to this brilliant French librarian and critic, whom I was fortunate enough to work with while she was studying for an MA in Children's Literature.

17. An excellent discussion of *Ce nains portent quoi???????* is provided by Marie Derrien in 'Radical Trends in French Picturebooks', *The Lion and the Unicorn*, Vol. 29, No. 2, April 2005, pp. 170–89.

18. The translations are mine, though *Ponctuation* includes English vocabulary in places; this seems to be more about design and acknowledging that alphabetical sign systems are transcultural than about creating a bilingual text.

4   Useful Idiots: Interactions Between Youth Culture and Children's Literature

1. Chapter 5 of *Girls Only? Gender and Popular Children's Fiction in Britain 1880–1910* (Reynolds, 1990) contains a discussion of critical views about the need for a special literature for adolescent girls.

2. Class, education, and affluence affect the extent to which children and parents communicate in Chambers's work, so Barry, Hal's more affluent lover, has a much more open relationship with his mother. In the later *Postcards from No Man's Land* (1999), Jacob Todd encounters much more liberal attitudes to sex and sexuality among the young and old alike when he travels to Holland, where he mixes with a more cosmopolitan set.

3. Jonathan Green's study of 1960s counterculture is symptomatic of this attitude in the way it criticises current youth culture for being 'an ultimately plagiaristic form of creativity, a mix 'n' match recycling of periods of real originality, as if no one has the energy or talent for genuine advance' (448).

5   Self-harm, Silence, and Survival: Despair and Trauma in Children's Literature

1. Nicholas Tucker's article on 'Depressive Stories for Children' in *Children's Literature in Education*, vol. 37, no. 3, Autumn 2006, pp. 199–209 provides an overview of

the arguments in favour of optimistic endings in children's books as well as some examples of books that deal with darker material.

2. I have some anecdotal evidence of the efficacy of reading such books with young people. Over the past three years I have taught books about self-harming, including those discussed in this chapter, to undergraduate students, some of whom were obviously actively cutting themselves and/or anorexic. I received more essays on this topic than on any other we covered, some of them extremely thoughtful and thoroughly researched. Students came to see me individually about their topics and some have continued to send me books subsequently. Several let it be known that they had found the books helpful and one, who was hospitalised repeatedly as an undergraduate, is now well and doing excellent postgraduate work. That student credits a specific book – Bella Bathurst's *Special* (2002) – with breaking her dependence on self-harming.

3. See http://www.mentalhealth.org.uk; statistics for the United States are comparable.

4. Unless otherwise stated, the translations from *Petit-Âne* are mine.

5. The endpapers encourage such a reading by reminding readers of the widely held belief (often found in children's stories) that when children go to sleep, their toys come alive. The first endpapers suggest that this is what is taking place, as the moon looks through the window into the nursery to show Ourson riding on Petit-Âne, and the pair starting simultaneously to emerge from framed pictures of them on the walls. The closing endpapers show all the characters (not just Petit-Âne) with their eyes closed, suggesting that morning is coming and their time for play is over.

6. The Priory Group's study into *Adolescent Angst* (2006) found that over one million adolescents (17% generally; 25% of girls) have wanted to self-harm and over 800,000 (13%) have actually self-harmed (15).

7. The 2001 census showed that 0.9% or 68,000 5–15 year olds were depressed. More recent studies show serious depression in children over twelve at between 1.4 and 5% (Tickle, 2006: 6).

8. The problem is not unique to schools and other places where young people mix in large numbers; *Adolescent Angst* reports that 10% of British youngsters experience violence and bullying at home (16).

9. See, for instance, the reports of the death of a twelve-year-old British schoolgirl, Georgie Phelan, who hanged herself on Christmas Day 2004 after a sustained campaign against her by bullies at school.

10. Although successful suicide attempts remain rare, they account for a fifth of all death of young people (Searle: 321), and 16% of adolescents report having considered suicide (*Adolescent Angst*, 17).

11. Correspondence with Professor Ron Best, Roehampton University, leading the Nuffield-funded project on self-harm in schools on 16 June 2003 and 10 July 2003.

12. In 2006 the Royal College of Nursing also proposed and is piloting schemes where self-harmers who cut themselves can arrange to be supervised in hospital when they feel the need to cut.

13. A.M. Vrettos's *Skin* (2006) is one of the few books to deal with the death of an anorexic character. Also unusually, it is told from the point of view of a sibling who is also caught up in the family problems that seem to have triggered the anorexia.

6 Baby, You're the Best: Sex and Sexuality in Contemporary Juvenile Fiction

1. Rose makes the point that this insistence on innocent childhood is particularly active in the domain of children's literature; elsewhere in western culture, images

of and discourses associated with what Anne Higonnet (1998) has termed the 'knowing child' are extremely active. Moral panics about the behaviour of the young periodically infuse the media and political debate (see Chapter 7).

2. For a discussion of the value placed on reading by young people in the United Kingdom, see Kimberley Reynolds, 'Reluctant Readers and Risk Taking' in Kimberley Reynolds and Susan Hancock (eds), *Young People's Reading at the End of the Century*. London: Book Trust, 1996, pp. 220–229. In its series of case notes, the UK child support service, Childline, has published its findings on *Alcohol and teenage sexual activity* which show that despite formal sex education classes and related information, many young people are badly informed about many aspects of sexual activity including contraception, their legal position, and how to practise safe sex.

3. See R. Burack, 'Teenage sexual behaviour: attitudes towards and declared sexual activity' in the *British Journal of Family Planning*, Vol. 24, no. 4, 1999, pp. 145–8 accessed via *www.ncbi.nlm.nih.gov/entrez/query* 28/04/2006.

4. By the time of its thirtieth anniversary celebrations, *Forever* had sold 3.5 million copies worldwide (Crown, 2005: 2).

5. Writing in the *New York Review of Books* on the twenty-fifth anniversary of Blume's book *Tales of a Fourth Grade Nothing*, Michael Oppenheimer, Mellon Fellow of American religious history at Yale University observed: 'when I got to college, there was no other author, except Shakespeare, whom more of my peers had read. We had learned about puberty from *Are You There, God? It's Me, Margaret* ... about sex from *Forever*; about divorce from *It's Not the End of the World*' (44).

6. Later he changed his views as he discusses in 'My Affair with Judy ...' in Chris Powling (ed.) in *The Best of 'Books for Keeps'*, London: Bodley Head, 1994, pp. 177–81 (first published in *Books for Keeps*, 27 July 1984.

7. In Britain, teenage pregnancy rates are falling in the 16 + age group but rising among thirteen to fifteen-year-olds (Burack, 1999).

8. The Childline findings suggest that girl on girl peer pressure is now as important as boy on girl – Retting makes a point of showing that Kelly Ann feels that she needs to apologise for still being a virgin to her girlfriends, who are eager for her to join them in being sexually active.

9. One of those who doesn't get to do it is Prue, the central character in Jacqueline Wilson's *Love Lessons* (2006). Wilson explores the attraction between talented but unworldly Prue who has been home-educated by her domineering father until he has a major stroke, and her new art teacher, Rax. The two need each other and Prue is desperate to secure Rax, but unlike the other pupil–teacher relationships discussed, Wilson does not allow her characters to start a sexual relationship. Rax determines not to jeopardise his marriage and disentangles himself. The reader is left with the sense that this is the best thing for Prue who is already being sought out by an attractive boy from her class and shows signs of being able to fit in better with her peers.

7   Frightening Fiction: The Transformative Power of Fear

1. Iona and Peter Opie (eds), *The Oxford Dictionary of Nursery Rhymes*. Oxford: Oxford University Press, 1951, no. 322, p. 286.

2. See Bottigheimer, 1996 for a full discussion of the death of children in the Bible.

3. Gillian Avery discusses martyrdom in books for children in 'Intimations of Mortality: The Puritan and Evangelical Message to Children' in Gillian Avery and

Kimberley Reynolds (eds) *Representations of Childhood Death*. Basingstoke: Macmillan, 2000.

4. Gammon (2000) discusses this and other ballads about the death of children interestingly and at length.

5. I am grateful to Jane Wickenden for calling this example to my attention.

6. An early example in children's literature of the use of such devices is Mary Martha Sherwood's 'Story on the Sixth Commandment' from *The History of the Fairchild Family* (1818). After discovering his children fighting over a doll, Mr. Sherwood takes them to a deep dark wood where they are shown a rotting corpse on a gibbet. It is not just the events of this tale that makes it so memorable but the use of narrative devices from ghost stories and gothic fiction.

7. In an informal Internet survey (children-literature-uk@JISCMAIL.AC.UK, September 2005), adults involved with children's literature in a variety of capacities volunteered information about the books they and the children with whom they work have found frightening. Only one mentioned a book specifically marketed as 'frightening fiction' (Stephen King's *Carrie*); the books that had frightened most readers were *Alice in Wonderland*, Andersen's *The Red Shoes*, *The New Mother*, *The Tale of Tom Kitten* (several works by Potter, including *Peter Rabbit*, were mentioned), and Roald Dahl's *The Witches*.

8. One respondent observed:

> ... remembering scary literature has recalled to me accompanying circumstances and settings with startling clarity. ... I can even remember where in each form-room I was sitting when I read *Moonfleet* and *Flannan Isle*. (02/09/2005 21:10:34)

9. Andrew Burn's (2004) comparative study of book, film, and game versions of *Harry Potter and the Philosopher's Stone* demonstrates this shift very effectively.

8 Back to the Future? New Forms and Formats in Juvenile Fiction

1. The term 'transliteracies' comes from a five-year project at the University of California which is researching the technological, social, and cultural practices of online reading. See Thomas, 2005 for a discussion of transliteracy and academic research. Details of the project can be found at http://transliteracies. english. ucsb.edu.

2. See Reid-Walsh (2006) for a discussion of the harlequinade. Sabuda's work in fact displays characteristics of hypermedia through its incorporation of small books within pages of his books, each of which takes readers off on complementary textual journeys.

3. Although more limited in their appeal, adventure gamebooks too have an online life; reader–players can currently select from a menu of online titles featuring scenarios ranging from romance in the Canadian wilderness through encounters with animals in the jungle, to 'The Trans-Morbid Adventure', described as 'An extended and humorous choose-your-own-adventure with many ways of not surviving' (see, for instance, http://dmoz.org/Games/Video_Games/Adventure/ Browser_Based/Choose_Y ... ,).

4. I am indebted to Mark Vasey-Saunder, Chaplain at the University of Newcastle and inveterate game-player, for much of my understanding of gaming.

5. Mummery (2005) looks at the interaction between writers and games from the point of view of the writer.
6. Several versions of digital or electronic paper are currently available. These facilitate collaborative access to documents online. More relevant to the future of narrative is the vision of an e-book technology in which each ultra-thin page of text serves as a screen that can be instantly updated (http://computing-dictionary.the freedictionary.com, accessed 12/07/2006).
7. Sainsbury (2006) suggests that Romain Victor-Pujebet's CD-ROM version of *Robinson Crusoe* is breaking new ground in its use of the narrative possibilities of digital media.
8. See Noga Applebaum's unpublished MA dissertation for detailed evidence to support this claim: 'Children and IT: Computers, internet and virtual realities in contemporary literature for young people', Roehampton University, 2003.
9. The word 'gramarye' means both 'grammar' and 'magic'; additionally, in the medieval period, before literacy was widespread and it was still common for people to be read to from important documents, ' "good reading" was collective and public, and silent reading often provoked suspicion' (Thomas, 2005: 28).
10. I am grateful to Nadia Crandall for calling this book to my attention.
11. This French children's book echoes Roland Barthes's *Camera Lucida* (1980) in which he points to the way photographs confer a kind of immortality on the deceased.
12. Books which take the opposite position and emphasise the dangers of 'a world without rules, without boundaries, where you can be anyone you want, or whoever you aren't', make up Jordan Cray's *Danger.com* series; see Harris, 2005: 119–21.
13. There are several books written in the form of email correspondence, but while these attempt to make the printed text look like messages on a computer screen, they otherwise progress like other novels written in the form of correspondence or journal entries. There is little in the way of stylistic innovation. Their emphasis on distinguishing between emails and other forms of communication (conversations, telephone calls, text messages and so on) does, however, call attention to the supposed medium in which the communication is taking place (Harris, 2005: 123–4).

Conclusion: The Foundations of Future Fictions

1. Perhaps following Peter Hollindale (1997) it should be known as 'childness literature', childness referring both to the adult's ability to remember childhood and recreate it fictionally for children, and children's sense of their developing selves.
2. For a discussion of the relationship between character migration and children's literature, see Susan Hancock's doctoral thesis, currently being prepared for publication: 'Poetics Plus: Miniature Literature as a Key to Decoding the Structures, Rhetoric and Underlying Topic of Children's Literature', University of Surrey Reohampton, 1999.

Bibliography

Adolescent Angst. London: The Priory Group, 2006.

Almond, David. *Clay*. London: Hodder, 2005.

Andersen, Hans Christian. 'The Little Match Girl' found at http://www.andersen. sdu.dk/vaerk/hersholt/TheLittleMatchGirl_e.html accessed on 19/03/2006.

Anderson, Chester G. *James Joyce*. London: Thames and Hudson, 1998.

Anderson, M.T. *Feed*. Cambridge, MA: Candlewick Press, 2002.

Anon. *Francis Fearful* in *Entertaining Memoirs of Little Personages* and *The Lilliputian Magazine; or, Children's Repository* (1775) located at http://www.cts.dmu.ac.uk/ AnaServer?hockliffe + 66578 + imager.anv accessed on 15/02/2006.

Applebaum, 2008. 'Interfaces of Technology and Children's Literature through the Dimension of Science Fiction Written for Young People'. PhD thesis that is due to be completed in 2008 at Roehampton University.

Appleyard, Joseph A. *Becoming a Reader: The Experience of Fiction from Childhood to Adulthood*. Cambridge: Cambridge University Press, 1994 (first published in 1991).

Ariès, Philippe. *Centuries of Childhood*. Translated by Robert Baldick. London: Pimlico, 1996 (first published in 1962).

ArtShock: The Human Canvas, Channel 4 (UK), 14 March 2006.

Atkins, Barry. *More than a Game: The Computer Game as Fictional Form*. Manchester and New York: Manchester University Press, 2003.

Atkins, Laura. 'Creepy Kids: Childhood and Knowing in Two Films of the Uncanny' in Kimberley Reynolds (ed.) *Children's Literature and Childhood in Performance*. Lichfield: Pied Piper Publishing, 2003, pp. 38–44.

Auerbach, Nina. *Our Vampires, Ourselves*. London: University of Chicago Press, 1995.

Averill, Esther. 'Avant-Gardes and Traditions in France' in Bertha E. Mahoney and Elinor Whitney (eds) *Contemporary Illustrators of Children's Books*. Detroit, MI: Gale Research Company, 1978 (first published in 1930), pp. 89–96.

Aycock, Alan. 'Virtual play: Baudrillard online' in *The Arachnet Electronic Journal on Virtual Culture*, vol. 1, no. 7, 30 November 1993, 10 pages.

Baer, Elizabeth R. 'A New Algorithm in Evil: Children's Literature in a Post-Holocaustal World' in *The Lion and the Unicorn*, vol. 23, no. 4, 2000, pp. 378–401.

Bakhtin, Mikhail. *Rabelais and His World*. Bloomington, IN: Indiana University Press, 1984.

Barker, Martin and Julian Petley (eds) *Ill Effects: The Media/Violence Debate*. London and New York: Routledge, 2001 (first published 1997).

Barthes, Roland. *The Pleasure of the Text*. Translated by Richard Miller. New York: Hill and Wang, 1975 (first published 1973).

——. 'Toys' in *Mythologies*. Translated by Annette Lavers. New York: Hill and Wang, 1984.

Bathurst, Bella. *Special*. London: Picador, 2002.

Baudrillard, Jean. 'Baudrillard on the New Technologies: An Interview with Claude Thibaut' on *http:/www.uta.edu/English/apt/collab/texts/newtech.html*

——. 'Simulacra and Simulations' in Mark Poster (ed.) *Jean Baudrillard: Selected Writings*. Stanford, CA: Stanford University Press, 1998.

——. *The Consumer Society: Myths and Structures*. London: Sage, 1998.

Beckett, Sandra. *Recycling Red Riding Hood*. New York and London: Routledge, 2002.

Beja, Morris. *James Joyce. A Literary Life*. Basingstoke: Macmillan, 1992.

Belloc, Hilaire and Edward Gorey. *Cautionary Tales for Children*. Orlando, FL: Harcourt Children's Books, 2002.

Belsey, Catherine. *Culture and the Real*. Abingdon and New York: Routledge, 2005.

Berghaus, Günter. *Avant-Garde Performance: Live Events and Electronic Technologies*. Basingstoke: Palgrave, 2005.

Bettelheim, Bruno. *The Uses of Enchantment: The Meaning and Importance of Fairy Tales*. London: Penguin, 1978.

Blackford, Holly Virginia. *Out of this World: Why Literature Matters to Girls*. New York: Teachers College Press, 2004.

Bloch, Dorothy. *'So the Witch Won't Eat Me': Fantasy and the Child's Fear of Infanticide*. London: Burnett Books in association with André Deutsch, 1978.

Bloom, Clive. *Creepers: British Horror and Fantasy in the Twentieth Century*. London: Pluto Press, 1993.

Blount, Margaret. *Animal Land: The Creatures of Children's Fiction*. New York: Morrow, 1975.

Blume, Judy. *Forever*. London: Pan, 1986.

Bolter, Jay David and Richard Grusin. *Remediation; Understanding New Media*. Cambridge, MA, and London: MIT Press, 1999.

Bosmajian, Hamida. 'Narrative Voice in Young Readers' Fictions about Nazism, the Holocaust, and Nuclear War' in Charlotte F. Otten and Gary D. Schmidt (eds) *The Voice of the Narrator in Children's Literature: Insights from Writers and Critics*. New York: Greenwood Press, 1989, pp. 308–24.

——. *Sparing the Child: Grief and the Unspeakable in Youth Literature about Nazism and the Holocaust*. New York: Routledge, 2002.

Bottigheimer, Ruth B. *The Bible for Children: From the Age of Gutenberg to the Present*. London and New Haven, CT: Yale University Press, 1996.

Bowers, Maggie Ann. *Magic(al) Realism*. London and New York: Routledge, 2004.

Bradshaw, Jonathan (ed.) *The Well-Being of Children*. London: Save the Children and the University of York, 2002.

Brennock, Mark. '55% of Young Know Peer Suicide Attempts' in *The Irish Times*, 20 September 2003, p. 1.

Brook, Peter. 'Towards Supreme Fictions' in Peter Brook (ed.) *Yale French Studies: The Child's Part*. 1969, pp.

Brooks, Karen. 'Nothing Sells like Teen Spirit: The Commodification of Youth Culture' in Kerry Mallan and Sharyn Pearce (eds) *Youth Cultures: Texts, Images, and Identities*. Westport, CT: Praeger, 2003, pp. 1–16.

Brooks, Kevin. *Kissing the Rain*. Frome, Somerset: The Chicken House, 2004.

Bunyan, John. 'Upon the Disobedient Child' in his *A Book for Boys and Girls; or, Country Rhymes for Children* (1686), found at http://rpo.library.utoronto.ca/poem/ 307.html

Burack, R. 'Teenage Sexual Behaviour: Attitudes towards and Declared Sexual Activity' in *The British Journal of Family Planning*, vol. 24, no. 4, 1999, pp. 145–8. Accessed via www.ncbi.nlm.nih.gov/entrez/query on 28/04/2006.

Burchill, Julie. *Sugar Rush*. London: Young Picador, 2004.

Burgess, Melvin. *Doing It*. London: Penguin, 2004.

——. *Junk*. London: Penguin, 1997.

——. *Lady: My Life as a Bitch*. London: Andersen Press, 2001.

——. 'Sympathy for the Devil' http://web.onetel.net.uk/~melvinburgess' accessed on 12/04/2006.

Burman, Erica. 'The Pedagogics of Post-Modernity: The Address to the Child as Political Subject and Object' in Karín Lesnik-Oberstein (ed.) *Children in Culture: Approaches to Childhood*. Basingstoke: Macmillan, 1998, pp. 55–88.

Burn, Andrew. 'Potterliteracy: Cross-media Narratives, Cultures and Grammars' in *Papers*, vol. 14, no. 2, 2004, pp. 5–17.

Butler, Judith. *The Psychic Life of Power.* Stanford, CA: Stanford University Press, 1997.

Card, Orson Scott. *Ender's Game.* London: Atom Books, 2002.

Carpenter, Humphrey. *Secret Gardens: A Study of the Golden Age of Children's Literature.* London: George Allen and Unwin, 1985.

——. 'Excessively Impertinent Bunnies: The Subversive Element in Beatrix Potter' in Gillian Avery and Julia Briggs (eds) *Children and Their Books: A Celebration of the Life and Work of Iona and Peter Opie.* Oxford: Clarendon Press, 1989.

Carpenter, Humphrey and Mari Prichard. *The Oxford Companion to Children's Literature.* Oxford and New York: Oxford University Press, 1984.

Carpentier, Alejo. 'On the Marvelous Real in America' in Lois Parkinson Zamora and Wendy B. Faris (eds) *Magical Realism: Theory, History, Community.* Durham, NC, and London: Duke University Press, 1995, pp. 83–8.

Carr, Diane. 'Play dead: genre and affect in *Silent Hill* and *Planescape Torment*' in *Game Studies*, vol. 3, no. 1, May 2003. Accessed at *http:www.gamestudies.org/0301/carr/* on 13/02/2006.

Carroll, Lewis. *The Annotated Alice* (ed.) Martin Gardner. Harmondsworth: Penguin, 1970.

Carson, Rachel. *The Silent Spring.* London: Penguin, 2000.

Caruth, Cathy. *Unclaimed Experience: Trauma, Narrative and History.* Baltimore, MD: Johns Hopkins University Press, 1996.

Castle, Luanne. 'Higgledy Piggledy, Gobbledygoo: The Rotted Residue of Nursery Rhyme in Sylvia Plath's Poetry' in Betty Greenway (ed.) *Twice-Told Tales: The Influence of Childhood Reading on Writers for Adults.* London and New York: Routledge, 2005, pp. 109–24.

Chambers, Aidan. *Breaktime.* London: Bodley Head, 1992.

——. *Dance on My Grave.* London: Bodley Head, 1992.

——. *Postcards from Noman's Land.* London: Bodley Head, 1999.

——. *This is All. The Pillow Book of Cordelia Kenn.* London: Bodley Head, 2005.

Chester, G.K. *Autobiography.* London: Arrow Books, 1959.

Chevalier, Noel. 'The Liberty Tree and the Whomping Willow: Political Justice, Magical Science, and Harry Potter' in *The Lion and the Unicorn*, vol. 29, no. 3, September 2005, pp. 397–415.

Child, Lauren. *What Planet Are You from Clarice Bean?* London: Orchard Books, 2002.

Clark, Stuart. *Thinking with Demons: The Idea of Witchcraft in Early Modern Europe.* Oxford: Oxford University Press, 1999.

Coats, Karen. *Looking Glasses and Neverlands: Lacan, Desire, and Subjectivity in Children's Literature.* Iowa City: University of Iowa Press, 2004.

Coghlan, Valerie. 'Bellsybabble for the Childers: James Joyce's *The Cat and the Devil*'. Unpublished paper delivered at the 'Representations of Otherness' conference, Kobe, Japan, 31 March 2005.

Colbert. June. *The King of Large.* Melbourne: Lothian Books, 2004.

Cole, Babette. *Hair in Funny Places.* London: Red Fox, 2001.

——. *Mummy Laid an Egg.* London: Red Fox, 2000.

——. *Mummy Never Told Me.* London: Red Fox, 2004.

Colfer, Eoin. *Artemis Fowl: The Arctic Incident.* London: Puffin, 2003 (first published 2002).

Colley, Ann. 'Edward Lear's Limericks and the Reversals of Nonsense' in *Victorian Poetry*, vol. 26, 1988, pp. 285–99.

Cordle, Daniel. 'Metaphor Mongering: Science, Writing and Science Writing' in *English Subject Centre Newsletter*, Issue 9, November 2005, pp. 5–9.

Corimer, Robert. *The Chocolate War.* London: Fontana, 1978.

Crandall, Nadia. 'Cyberspace and the Gothic Novel'. Unpublished MA essay, Roehampton University (2004); a revised version will appear in Karen Coats and Rod McGillis (eds) *The Gothic in Children's Literature: Haunting the Borders*. New York: Routledge, forthcoming, 2007.

Crown, Sarah. 'Teen Spirit' in *The Guardian*, 8 June 2005. Accessed via http://guardian.co.uk/departments/childrenandteens/story/0 on 25/07/2006.

Cullinan, Bernice E. and Diane G. Person (eds) *The Continuum Encyclopedia of Children's Literature*. New York and London: Continuum, 2001.

Cullingford, Cedric. *Children's Literature and its Effects*. London and Washington, DC: Cassell, 1998.

Davidoff, Leonore. 'Class and Gender in Victorian England' in Judith Newton, Mary Ryan and Judith Walkowitz (eds) *Sex and Class in Women's History*. London: Routledge and Kegan Paul, 1983.

Debattista, Marina. 'Eugene Ionesco's Writing for Children' in *Bookbird*, vol. 43, no. 4, 2005, pp. 15–21.

De Maeyer, Gregie. *Jules*. Illustrated by KoenVanmechelen. Paris: Mango, 1996.

Derrien, Marie. 'In Search of the Future of the Book: Exploring French Picturebooks'.Unpublished Masters dissertation of the University of Surrey, UK, 2004.

——. 'Radical Trends in French Picturebooks' in *The Lion and the Unicorn*, vol. 29, no. 2, April 2005, pp. 170–89.

——. 'Keep out of the reach of the adults? The adult impossibility of children's fiction.' Unpublished paper presented as part of the MA in Children's Literature, Roehampton University, 2003.

Dickinson, Peter. *The Weathermonger*. Harmondsworth: Puffin, 1968.

——. *Heartsease*. Harmondsworth: Puffin, 1969.

——. *The Devil's Children*. Harmondsworth: Puffin, 1970.

Dresang, Eliza. *Radical Change: Books for Youth in a Digital Age*. New York: H. Wilson, 1999.

Drucker, Elina. 'Images within Images' in Tove Jansson's *The Book about Moomin, Mymble and Little My*. Unpublished paper delivered at the NorChilNet workshop, 'Children's Literature: Art or Pedagogy?', Reykjavik, 5–10 October 2004.

Dusinberre, Juliet. *Alice to the Lighthouse: Children's Books and Radical Experiments in Art*. Basingstoke: Macmillan, 1987.

Eccleshare, Julia. 'Teenage Fictions: Realism, Romances, Contemporary Problem Novels' in Peter Hunt (ed.) *International Companion Encyclopedia of Children's Literature*, vol. 1, 2nd edition. London and New York, 2004, pp. 542–55.

Eckley, Grace. *Children's Lore in 'Finnegans Wake'*. Syracuse, NY: Syracuse University Press, 1985.

Ellmann, Richard (ed.) *Selected Letters of James Joyce*. London: Faber and Faber, 1975.

Evans, Alison. 'The Global Playground: Fan Fiction in Cyberspace'. Unpublished MA dissertation, Roehampton University, 2006.

Fanelli, Sara. *Dear Diary*. London: Walker Books, 2000.

Farr, Liz. 'Paper Dreams and Romantic Projections: The Nineteenth-Century Toy Theatre, Boyhood and Aesthetic Play' in Dennis Denisoff (ed.) *Small Change: Nineteenth-Century Childhood and the Rise of Consumer Culture*. Burlington: Ashgate (forthcoming).

Fass, Paula S. (ed.) *Encyclopedia of Children and Childhood in History and Society*. New York: Macmillan, 2003.

Felman, Shoshana. ' "Don't You See I'm Burning?" Or Lacan and Philosophy' in *Writing and Madness*. Ithaca, NY: Cornell University Press, 1985, pp. 134–40.

Figes, Eva. *Tales of Innocence and Experience: An Exploration*. London: Bloomsbury, 2003.

Fine, Anne. 'Filth, Whichever Way You Look At It' in *The Guardian*, 29 March 2003.

——. *The Road of Bones*. London: Doubleday, 2006.

Fish, Stanley. *Surprised by Sin: The Reader in Paradise Lost*. Boston, MA: Harvard University Press, 1967.

Fiske, John. *Reading the Popular*. London: Unwin Hyman, 1989.

Foucault, Michel. *Discipline and Punish: The Birth of the Prison*. London: Vintage, 1995.

Forde, Catherine. *Fat Boy Swim*. London: Random House, 2004.

Fox, Helen. *Eager*. London: Hodder Children's Books, 2003.

Frank, E.R. *America is Me*. London and New York: Simon and Schuster, 2002.

——. *Life is Funny*. New York: DK Publishing, 2000.

Freeman, Hilary. 'Girls Who Cut' in *The Guardian*, 2 September 2003, pp. 10–11.

Freud, Sigmund. 'The Uncanny' in vol. 14, *The Pelican Freud Library*. Translated by James Strachey. Harmondsworth: Penguin Books, 1985 (first published 1919), pp. 339–68.

Freud, Sigmund. 'Creative Writers and Daydreaming' in Peter Gay (ed.) *The Freud Reader*, New York: Norton, 1989, pp. 436–43.

Gaiman, Neil. *Coraline*. London: Bloomsbury, 2002.

——. *The Wolves in the Walls*. London: Bloomsbury, 2003.

Gammon, Vic. 'Child Death in British and North American Ballads from the Sixteenth to the Twentieth Centuries' in Gillian Avery and Kimberley Reynolds (eds) *Representations of Childhood Death*. Basingstoke: Macmillan, 2000, pp. 29–51.

Gardner, Martin. *The Annotated Alice*. Harmondsworth: Penguin, 1996.

Genette, Gerard. *Paratexts: Thresholds of Interpretation*. Cambridge: Cambridge Unversity Press, 2001.

Geras, Adèle. *The Tower Room*. London: HarperCollins, 1992.

Gibbons, Alan. *Shadow of the Minotaur*. London: Orion Children's Books, 2002.

Gill, Michele. 'Just Telling It Like It Is? Representations of Teenage Fatherhood in Contemporary Western Young Adult Fiction' in *Papers*, vol. 16, no. 1, 2006, pp. 41–50.

Gmuca, Jacqueline L. 'Transmutations of Folktale and School Story in *A Portrait of the Artist as a Young Man*' in Betty Greenway (ed.) *Twice-Told Children's Tales: The Influence of Childhood Reading on Writers for Adults*. New York and London: Routledge, 2005, pp. 207–19.

Godden, Rumer. 'An Imaginary Correspondence' in *Horn Book Magazine*, 38, August 1963, pp. 197–206.

Goldthwaite, John. 'Do You Admire the View? The Critics Go Looking For Nonsense' in *Signal 67*, January 1992, pp. 41–66.

Goodall, Janet. 'Grieving Parents, Grieving Children' in Gillian Avery and Kimberley Reynolds (eds) *Representations of Childhood Death*. Basingstoke: Macmillan, 2000, pp. 225–38.

Greene, Graham. 'Beatrice Potter' in Sheila Egoff (ed.) *Only Connect*, 3rd edition. Toronto: Oxford University Press, 1996, pp. 258–65.

Green, Jonathan. *All Dressed Up: The Sixties and the Counterculture*. London: Pimlico, 1998.

Greenlaw, Lavinia. 'If Coke Were a Person, What Would He Be Like?', *The Guardian*, 17 May 2003, p. 13.

Greenway, Betty (ed.) *Twice-Told Tales: The Influence of Childhood Reading on Writers for Adults*. London and New York: Routledge, 2005.

Grimm, Wilhelm. *Dear Mili*. Translated by Ralph Manheim. Illustrated by Maurice Sendak. New York: Farrar, Straus and Giroux, 1988.

Grixti, Joseph. *Terrors of Uncertainty: The Cultural Contexts of Horror Fiction*. London: Routledge, 1989.

Hamm, Steve. 'GameBoy' in *BusinessWeek*, 10 October 2005, pp. 86–94.

Haraway, Donna. 'A Manifesto for Cyborgs: Science, Technology and Feminism in the 1980s' in Linda Nicholson (ed.) *Feminism/Postmodernism*. London and New York: Routledge, 1990 (first published in 1985), pp. 464–81.

Harris, Marla. 'Contemporary Ghost Stories: Cyberspace in Fiction for Children and Young Adults' in *Children's Literature in Education*, vol. 36, no. 2, June 2005, pp. 111–28.

Hasegawa, Shuhei. *Sleepless*. Tokyo: Shoton, 1996.

Hayden, Peter. 'The Child in Children's Literature'. Unpublished MA dissertation for the University of Sussex, 1989.

Healy, Melissa. 'Is Video Killing Catching?' *The Hartford Courant*, 22 September 2005, pp. D3–4.

Heffernan, John. *My Dog*. Illustrated by Andrew Mclean. Hunters Hill, NSW: Margaret Hamilton, 2001.

Hegerfeldt, Anne. 'Magic Realism, Magical Realism, 1960'. Accessed at www. LitEncyc.com. On 22/09/2004, 4 pages.

Heinrich Hoffman's *Struwwelpeter* (1845; English translation, 1848), found at http://www.fln.vcu.edu/struwwel/struwwel.html

Heller, Terry. *The Delights of Terror: An Aesthetics of the Tale of Terror*. Chicago, IL: University of Illinois Press, 1987.

Heyman, Michael. 'The Performative Letter, from Medieval to Modern' in *Children's Literature Association Quarterly*, vol. 30, no. 1, Spring 2005, pp. 100–07.

Higonnet, Anne. *Pictures of Innocence: The History and Crisis of Ideal Childhood*. London: Thames and Hudson, 1998.

Higonnet, Margaret. 'Narrative Fractures and Fragments' in *Children's Literature*, vol. 15, 1987, pp. 37–53.

Hildick, Wallace and Leonard Woolf. Private correspondence, in the Monk's House Papers in the Special Collections section of the University of Sussex Library.

Hill, Amelia. 'Teenagers' Epidemic of Self-harm' in *The Observer*, 26 March 2006, p. 13.

Hinton, S.E. *Rumble Fish*. London: HarperCollins, 1992.

Hoban, Russell. *The Mouse and His Child*. Penguin: Puffin, 1993.

Hollindale, Peter. *Signs of Childness in Children's Books*. Stroud: Thimble Press, 1997.

Honigsbaum, Mark. 'Sense of Failure: The Scale of Teenage Self-harm' in *The Guardian*, 28 November 2005, p. 5.

Howarth, Lesley. *Ultraviolet*. London: Puffin, 2001.

Hughes, Felicity, A. 'Children's Literature: Theory and Practice' in Peter Hunt (ed.) *Children's Literature: The Development of Criticism*. London: Routledge, 1990.

Hughes, Richard. *The Spider's Palace and Other Stories*. Harmondsworth: Puffin, 1972 (first published in 1931).

Hunt, Peter. *Children's Literature*. Oxford: Blackwell, 2001.

——. (ed.) *Children's Literature: The Development of Criticism*. London: Routledge, 1990.

——. *Criticism, Theory and Children's Literature*. Oxford: Basil Blackwell, 1991.

——. (ed.) *International Companion Encyclopedia of Children's Literature*, 2 vols. London: Routledge, 2004.

——. *An Introduction to Children's Literature*. Oxford: Oxford University Press, 1994.

——. *Literature for Children: Contemporary Criticism*. London: Routledge, 1992.

Inglis, Fred. *The Promise of Happiness: Value and Meaning in Children's Fiction*. Cambridge: Cambridge University Press, 1982 (first published in 1981).

Innocenti, Roberto and Ian McEwan. *Rose Blanche*. London: Jonathan Cape, 1995 (first published in a version with text by Christophe Gallaz, 1985).

Ionesco, Eugene. *Story Number 1*. Illustrated by Joel Naprstek. Translated by Calvin K. Towle. New York: Harlin Quist, 1978.

——. *Story Number 2*. Illustrated by Gerard Failly. Translated by Calvin K. Towle. New York: Harlin Quist, 1978.

——. *Story Number 3*. Illustrated by Philippe Corentin. Translated by Ciba Vaughan. New York: Harlin Quist, 1971.

Jackson, Rosemary. *Fantasy; The Literature of Subversion*. London and New York: Routledge, 1981.

Jameson, Fredric. *Archaeologies of the Future: The Desire Called Utopia and Other Science Fictions*. London: Verso, 2005.

——. 'Cognitive Mapping' in Michael Hardt and Kathi Weeks (eds) *The Jameson Reader*. Oxford: Basil Blackwell, 2000, pp. 277–87.

Jansson, Tove. *The Book about Moomin, Mymble and Little My*. English version by Sophie Hannah. London: Sort of Books, 2004.

Jardin, Alexandre. *Cybermaman*. Paris: Gallimard Jeunesse, 1997.

Johnstone, Nick. 'Blue Notes' in *The Guardian*, 8 June 2004, p. 9.

——. 'This Band-Aid Won't Stop the Bleeding' in *The Guardian*, 30 July 2004. Accessed at http://society.guardian.co.uk/mentalhealth/comment, on 05/06/2006.

Juster, Norton. *The Phantom Tollbooth*. New York: Alfred A. Knopf, 1989 (first published in 1961).

Kafka, Franz. 'In the Penal Settlement' in *Metamorphosis and Other Stories*. Translated by Willa and Edwin Muir. Harmondsworth: Penguin, 1978 (first published in 1919).

——. *Wedding Preparations in the Country and other Prose Writing*. Translated by Ernst Kaiser and Eithne Wilkins. London: Secker and Warburg, 1973.

Kaminski, Winfred. 'Literature for Young People: Between Liberation and Suppression' in *Children's Literature Association Quarterly*, vol. 11, no. 4 (Winter 1986–7), pp. 201–04.

Kaum, Eva. 'For All of Us Can be Transformed: A Study of the Ordinary and the Extraordinary Worlds in David Almond's Teenage Novels'. Unpublished MA dissertation, Roehampton University, 2001.

Kaysan, Elizabeth. *Girl Interrupted*. London: Virago, 2000.

Kebbe, Jonathan. *Noodle Head*. London: Corgi, 2005.

Kelleher, Joe. 'Face to Face with Terror: Children in Film' in Karin Lesnik-Oberstein (ed.) *Children in Culture: Approaches to Childhood*. Basingstoke: Macmillan, 1998, pp. 29–54.

Kember, Sarah. *Virtual Anxiety: Photography, New Technologies and Subjectivity*. Manchester and New York: Manchester University Press, 1998.

Kertzer, Adrienne. *My Mother's Voice: Children, Literature and the Holocaust*. Peterborough, ON: Broadview Press, 2002.

Kettlewell, Caroline. *Skin Game*. New York: Griffin St. Martin's, 1999.

Kharms, Daniil. It Happened Like This: Stories and Poems. Translated by Katya Arnold. New York: Farrar, Straus and Giroux, 1998.

Kidd, Kenneth. ' "A" is for Auschwitz: Psychoanalysis, Trauma Theory, and the "Children's Literature of Atrocity" ' in *Children's Literature*, vol. 33, 2005, pp. 120–49.

Kincaid, James R. *Child-Loving: The Erotic Child and Victorian Culture*. London: Routledge, 1992.

Kingsley, Jo and Alice Kingsley. *Alice in the Looking Glass: A Mother and Daughter's Experience of Anorexia*. London: Piatkus, 2005.

Knoepflmacher, U.C. 'The Critic as Former Child: A Personal Narrative' in *Papers*, vol. 12, no. 1, April 2002, pp. 5–9.

Koertge, Ron. *Where the Kissing Never Stops*. London: Walker, 2006.

Kostick, Conor. *Epic*. Dublin: The O'Brien Press, 2004.

Kozlov, Serge. *Petit-Âne*. Illustrated by De Vitaly Statzynsky. French translation by Pavlik de Bennigsen. Paris: Ipomée-Albin Michel, 1995.

Kress, Gunther. 'Interpretation or Design: From the World Told to the World Shown' in Morag Styles and Eve Bearne (eds) *Art, Narrative and Childhood*. Stoke on Trent: Trentham Books, 2003, pp. 137–54.

Kristeva, Julia. *Powers of Horror: An Essay on Abjection*. Translated by L.S. Roudiez. New York: Columbia University Press, 1982.

Kuznets, Lois. *When Toys Come Alive: Narratives of Animation, Metamorphosis, and Development*. New Haven, CT, and London: Yale University Press, 1994.

Lacan, Jacques. *The Four Fundamental Concepts of Psychoanalysis: The Seminar of Jacques Lacan, Book XI*. Edited by Jacques Alain Miller. Translated by Alan Sheridan. New York: W.W. Norton, 1998.

Lamb, Kathryn. *Brothers, Boyfriends and Babe Magnets*. London: Piccadilly Press, 2006.

Lathey, Gillian. *The Impossible Legacy: Identity and Purpose in Autobiographical Children's Literature Set in the Third Reich and the Second World War*. Bern: Peter Lang, 1999.

Leatham, Victoria. *Bloodletting*. London: Alison and Busby Ltd., 2005.

Lecercle, Jean-Jacques. *The Philosophy of Nonsense: The Intuitions of Victorian Nonsense*. London: Routledge, 1994.

Lefebvre, Benjamin. 'From *Bad Boy* to Dead Boy: Homophobia, Adolescent Problem Fiction, and Male Bodies that Matter' in *Children's Literature Association Quarterly*, vol. 30, no. 3, Fall 2005, pp. 288–313.

L'Engle, Madeleine. *A Swiftly Tilting Planet*. New York: Farrar, Straus and Giroux, 1978.

——. *Many Waters*. New York: Farrar, Straus and Giroux, 1986.

——. *Wind in the Door*. New York: Farrar, Straus and Giroux, 1973.

——. *A Wrinkle in Time*. New York: Farrar, Straus and Giroux, 1962.

Lennon, Tom. *When Love Comes to Town*. Dublin: O'Brien Press, 1993.

Lesnik-Oberstein, Karin. 'Childhood and Textuality: Culture, History, Literature' in Karín Lesnik-Oberstein (ed.) *Children in Culture: Approaches to Childhood*. Basingstoke: Macmillan, 1998, pp. 1–28.

——. *Children's Literature: Criticism and the Fictional Child*. Oxford: Clarendon Press, 1994.

——. *Children's Literature: New Approaches*. Basingstoke and New York: Palgrave Macmillan, 2004.

Levithan, David. *Boy Meets Boy*. London: HarperCollins, 2003.

Livingstone, Sonia and Magdalena Bober. *UK Children Go Online*. London: London School of Economics, 2005.

Loy, Mina. 'Gertrude Stein'. Accessed at http://www2.english.uiuc.edu/finnegan/English%20256/gertrude_stein.htm. on 14/02/2006.

Lunden, Anne. *Constructing the Canon of Children's Literature: Beyond Library Walls and Ivory Towers*. New York: Routledge, 2004.

Lurie, Alison. *Don't Tell the Grown-Ups: Subversive Children's Literature*. London: Bloomsbury, 1990.

——. (ed.) *The Oxford Book of Fairy Tales*. Oxford: Oxford University Press, 1993.

Mackey, Margaret. *Literacies Across Media: Playing the Text*. London and New York: Routledge, 2002.

——. 'Playing in the Phase Space: Contemporary Forms of Fictional Pleasure' in *Signal*, no. 88, January 1999, pp. 16–33.

Magistral, Tony and Morrison Michael (eds) *A Dark Night's Dreaming: Contemporary American Horror Fiction*. Columbia, SC: University of South Carolina Press, 1996.

Mahy, Margaret. *Alchemy*. London: CollinsFlamingo, 2002.

——. *The Changeover*. Harmondsworth: Puffin, 1995 (first published in 1984).

Malcolm, Noel. *The Origins of English Nonsense*. London: Harper Collins, 1997.

Mallan, Kerry and Sharyn Pearce. *Youth Cultures: Texts, Images, Identities*. Westport, CT: Praeger, 2003.

Mantel, Hilary. 'Some Girls Want Out' in *London Review of Books*, 4 March 2004, p. 15.

Markley, Robert. 'Shreds and Patches: The Morphogenesis of Cyberspace' in *Configurations*, 2.3, 1994, pp. 433–9.

Marshall, Elizabeth. 'Borderline Girlhood: Mental Illness, Adolescence, and Femininity in *Girl, Interrupted*' in *The Lion and the Unicorn*, vol. 30, no. 1, January 2006, pp. 117–33.

Masaki, Tomoko. *A History of Victorian Popular Picture Books: The Aesthetic, Creative, and Technological Aspects of the Toy Book through the Publications of the Firm of Routledge 1852–1893*. Tokyo: Kazamashobo, 2006.

McCallum, Robyn. *Ideologies of Identity in Adolescent Fiction: The Dialogic Construction of Subjectivity*. New York and London: Garland, 1999.

McCarron, Kevin. 'Point Horror and the Point of Horror' in Anne Hogan (ed.) *Researching Children's Literature*. Southampton: LSU College of Higher Education, 1994.

——. 'Point Horror and the Point of Horror' in Kimberley Reynolds, Geraldine Brennan and Kevin McCarron (eds) *Frightening Fiction*. London: Continuum, 2001, pp. 19–52.

McCormick, Patricia. *Cut*. London: CollinsFlamingo, 2000.

McGuire, Ann. 'Simplification: The Sims and Utopianism' in *Papers*, vol. 14, no. 2, 2004, pp. 54–64.

McHale, Brian. 'Making (non)sense of postmodernist poetry' in Michael Toolan (ed.) *Language, Text and Context*. London and New York: Routledge, 1992, pp. 6–33.

McRobbie, Angela. *Feminism and Youth Culture: From 'Jackie' to 'Just Seventeen'*. London: Macmillan, 1991.

——. (ed.) *Zoot Suits and Second-Hand Dresses: An Anthology of Fashion and Music*. London: Macmillan, 1989.

Menand, Louis. 'How to Frighten Small Children: The Complicated Pleasures of Kids' Books' in *The New Yorker*, 6 October 1997, pp. 112–21.

Mickenberg, Julia. L. *Learning from the Left: Children's Literature, the Cold War, and Radical Politics in the United States*. New York: Oxford University Press, 2006.

Mitterauer, Michael. *A History of Youth*. Translated by G. Dunphy. Oxford: Blackwell, 1992 (first published in 1986).

Morrison, Blake. 'Sonnet' in the *Times Literary Supplement*, 3 April 1987.

Muir, Percy. *English Children's Books 1600 to 1900*. London: B.T. Batsford, 1985 (1st edition 1969).

Mummer, Jim. Letter in *UK Writer*, New Year 2005, pp. 24–5.

Murail, Elvire, Lorris and Marie-Aude. Translated by Sarah Adams. *Golem 1: Magic Berber*. London: Walker Books, 2005.

Murail, Elvire. *Golem 2: Joke*. London: Walker Books, 2005.

——. *Golem: 3: Natasha*. London: Walker Books, 2005.

——. *Golem 4: Mr. William*. London: Walker Books, 2005.

——. *Golem 5: Alias*. London: Walker Books, 2005.

Murray, Janet. *Hamlet on the Holodeck: The Future of Narrative in Cyberspace*. New York: The Free Press, 1997.

Natov, Roni. *The Poetics of Childhood*. London and New York: Routledge, 2003.

Nelson, Claudia. 'Adult Children's Literature in Nineteenth-Century Britain' in Dennis Denisoff (ed.) *Small Change: Nineteenth-Century Childhood and the Rise of Consumer Culture*. Burlington: Ashgate (forthcoming n.d.).

Neustatter, Angela. 'Changing Shapes' in *Young Minds Magazine*. Accessed at http://www.YoungMinds/Magazine/Changing shapes on 22/09/2004.

Newton, Michael. 'Tsk, Ukh, Hmmm' in *London Review of Books*, 25 February 2006, pp. 25–6.

Nicholls, Peter. *Modernisms: A Literary Guide*. Basingstoke: Macmillan, 1995.

Nikolajeva, Maria. *Children's Literature Comes of Age: Toward a New Aesthetic*. New York and London: Garland, 1996.

——. *The Magic Code: The Use of Magical Patterns in Fantasy for Children*. Stockholm: Almqvist and Wiskell International, 1988.

——. 'Exit Children's Literature?' in *The Lion and the Unicorn*, vol. 22, 1998, pp. 221–36.

Nodelman, Perry. 'The Case of Children's Fiction: Or the Impossibility of Jacqueline Rose' in *Children's Literature Association Quarterly*, vol. 10, no. 3, 1985, 98–103.

——. *The Pleasures of Children's Literature*, 2nd edition. White Plains, NY: Longman, 1996.

Nodelman, Perry and Mavis Reimer. *The Pleasures of Children's Literature*, 3rd edition. Boston, MA: Allyn and Bacon, 2003.

Norton, Jody. 'Transchildren and the Discipline of Children's Literature' in *The Lion and the Unicorn*, vol. 23, no. 3, September 1999, pp. 415–36.

Oakes, Margaret, J. 'Flying Cars, Floo Powder, and Flaming Torches: the Hi-tech, Low-tech World of Wizardry' in Giselle Lisa Anatol (ed.) *Reading Harry Potter: Critical Essays*. Westport, CT: Praeger, 2003, pp. 117–28.

O'Har, George M. 'Magic in the Machine Age' in *Technology and Culture*, vol. 41, no. 4, 2000, pp. 862–4.

O'Malley, Andrew. *The Making of the Modern Child: Children's Literature and Childhood in the Late Eighteenth Century*. New York and London: Routledge, 2003.

Opie, Iona and Peter Opie. *The Oxford Dictionary of Nursery Rhymes*. Oxford and New York: Oxford University Press, 1997 (first published 1951).

Oppenheimer, Marc. 'Why Judy Blume Endures' in *The New York Review of Books*, 16 November 1997, p. 44.

O'Prey, Paul. *A Reader's Guide to Graham Greene*. London: Thames and Hudson, 1988.

Ostashevsky, Eugene. 'OBERIU: Russian Absurdism of the 1930s' reproduced at http://www.newamericanwriting.com/20/eostashevsky.htm. Accessed on 13/02/2006.

O'Sullivan, Emer. *Comparative Children's Literature*. Translated by Anthea Bell. London and New York: Routledge, 2005.

——. '*Rose Blanche, Rosa Weiss, Rosa Blanca*: A Comparative View of a Controversial Picture Book' in *The Lion and the Unicorn*, vol. 29, no. 2, April 2005, pp. 152–70.

Pacoviska, Kveta. *Un Livre Pour Toi*. Paris: Éditions du Seuil, 2004.

——. *Ponctuation*. Paris: Éditions du Seuil, 2004.

Paddock, Terri. *Come Clean*. London: HarperCollins, 2004.

Pankenier, Sarah. 'Play for Play's Sake: Daniil Kharms' Ant-Pedagogical Poetics'. Unpublished paper delivered at the NorChilNet workshop, 'Children's Literature: Art or Pedagogy?', Reykjavik, 5–10 October 2004.

——. '*in fant non sens*: The Infantilist Aesthetic of the Russian Avant-Garde, 1909–39'. Unpublished PhD thesis from Stanford University in California, 2006.

Paul, Lissa. 'Sex and the Children's Book' in *The Lion and the Unicorn*, vol. 29, no. 2, April 2005, pp. 222–35.

——. ' "Writing poetry for children is a curious occupation": Ted Hughes and Sylvia Plath' in *The Horn Book Magazine*, May/June 2005. In http://www.hbook.com/publications/magazine/articles/may05_paul.asp. Accessed on 16/02/2006.

Pausewang, Gudrun. *Fall-Out*. Translated by Patricia Crampton. London: Penguin, 1994.

Pearce, Sharyn. 'Today's Boys: New Millennium Guides to Masculinity and Sexuality' in *CREArTA*, vol. 2, no. 1, Southern Winter, 2001, pp. 61–70.

Pef. *Une si Jolie Poupee*. Paris: Gallimard, 2001.

Peters, John, D. *Speaking into the Air: A History of the Idea of Communication*. Chicago, IL: University of Chicago Press, 1999.

Peters, Julie Anne. *Luna: A Novel*. New York and Boston, MA: Little, Brown, and Company, 2004.

Philbrick, Rodney. *The Last Book in the Universe*. New York: Scholastic, 2000.

Plotz, Judith. '*Haroun* and the Politics of Children's Literature' in *Children's Literature Association Quarterly*, vol. 20, no. 3, Fall 1995, pp. 100–4.

Pratchett, Terry. *Only You Can Save Mankind*. London: Corgi, 2004.

Pullman, Philip. Carnegie Medal acceptance speech found at http://www.randomhouse.com/features/pullman/philippullman/speech.html. Accessed on 30/05/2006.

——. *Clockwork, or All Wound Up*. London: Corgi Yearling, 1997.

Quilgars, Deborah. 'The Mental Health of Children' in Jonathan Bradshaw (ed.) *The Well-being of Children in the UK*. London: Save the Children with the University of York, 2002, pp. 346–62.

Rabinowitz, Rebecca. 'Messy New Freedoms: Queer Theory and Children's Literature' in Sebastian Chapleau (ed.) *New Voices In Children's Literature Criticism*. Lichfield: Pied Piper Publishing, 2004.

Ragland, Ellie. 'Lacan, the Death Drive and the Dream of the Burning Child' in Sarah Webster Goodwin and Elisabeth Bronfen (eds) *Death and Representation*. Baltimore, MD, and London: Johns Hopkins University Press, 1993, pp. 80–102.

Rai, Bali. *(Un)arranged Marriage*. London: Random House, 2001.

Redford, John. *Wit and Science*. Oxford: Malone Society Reprints, 1951.

Rees, David. *The Marble in the Water: Essays in Contemporary Writers of Fiction for Children and Young Adults*. Boston: Horn Book, 1980.

Reid Walsh, Jacqueline. 'Playing in the Text: Pantomime and Children in Late Eighteenth-Century Britain' in The *British Journal for Eighteenth-Century Studies*, vol. 29, no. iii, 2006, pp. ??Please provide page numbers.

Rennison, Louise. ' ... *then he ate my boy entrancers.*' London: HarperCollins, 2005.

——. *... and that's when it fell off in my hand.' Further fabbitty-fab confessions of Georgia Nicolson*. London: HarperCollins, 2005.

Retting, Liz. *My Now or Never Diary by Kelly Ann*. London: Corgi, 2006.

Reynolds, Kimberley. 'Alchemy and Alco Pops: Breaking the Ideology Trap' in Celia Keenan and Mary Shine Thompson (eds) *Studies in Children's Literature 1500–2000*. Dublin: Four Courts Press, 2004, pp. 138–47.

——. (ed.) 'Children's Literature in Performance' in *Children's Literature and Childhood in Performance*. Lichfield: Pied Piper Publishing, 2003, pp. 3–10.

——. 'Fatal Fantasies: The Death of Children in Victorian and Edwardian Fantasy Writing' in Gillian Avery and Kimberley Reynolds (eds) *Representations of Childhood Death*. Basingstoke: Macmillan, 2000.

——. *Children's Literature in the 1890s and the 1990s*. Plymouth: Northcote House in association with the British Council, 1994.

——. *Girls Only? Gender and Popular Children's Fiction in Britain, 1880–1910*. Hemel Hempstead: Harvester, 1990.

Reynolds, Kimberley, Geraldine Brennan and Kevin McCarron. *Frightening Fiction*. London and New York: Continuum, 2001.

Reynolds, Kimberley and Nicola Humble. *Victorian Heroines: Representations of Femininity in Nineteenth-Century Literature and Art*. Hemel Hempstead: Harvester, 1993.

Reynolds, Kimberley and Nicholas Tucker. *Children's Book Publishing in Britain Since 1945*. Aldershot: Ashgate, 1998.

Robson, Catherine. *Men in Wonderland: The Lost Girlhood of the Victorian Gentleman*. Princeton and Oxford: Oxford University Press, 2001.

Rose, Jacqueline. *The Case of Peter Pan, or, The Impossibility of Children's Fiction*. Basingstoke and London: Macmillan, 1984.

Rose, Malcolm. *The Obtuse Experiment*. London: Scholastic, 1993.

Rose, Steve. 'Who's nasty now?' in *The Guardian*, 9 September 2005, p. 11.

Rosen, Michael. *Don't Put Mustard in the Custard*. Illustrated by Quentin Blake. London: Andre Deutsche, 1985.

——. *Michael Rosen's Sad Book*. Illustrated by Quentin Blake. London: Walker, 2004.

Rossof, Meg. *How I Live Now*. London: Penguin, 2004.

Rowling, J.K. *Harry Potter and the Half-Blood Prince*. London: Bloomsbury, 2005.

Rudd, David. 'Children's Literature and the Return to Rose' on *Working Papers on the Web* (www.shu.ac.uk/wpw/). Sheffield Hallam University: Autumn, 2006.

——. 'Theories and Theorising: The Condition of Possibility of Children's Literature' in Peter Hunt (ed.) *International Companion Encyclopedia of Children's Literature*, 2nd edition, vol. 1, London: Routledge, 2004, 29–43.

Rudge, Ian. 'Magic Realism in Children's Literature: A Narratological Reading' in *New Review of Children's Literature and Librarianship*, vol. 10, no. 2, November 2004, pp. 127–40.

Rushdie, Salman. *Haroun and the Sea of Stories*. London: Granta Books, 1991.

Russell, David L. 'Hope among the Ruins: Children, Picture Books, and Violence' in *Paradoxa*, vol. 2, no. 3–4, 1996, pp. 346–56.

Rustin, Margaret and Michael Rustin. *Narratives of Love and Loss: Studies in Modern Children's Fiction*, revised edition. London and New York: Karnac, 2001.

Sabuda, Robert. *Alice in Wonderland*. New York: Simon and Schuster, 2003.

Sabuda, Robert and Matthew Reinhart. *The Wonderful Wizard of Oz*. New York: Simon and Schuster, 2000.

——. *Encyclopedia Prehistorica: Dinosaurs*. London: Walker Books, 2005.

Sachar, Louis. *Holes*. London: Bloomsbury, 2000.

Sandoval, Angelina 'Dancing with Zombies at the Silent Hill Hotel', http://pc.gamezone.com/news/10_19_04_10_19AM.htm. Accessed on 22/07/05.

Sainsbury, Lisa. 'Game On: Adolescent Texts to Read and Play' in Kerry Mallan and Sharyn Pearce (eds) *Youth Cultures: Texts, Images and Identities*. Westport, CT, and London: Praeger, 2003, pp. 155–67.

——. 'The Postmodern Carnival of Children's Literature: Necessary Playgrounds and Subversive Space in the Protean Body of Children's Literature'. Unpublished doctoral thesis, University of Surrey, 1998.

——. 'Rousseau's Raft: The Remediation of Narrative in Romain Victor- Pujebet's CD-ROM Version of *Robinson Crusoe*' in Fiona Collins and Jeremy Ridgman (eds) *Children's Literature in Performance and the Media*. Oxford: Peter Lang, 2006, pp. 207–26.

Saint-Exupéry, Antonie, de. *The Little Prince*. Can be viewed at http://www.angelfire.com/hi/littleprince/frames.html.

Sarland, Charles. 'Attack of the Teenage Horrors: Theme and Meaning in Popular Series Fiction', in *Signal 73*, 1994, pp. 48–61.

——. *Young People Reading: Culture and Response*. Milton Keynes: Open University Press, 1991.

Searle, Beverley. 'Youth Suicide' in Jonathan Bradshaw (ed.) *The Well-being of Children in the UK*. London: Save the Children with the University of York, 2002, pp. 321–30.

Sendak, Maurice. *Where the Wild Things Are*. New York: HarperCollins, 2003.

Sconce, Jeffrey. *Haunted Media: Electronic Presence from Telegraphy to Television*. Durham, NC: Duke University Press, 2000.

Sewell, Elizabeth. *The Field of Nonsense*. London: Chatto and Windus, 1952.

——. 'Nonsense Verse and the Child' in *The Lion and the Unicorn*, vol. 4, no. 2, 1980, pp. 30–48.

Shaffer, David Williamson. 'Epistemic Frames and Islands of Expertise: Learning from Infusion Experiences' in Yasmin Kafai et al. (eds) *Proceedings of the Sixth International Conference of the Learning Sciences*. Mahwah, NJ: Erlbaum, 2004, pp. 521–8.

Shaffer, David Williamson, Kurt Squire R., Richard Halverson and James P. Gee. 'Video games and the future of learning' in *Phi Delta Kappa*, October 2005, pp. 105–11.

Sheehy Skeffington, Tricia. 'Helping harmed teenagers' in *The Irish Times*, 22 September 2003.

Shires, Linda M. 'Fantasy, Nonsense, Parody, and the Status of the Real: The Example of Lewis Carroll' in *Victorian Poetry*, vol. 76, no. 7, 1988, pp. 267–83.

Showalter, Elaine. *Hystories: Hysterical Epidemics and Modern Culture*. London: Picador, 1997.

——. *Sexual Anarchy: Gender and Culture at the fin de siecle*. London: Virago, 1992 (first published in 1990).

Singer, Nicky. *Doll*. London: CollinsFlamingo, 2002.

Sinyard, Neil. *Graham Greene: A Literary Life*. Basingstoke: Palgrave, 2003.

Smith, Gerilyn, Dee Cox and Jacqui Saradin. *Women and Self-Harm*. London: The Women's Press, 1998.

Spandler, Helen. *Who's Hurting Who? Young People, Self-harm and Suicide*. Gloucester: Handsell, 2001 (originally published by 42nd Street, 1998).

Spufford, Francis, *The Child that Books Built*. London: Faber and Faber, 2002.

Staunch, Barbara. *Why Are they so Weird? What's Really Going on in a Teenager's Brain?* London: Bloomsbury, 2003.

Stein, Gertrude. *The World is Round*. Illustrated by Roberta Arenson. New York: Barefoot Books, 1993.

Stephens, John. *Language and Ideology in Children's Fiction*. London: Longman, 1992.

——. 'Performativity and the Child Who May Not Be a Child', Francelia Butler Memorial Lecture at 'Performing Childhood', Children's Literature Association Conference, Winnipeg, Canada, 10 June 2005.

Stephens, John and Robyn McCallum. *Retelling Stories, Framing Culture: Traditional Stories and Metanarratives in Children's Literature*. London and New York: Garland, 1998.

——. ' "There are Worse Things than Ghosts": Reworking Horror Chronotopes in Australian Children's Fiction,' in Adrienne E. Gavin and Christopher Routledge (eds) *Mystery in Children's Literature: From the Rational to the Supernatural*. Basingstoke: Palgrave Macmillan, 2001, pp. 165–83.

Stevenson, Randall. *Modernist Fiction; An Introduction*. Hemel Hempstead: Harvester Wheatsheaf, 1992.

Stivers, Richard. *Technology as Magic: The Triumph of the Irrational*. New York: Continuum, 1999.

Storr, Catherine. *Marianne Dreams*. London: Faber, 2000.

Strong, Marilee. *A Bright Red Scream: Self-Mutilation and the Language of Pain*. London: Virago, 1998.

Tan, Shaun. *The Red Tree*. Melbourne: Lothian Books, 2004.

Tashjian, Janet. *The Gospel According to Larry*. New York: Laurel Leaf Books, 2003.

Thomas, Donald. *Lewis Carroll: A Portrait with Background*. London: John Murray, 1996.

Thomas, Sue. 'Transliteracy - Reading in the Digital Age' in The *English Subject Centre Newsletter*, Issue 9, November 2005, pp. 26–30.

Thompson, Jonathan and Sophie Goodchild. 'Teen UK. A Generation Sitting on a Mental Health Time Bomb' in *The Independent on Sunday*, 27 November 2005, pp. 6–7.

Thomson, Stephen. 'The real adolescent: performance and negativity in Melvin Burgess's *Junk*' in *The Lion and the Unicorn*, no. 23, 1999, pp. 22–9.

Tickle, Louise. 'Fear and sadness in the classroom' in *The Guardian*, 18 July 2006, p. 6.

Tigges, Wim. *An Anatomy of Literary Nonsense*. Amsterdam: Rodopi, 1988.

Todorov, Tzvetan. *The Fantastic: A Structural Approach to a Literary Genre*. Translated by R. Howard. Cleveland and London: The Press Case of Western Reserve University, 1973.

Townsend, John Rowe. *Written for Children: An Outline of English-Language Children's Literature*. London: Kestrel Books, 1983.

Trites, Roberta Seelinger. *Disturbing the Universe: Power and Repression in Adolescent Literature*. Iowa City: University of Iowa Press, 2000.

Trodd, Anthea. *A Reader's Guide to Edwardian Literature*. Hemel Hempstead: Harvester Wheatsheaf, 1991.

Tucker, Nicholas. *The Child and the Book: A Psychological and Literary Exploration*. Cambridge: Cambridge University Press, 1991 (first published in 1981).

——. 'Depressive Stories for Children' in *Children's Literature in Education*, vol. 37, no. 3, Autumn 2006, pp. 199–209.

——. *Suitable for Children? Controversies in Children's Literature*. Berkeley and Los Angeles: University of California Press, 1976.

Turkle, Sherry. *Life on the Screen: Identity in the Age of the Internet*. New York: Simon and Schuster, 1995.

Twitchell, J.B. *Dreadful Pleasures: An Anatomy of Modern Horror*. Oxford: Oxford University Press, 1985.

Ungerer, Tomi. *Le Nuage Bleu*. Paris: École des Loisirs, 2003 (first French edition 2000; originally published in German as *Die blaue Wolke*).

Vasey-Saunders, Mark. Private email correspondence, 24/10/2005.

Vice, Sue (ed.) *Beyond the Pleasure Dome: Writings and Addiction from the Romantics*. London: Futura, 1997.

Vigeurs, Susan T. 'Nonsense and the Language of Poetry' in *Signal*, no. 42, September 1983, pp. 137–49.

Vrettos, A.M. *Skin*. London: Egmont, 2006.

Wall, Barbara. *The Narrator's Voice: The Dilemma of Children's Fiction*. London: Macmillan, 1991.

Walter, Virginia and Susan March F. 'Juvenile Picture Books about the Holocaust: Extending the Definitions of Children's Literature' in *Publishing Research Quarterly*, vol. 9, Fall, 1993, pp. 36–51.

Warner, Marina. 'Dark Arts', *The Guardian*, 14 October 2004, pp. 6–7.

——. ' "Eyes like Carbuncles": The Spell of Fairytale Now'. Lecture for 'Hans Christian Andersen 1805–1875: A Celebration and Reappraisal' at the British Library, 8 August 2005.

——. 'Knowing Your Daemons: Metamorphosis from the Arabian Nights to Philip Pullman' in Emer O'Sullivan, Kimberley Reynolds, and Rolf Romoren (eds) *Children's Literature Global and Local: Social and Aesthetic Perspectives*. Oslo: Novus Press, 2005, pp. 25–43.

——. *No Go the Bogeyman: Scaring, Lulling, and Making Mock*. London: Chatto and Windus, 1998.

——. *Only Make Believe: Ways of Playing*, catalogue (eds John Leslie and Antonia Harrison) to the exhibition at Compton Verney, 25 March-5 June, 2005. Compton Verney, Warwickshire, 2005.

Watson, Victor (ed.) *The Cambridge Guide to Children's Books in English*. Cambridge: Cambridge University Press, 2001.

Weinreich, Torben. *Children's Literature - Art or Pedagogy?* Copenhagen: Rothskilde University Press, 2000.

Westall, Robert. *Falling into Glory*. London: Methuen, 1993.

Wiesner, David. *The Three Pigs*. Boston: Clarion Books, 2001.

Wilce, Hilary. 'Dear Judy, you're brilliant' in *The Times Educational Supplement Review*, 4 February 1994, pp. 1–2.

Wilson, Jacqueline. *Love Lessons*. London: Corgi, 2006.

Winick, Judd. *Pedro and Me: Friendship, Loss and What I Learned*. New York: Holt, 2000.

Wittlinger, Ellen. *Hard Love*. New York: Simon and Schuster, 1999.

Zipes, Jack. *Fairy Tales and the Art of Subversion: The Classical Genre for Children and the Process of Civilization*. New York: Routledge, 1991 (first published in 1983).

Zornado, Joseph. *Inventing the Child: Culture, Ideology and the Story of Childhood*. London: Garland, 2000.

Web sites

http://www.childline.org.uk/. Accessed 22/09/2004.

http://www.chl.kiev.ua/ev/ermosob/sob_11e.html. Accessed 20/02/2006.

http://digital.library.mcgill.ca/russian/intro.htm. Accessed 17/03/2006.

http://dmoz.org/Games/Roleplaying/Gamebooks/desc.html. Accessed 24/10/2005.

http://www.iisg.nl/collections/sovietchildren/2099c-23.html. Accessed 20/02/2006.

http://pc.ign.com/mail/2003–11-03.htm. Accessed 22/07/05.

http://www.selfharmuk.org/facts. Accessed 05/06/2006.

http://en.wikipedia.org/wiki/Fan_fiction. Accessed 07/07/2006.

http://www. sevaj.dk/kharms/stories/summerd.htm. Accessed 03/03/2006.

Index